ADAM SMITH
IN HIS TIME
AND OURS

ADAM SMITH
IN HIS TIME
AND OURS

DESIGNING
THE DECENT
SOCIETY

JERRY Z. MULLER

THE FREE PRESS
A Division of Macmillan, Inc.
New York

Maxwell Macmillan Canada
Toronto

Maxwell Macmillan International
New York   Oxford   Singapore   Sydney

The Free Press
A Division of Macmillan, Inc.
866 Third Avenue, New York, N.Y. 10022

Maxwell Macmillan Canada, Inc.
1200 Eglinton Avenue East
Suite 200
Don Mills, Ontario M3C 3N1

Macmillan, Inc. is part of the Maxwell Communication
Group of Companies.

Printed in the United States of America

printing number
1 2 3 4 5 6 7 8 9 10

Library of Congress Cataloging-in-Publication Data

Muller, Jerry Z.
    Adam Smith in his time and ours: designing the decent society /
by Jerry Z. Muller.
        p.   cm.
    ISBN 0-02-922234-6
    1. Smith, Adam, 1723-1790.   2. Economics—Moral and ethical
aspects.   I. Title.
HB103.S6M83   1993
330.15′3—dc20   92-29066
                                                    CIP

For Sharon

"the chief part of human happiness arises from the consciousness of being beloved"

ADAM SMITH,
The Theory of Moral Sentiments

"He is certainly not a good citizen who does not wish to promote, by every means in his power, the welfare of the whole society of his fellow-citizens."

ADAM SMITH, The Theory of Moral Sentiments

"What institution of government could tend so much to promote the happiness of mankind as the general prevalence of wisdom and virtue? All government is but an imperfect remedy for the deficiency of these . . ."

ADAM SMITH, The Theory of Moral Sentiments

Contents

Introduction
Back to Adam?

"Economic activity in a market system must occur at the expense of consumers, because it is motivated by the search for private gain."

"A system based on the pursuit of self-interest cannot benefit society as a whole."

"A rational economic system is based on a comprehensive plan that directs resources to where they are most needed."

All three propositions seem to be self-evident truths: Public benefits are the result of altruistic intentions expressed through deliberate planning. Historically, all three were widely believed —perhaps they still are. Yet all three are false, because the consequences of social actions often differ substantially from the intentions of those who perform them.

In *An Inquiry into the Nature and Causes of the Wealth of Nations* Adam Smith explored the implications of the counterintuitive notion that the pursuit of self-interest may in fact result in public benefits. That proposition is central to social science and policy analysis, for it enables us to anticipate more accurately the outcomes of deliberate policies. In dispelling false though intuitively compelling assertions about the relationship between intentions and outcomes, Smith wrote the great primer of social scientific literacy.

It is as the founder and systematizer of capitalist economics that Adam Smith is best known. By explaining why a market economy is best able to meet the economic needs of consumers, he provided what is still the most cogent defense of capitalism. One purpose of this book is to acquaint those who condemn the pursuit of self-interest on moral grounds with the arguments of the most sophisticated and nuanced exponent of the social and moral uses of self-interest. Another purpose is to remind contemporary devotees of self-interest of the distance between Smith's position and theirs.

Those who are most likely to cite Smith's authority often misunderstand the substance of his thought. His name is invoked by those who claim that the public good springs automatically out of the pursuit of self-interest, who regard government as the enemy of liberty, and who cite Smith's principal of "natural liberty" to defend the legalization of everything from pornography to guns to hard drugs. Many of those who style themselves Smithians substitute what they believe him to have said for what he actually said.

Far from being an individualist, Smith believed that it is the influence of society that transforms people into moral beings. He thought that people often misjudge their own self-interest. He never used the term "laissez-faire," and he believed that governmental expenses were bound to increase as civilization advanced. He regarded the attempt to explain all human behavior on the basis of self-interest as analytically misguided and morally pernicious. In the society he intended to promote, men and women were freer from the traditional, direct controls of political lords and state churches. But that had been made possible, he showed, only by the growth of central government, and it would only be desirable when coupled with a panoply of social institutions which fostered self-control. The "liberty" Smith advocated was not "freedom" from all control, but freedom to control one's own passions. That freedom would be learned from and encouraged by such social institutions as the market, the family, religious communities, and the law.

Adam Smith is best known as an advocate of "natural liberty." But the understanding of what liberty means and of why it is worth having has changed radically from his day to ours. If Smith's association of liberty with institutionally fostered self-control sounds strange to us, it is because we have adopted the assumption that the most "authentic" self is the self that is least inhibited by external standards, and so many have come to identify liberty with the absence of legal constraint, social constraint, and even self-restraint—with unbounded will and unconstrained desire; and imagine that Adam Smith offered the ultimate rationale for "doing as one likes." This book may disabuse them of that view and may even lead them to consider whether Smith was right after all about the links between political liberty, institutionally fostered self-control, and the moral development of the individual.

Marxism may be ready for interment, but contemporary liberalism and conservatism are hardly in good health. Liberals tend to promote the expansion of "rights" and entitlements, and refuse, on principle, to distinguish between forms of conduct that are worthy of government support and those that should be discouraged. Skeptical conservatives (and some liberals) have come to question these preoccupations. How, they ask, can government promote the common good if politics is little more than the struggle among competing groups for rights and entitlements? If citizens can make claims on the state without the state making claims on them, and if the role of social institutions in creating self-controlled individuals is beyond the ken of the state, should we be surprised at the emergence of men ever less inclined and less able to limit their own desires? And if the inability of men to limit their desires makes them dangerous to others, is it astonishing that citizens look to the state primarily to protect them from the threat posed by other citizens?

Conservatives declare their commitment to the conservation of traditional cultural and social institutions. When liberals urge the enlargement of rights, conservatives cite the importance of responsibilities. When the liberals warn that the state is interfering with the inalienable right of citizens to experiment with various lifestyles, conservatives respond that failed experiments lead to wrecked lives, and that the state should safeguard the institutions that have withstood the test of time. Conservatives are apt to regard the market, untrammeled by governmental restrictions, as among the tried and true institutions they seek to conserve. But what happens when the market, fueled by the profit motive, elevates desire beyond duty, and when the surest way to make a buck is to appeal to what conservatives regard as the lowest of desires? Might not forces within the market, or the attitudes it promotes, erode the very cultural and social institutions conservatives seek to preserve? Some conservatives, having concluded that government is the enemy, see no reason to devote intellectual energy to shape government policies that will promote their aims. Rather, they work to shrink the role of government and encourage reliance on the purportedly self-regulating forces of the market. Antipathy to government and faith in the market sometimes lead conservatives to believe that the best antidote to the failed policies of the liberals is no policy at all—a view that often has unanticipated, negative social costs.

It is understandable, then, that thoughtful liberals and conservatives find themselves dissatisfied with the typical options offered by contemporary political debate. When they look to the academy for intellectual clarification, they often search in vain. Universities are supposed to provide a home for disinterested but not uninterested reflection. Yet it sometimes seems that they are populated either by ideologically driven cheerleaders rooting for their own team or by specialists hawking popcorn in the disciplinary grandstands. More and more the academic left is becoming an epistemological left, with a preference for debates about words rather than about things. Elsewhere in the academy, the explanation of human affairs is increasingly dominated by one-sided models, such as game theory, which can be grasped with little knowledge of human history and then applied to ever broader areas, from the family to international relations.

To those who find themselves dissatisified with the state of contemporary liberalism and conservatism, with the propensity of many academics to dwell on matters that are of little concern beyond their ideological or disciplinary precincts or to offer unworldly answers to worldly questions, this book suggests that the beginning of a solution may lie in going back to Adam.

Smith addressed the broad questions that contemporary academics often lose sight of: the origins and institutional prerequisites of commercial society, and the social, political, military, and cultural effects of the market economy. Written at a time when moral philosophy encompassed the study of law, history, and what we know today as psychology, political science and anthropology, Smith's works are remarkable for their range and for the linkages they establish in the histories of legal, political, economic, military, religious, and familial institutions. The richness of Smith's vision comes from his ability to illuminate the relationships among those institutions and to do so with a common method of analysis.

Politicians and policy makers also stand to benefit from a deeper acquaintance with Smith the social scientist and moral philosopher. Seen as a whole, his work offers an alternative to many of the caricatured conceptions that find their way into political debate. It provides an antidote to the view that the sole role of the market and of government is to make men richer and that any attempt to make society more moral will lead either to despotism or to poverty. It offers a critical response both to those who believe that government is the enemy and to those who assume that the market is wasteful or immoral. It serves as a corrective both to those who regard self-interest as intrinsically immoral and to those who regard it as the last word on human motivation. Smith disputes both the notion that the pursuit of self-interest is incompatible with the public good and the notion that the public good is automatically served by the pursuit of self-interest. He offers a reasoned reproach both to elitists who disdain modern politics for its attention to the welfare of the populace, and to populists who believe that a modern polity can survive without elites motivated by a concern for the public interest and without the systematic knowledge required to make actions conform to intentions.

Brilliant and multifaceted a thinker as Adam Smith was, however, his work can provide few specific prescriptions for action two centuries after his death. But it suggests a way of looking at the social world that balances moral concern with a realistic appraisal of human nature and human institutions. Moreover, it suggests that the proper role of social scientists is to identify the institutional means by which the mixed passions of human nature can be harnessed in the pursuit of a more decent society.

Theorists at various points on the political spectrum criticize the propensity of policy makers to begin and end discussions of public policy with the purported "rights" of individuals and groups, as if summarizing those rights were tantamount to setting public goals.[1] So exclusive a focus on legal rights obscures the need to consider the institutions that make "rights" possible and that give them meaning. Smith's approach to questions of public policy is very different. He sets up the model of conduct which ought to be encouraged, examines the capacity of existing

institutions to promote such behavior, and suggests appropriate
ways to preserve or reform them to meet that goal.

Critics object that such a model is no longer relevant. A
modern, pluralist society, they claim, is incapable of arriving at
any consensus on what constitutes a virtuous existence and is
unwilling even to ask such a question. In its strong version, this
claim is certainly true: the multiplicity of convictions on what
constitutes a good life makes it impossible to arrive at a universally accepted model, and it is the absence of such a model that
makes it possible for disparate communities to coexist within a
liberal, capitalist society. But can such a society survive over the
long term without some minimal concurrence on what constitutes desirable behavior? Are there not standards of conduct that
society must foster if it is to thrive? Smith thought there were. He
believed that what he called a commercial society requires
institutions which foster prudence, self-control, respect for life
and property and, among some at least, concern for the common
good, the ability to recognize the likely outcome of one's actions,
and an awareness of the limits of what is knowable and foresee-
able. These concerns are once again at the forefront of political
theory and public policy.[2]

It was in the course of a project on capitalism in modern
European thought that I originally immersed myself in the
scholarship on Adam Smith and in his writings. As my understanding of Smith's thought deepened, I was struck time and
again by its contemporary relevance. That relevance lay less in
his specific policy recommendations than in his mode of thought,
which cannot be characterized as either liberal or conservative,
philosophical or economistic. Yet despite the wealth of scholarship that has been devoted to Smith, I knew of no book which
had captured that mode of thought, and demonstrated the
common denominator behind his works.

Smith's writings touch upon almost every aspect of social
life, in an approach I have termed "the institutional direction of
the passions." His purpose was to make people more decent by
designing social institutions which draw the passions toward
socially and morally beneficial behavior. This is the thread that
runs through all his works: how the market can be structured to
make the pursuit of self-interest benefit consumers; how the
passion for the approval of others can make us act more
selflessly; how public institutions can be structured to ensure that

they deliver the services they are mandated to provide; how our desires for sex and for progeny can be structured by the law to create family institutions that foster self-control; how institutions concerned with defense and taxation can be structured to avoid unnecessary wars, while averting military defeat which had so often destroyed civilized societies in the past.

The dominant image of Adam Smith is as an advocate of unhampered self-interest, an opponent of government, and an icon of individualism, rugged or not. Such distortions result from reading him through retrospective ideological lenses that transform him into a proto-libertarian, an avatar of "laissez-faire," a spokesman of the rising bourgeoisie, a conservative, or a public-choice theorist *avant la lettre*. Though his works include hints of these later constructs, the sum of his concerns is very different from any of them. Smith needs to be rescued from those who claim him as their intellectual progenitor.

This book is an essay in historical recovery. I have tried to recapture Adam Smith's moral and political philosophy of capitalism, his view of social science, and his conception of the roles of the merchant, the intellectual, and the legislator in a capitalist society.

Smith was a rich and complex thinker, and his books are fraught with purposes which appear paradoxical when read outside the historical context in which they were written and without regard to the audience to which they were addressed. *The Wealth of Nations*, which focuses on the analysis of market processes motivated by self-interest, was written by a Scottish professor of moral philosophy to arouse politicians to pursue the common good. It celebrates the virtues of "commercial society" while vilifying the merchant—who gave his name to "the mercantile system" which Smith endeavors to demolish. It identifies profit-seeking as the key coordinating mechanism of the economy but seeks to discourage high profits. A book intended to guide the actions of legislators emphasizes the unanticipated consequences of deliberate action. Smith's other major work, *The Theory of Moral Sentiments*, sets out to explain how people progress from the natural passion of self-love toward benevolence and altruism—this from the man who wrote, "It is not from the benevolence of the butcher, the brewer, or the baker, that we expect our dinner, but from their regard to their own interest." Smith's great work on law and political institutions, which was never completed but has come down to us in notes taken by his students, is devoted in large part to the history of the family, and to the history of military defense. Finally, the man who is often cited as an advocate of limited government and free trade spent the years following the publication of *The Wealth of Nations* as a collector of customs on imported goods.

For Smith, morals, economics, and government were closely intertwined. While his works are enduring classics of social science, they are also works of moral philosophy. His overarching goal was to improve human character, a civilizing project that led him to investigate the role of the state, law, family, churches, and the market in producing human beings capable of the self-discipline and benevolence required by a liberal capitalist society. For Smith, the greatest benefit of commercial society was that it created incentives for people to develop what he called the "imperfect, but attainable virtues" which provided the basis of a decent society: self-control, the ability to defer gratification, and the propensity to orient one's actions to the needs of others.

Compared to the classical philosophers or even the early modern humanists, Smith was less concerned with the welfare of the social and political elite than with the welfare—both material and moral—of the vast majority of society. He believed that the proper yardstick of the material wealth of the nation is not the government's economic resources or the wealth of its elites, but the purchasing power of the nation's consumers. Commercial society, he believed, made it possible for the mass of the populace to escape the demeaning relations of dependence characteristic of the past. Direct domination by political elites would be replaced by a network of institutions which promoted self-control among politically free citizens, while the rising level of material comfort would make it possible to expand sympathy and concern for others. It was this political philosophy which lay behind Smith's advocacy of higher wages, mass education, and other policies that conflicted with the conventional wisdom of the upper classes to whom his books were addressed. Smith was skeptical about the possibility of making everyone virtuous, but he was optimistic about lifting people to higher levels of morality by means of properly structured institutions, the rudiments of which Smith thought were already at hand in the commercial society of his day. He identified the institutions that performed the functions of discipline and moral regulation, suggested that certain institutions of the past could serve as models for institutional reform, and (more rarely) prescribed how new institutions should be structured. What he has to say about education, the family, and moral character is as trenchant as what he has to say about the market.

A welcome trend among intellectual historians insists that works of social and political thought can best be understood by placing them in their historical contexts. Some object that this approach robs great works of their timelessness and of the possibility that they may have something important to say to us today.[3] This book accommodates both views: understanding what is timeless and what is timely in Smith's work depends on our understanding it in the context of his own time.

This book begins by sketching the aspects of Smith's life, the elements of his milieu, and the traditions of intellectual inquiry which are most important for appreciating his moral and political philosophy of commercial society. Smith's life is lacking in dramatic events: or rather, the most dramatic events in Smith's life took place (as they do for most intellectuals) in his mind as he encountered new texts and new historical developments which he sought to order. My working assumption is that Smith's thought is relatively coherent, that *The Wealth of Nations* must be seen in the light of his other works, and that there is continuity between his writings and his career as a professor of moral philosophy, educator of the social and political elite, adviser to politicians, and civil servant. Seeing Smith in his historical context helps explain why he should have been motivated to undertake his "science of a legislator" with reasonable confidence in its efficacy.

To recover Smith's thought we must attend to the rhetorical elements of his writing and to his intended audience.[4] For Smith wanted not merely to inform and enlighten his readers but to *influence* them. To understand what Smith is saying in *The Wealth of Nations* we must be aware of who his intended audience was, what their concerns and assumptions were likely to have been, which contemporary experiences the book was intended to illuminate, and what practices he was trying to encourage or reform. Some of his most striking and radical formulations take on a rather different significance when seen in this light.

I have tried to avoid the condescension of posterity and have assumed that Smith might have thought differently and possibly better than any of us. My purpose has been to recapture what he *actually* said, which is inextricably linked with *how* he said it and *whom* he was addressing. Understanding Smith well is a necessary prerequisite to deciding what is living and what is dead in his thought. I have tried to avoid reading present-day concerns into Smith's work, but without committing the antiquarian sin of failing to recognize such concerns merely because they are expressed in the language of the past.

This book gathers the fruits of a rich harvest of Smith scholarship which I review in the Guide to Further Reading. The oldest secondary source on Smith's work, and the one I have found most useful, was written by his student Dugald Stewart. I have profited from the labors of more recent Smith scholars such as Jacob Viner, Nathan Rosenberg, Donald Winch, Istvan Hont, Knud Haakonssen, and Laurence Dickey, as well as from the demonstration effect of the works of Gertrude Himmelfarb, Albert O. Hirschman, and J. G. A. Pocock, whose very different modes of intellectual history I have tried to combine.[5] In some measure Smith scholarship has become a process of diminishing returns, in that it rediscovers or refines insights already available elsewhere. Actually, however, it is not so much a matter of saying more and more about less and less, but of saying more and more *about more and more* as we acquire a better understanding of the larger contexts in which Smith's thought took shape. The efflorescence of social and economic history in recent decades has made it possible to recapture more fully the referents of Smith's writings on the economy and society. Much new light has been cast on Smith's political, economic, and intellectual milieu—light which can be refocused to illuminate Smith's work more fully.

Joseph Schumpeter once remarked that *The Wealth of Nations* "does not contain a single analytic idea, principle, or method that was entirely new in 1776," but that its significance lies in its synthesis of prior ideas and information.[6] So too with this book: its purpose is to show the connections between the elements of Smith's thought and between what he wrote and what he did. For the most part, this book is expository rather than critical. My aim has been to reconstruct Smith's vision and to show how the various parts of his analysis relate to his overarching concerns and premises. Only at the end do I question the validity of his premises, his inferences, and his judgments.

To reveal the polemical point of Smith's argument, I have sketched the intellectual traditions with which he grappled. I have tried to recapture the cultural context of his thought without overemphasizing the genealogy of his ideas or detailing his debates with contemporary thinkers. Again, my purpose has been to familiarize readers with Adam Smith's social, political, and cultural universe so that they can read Smith's works through Smith's eyes.

I have made no attempt to trace the development of Smith's ideas over his lifetime. Smith rewrote his two major works both before their publication and after. One could write a developmental account of his thought by examining his unpublished lectures of the 1750s and 1760s, other precursors of *The Wealth of Nations*,[7] and successive editions of the book itself, and by comparing the successive editons of *The Theory of Moral Sentiments* published from 1759 to 1790. Most of the changes Smith made in *The Wealth of Nations* after its first publication in 1776 were not substantive. His changes in *The Theory of Moral Sentiments*, by contrast, are more extensive and more significant, so that the sixth and final edition of 1790 is a rather different book from the first edition.[8] I have chosen to deal only with the last editon of each text, as reflecting Smith's final views.

Smith is an uncommonly quotable writer, for he was acutely aware of the importance of rhetoric, of the effect of how we say what we say. And so Smith is quoted often in this book. I have occasionally altered his punctuation and spelling to conform to modern usage.

PART I

ADAM SMITH IN HIS TIME

CHAPTER ONE

Cosmopolitan Provincial: Smith's Life and Social Milieu

"HE SPEAKS HARSHLY, WITH BIG teeth, and he's ugly as the devil. He's Mr. Smith, author of a book I haven't read." So wrote Madame Riccoboni, a French novelist who first met Adam Smith in Paris in May 1766.[1] She soon changed her opinion. "He's a most absent-minded creature," she wrote to a friend in London, "but one of the most lovable." Later that year, after Smith had left Paris for London, she wrote to the actor David Garrick, "Scold me, beat me, kill me, but I like Mr. Smith, I like him greatly. I wish that the devil would carry off all of our men of letters, all of our philosophers, and bring Mr. Smith to me. Superior men seek him out."[2] Voltaire, the greatest propagandist of the French Enlightenment and the man who almost single-handedly created the role of the modern intellectual, agreed. "This Smith is an excellent man!" he wrote after meeting the Scottish philosopher. "We have nothing to compare with him, and I am embarrassed for my dear compatriots."[3] Along with men and women of letters and learning, the foremost politicians of Scotland, England, and France sought the advice of this less than handsome savant. Within a few years of its publication in 1776, his *Wealth of Nations* was being taught in universities as distant as Königsberg in eastern Prussia, and in the New World. Thomas Jefferson regarded it as the best book available on political economy. How can we account for the man whose book on the market was praised by contemporaries for "overturning all that interested Sophistry of Merchants, with which they have Confounded the whole Subject of Commerce"?[4]

Adam Smith spent most of his life in that great eighteenth-century incubator of intellectual innovation—Scotland. He was born in the small port town of Kirkcaldy on the east coast in 1723, sixteen years after the kingdom north of the Tweed was united with the British crown. Later he would reside in Edinburgh and Glasgow, in London and Oxford, in Paris and Toulouse, but each time he was pulled back to Kirkcaldy by the presence of his mother. She was a woman, Smith wrote, "who certainly loved me more than any other person ever did or ever will love me; and whom I certainly loved and respected more than I ever shall either love or respect any other person." Adam was her only child and she was his only parent, for he had come into the world some months after the death of his father, for whom he was named.[5]

Smith was born into a milieu in which property, patronage, education, and government service were closely linked, and those coordinates would continue to chart his social course thereafter.[6] In an age when customs duties on imports were a major source of government revenue, his father had served as Comptroller of Customs in Kirkcaldy, and he himself would spend the last decade of his life as Commissioner of Customs for Scotland.

Scotland was largely a rural society, at a comparatively low level of commercial and industrial development. The main industries in the Kirkcaldy region, coal mining and salt panning, were carried on by laborers who were legally bound for a period of time to their place of work. In another industry—nail-making—some employers paid their workers in nails, which local shopkeepers accepted as currency. Land ownership and political power were closely intertwined. Smith's maternal grandfather had been a substantial landowner and had sat in the Scottish Parliament. Smith's father was from a less notable but well-connected landed family, and his relatives held a variety of official posts in Scotland, including an uncle who was General Collector of Taxation.

Smith's father's career was based on service to and prefer-ment from aristocratic landowners, who dominated the govern-ment of Scotland. In return for their support of the British crown, these aristocrats dispensed government posts controlled by their patronage, thus forging a link between local elites and the growing bureaucracy. After receiving a legal education in Aberdeen, Smith Senior became private secretary to Hugh Campbell, Earl of Loudon, who rose to become Secretary of State for Scotland and who appointed Smith to a series of government offices. In 1714 the Earl's patronage led Smith Senior to the post of Comptroller of Customs in Kirkcaldy, where his superior was his cousin Hercules.

In the small, oligarchic society of Kirkcaldy, the young Adam Smith numbered among his friends James Oswald of Dunnikier, the largest landowner in the region. In a pattern typical of the upper reaches of the Scottish nobility, Oswald moved to London and assumed a position in the British ruling class.[7] He became first an MP and later Lord of Trade and Lord of the Treasury—and served as a source of information for his boyhood friend.[8]

At the age of fourteen, Smith was sent to the University of Glasgow. There he was deeply influenced by the lectures on moral philosophy given by Francis Hutcheson, by his first exposure to ancient Stoic thought, and by his reading of the great natural rights theorists of the late seventeenth century, Grotius, Pufendorf, and Locke. It was in Glasgow that Smith first confronted the great issues which were to drive Scottish moral philosophy in the eighteenth century. The first of those issues was how to reconcile classical and Christian demands for altruism and benevolence in human relations with recent arguments by Thomas Hobbes and Bernard Mandeville that egoism and self-interest were the driving force in society, and how to do so without resorting to the disputed authority of revelation. By the time Smith arrived at the university, Hutcheson had already written a short refutation of Mandeville's *Fable of the Bees*, which had held that socially beneficial actions could be traced to egoistic "private vices." In his lectures, Hutcheson developed his notion of the irreducible reality of a "moral sense" implanted in man by his creator, which led man to take pleasure in benevolent action and which provided the psychological basis of virtuous behavior. The second great issue, to which the natural rights theorists had paid serious attention and which loomed large in Hutcheson's lectures on moral philosophy, was the growth of commerce and its role in human affairs. Self-love and morality, and moral psychology and the nature of commerce, were to become the paramount themes of Smith's thought as well.

An outstanding student, Smith won a scholarship to Oxford, where he spent half a dozen years learning—but not from his teachers. The faculty made few demands on the students, Smith noted at the time. He later devoted substantial portions of *The Wealth of Nations* to a critical explanation of how the assured income of university faculties impaired their incentive to teach or pursue scholarly excellence. This was to be one of his many analyses of how institutions guide the passions, in this case to negative outcomes unanticipated by those who had endowed the Oxford faculty with an assured stream of income. The universities, he wrote, had become "the sanctuaries in which exploded systems and obsolete prejudices found shelter and protection, after they had been hunted out of every other corner of the world." The universities produced students "completely igno-rant of every thing which is the common subject of conversation among gentlemen and men of the world," he lamented.[9]

But Smith profited enormously from his years at Oxford despite its institutional structure, which turned out to have been quite advantageous for a man of his character. He had arrived at Oxford with a set of intellectual problems formulated in his undergraduate years at Glasgow and equipped with an excellent knowledge of Greek and Latin. With prodigious intellectual energy, fueled perhaps by his fear of what he imagined to be his propensity to laziness, Smith set about educating himself, de-vouring the resources of Oxford's great libraries. His surviving writings from the 1740s and the lectures he gave after his return to Kirkcaldy show that he had immersed himself in the Greek and Latin classics, in modern French and English literature, in recent science and some contemporary philosophy. His main work during these early years, "The Principles which Lead and Direct Philosophical Enquiries; Illustrated by the History of Astronomy," is a remarkable exploration of the psychological basis of scientific inquiry, which he traced to the mind's craving for order and tranquillity. This craving was upset by the confron-tation with new facts which did not fit into previously accepted explanatory systems. Scientific inquiry (for Smith, science and philosophy were one and the same) was motivated by the resulting discomfort, which was alleviated only when a new explanatory system brought the known facts together with greater simplicity and comprehensiveness.[10]

Smith began to make his name in the intellectual world in

1748 when he gave a series of lectures in Edinburgh sponsored by his friend James Oswald and by Henry Home. Home was a distinguished jurist, man of letters, and improving landlord who tried to put commercial agriculture on a more scientific basis, experimenting with everything from crop selection to mulching and manure. To an audience made up of students of law and theology and prominent citizens of the town, Smith lectured on rhetoric, belles lettres, and jurisprudence.

The success of his lectures led to a professorship at the University of Glasgow in 1751, where at the age of twenty-eight he was appointed to the chair of logic and rhetoric and then to the chair of moral philosophy. Smith's lectures on ethics formed the basis of his first book, *The Theory of Moral Sentiments*, published in 1759. Even before completing that book, he had begun to lecture on "jurisprudence," a topic which included not only the principles of law but the principles of government and political economy as well. The portions of these lectures dealing with political economy and military defense eventually found their way, in modified form, into *The Wealth of Nations*. The portions on law and government were to have been the basis of a third major work. Smith tinkered with the manuscript for years, but, unable to complete it to his own satisfaction, he insisted on his deathbed that it be burned rather than released to the public in its imperfect form. Fortunately, two sets of student notes on these lectures have survived. One set, probably stemming from Smith's lectures of 1763–64, was discovered and published in the late nineteenth century. A second, more extensive set of notes taken a year earlier was discovered in 1958 and was published in 1978 together with the first set as *Lectures on Jurisprudence*. In these remarkably erudite lectures, Smith traced the historical development of the legal and political institutions which made possible what he called "civilization"—a combination of commerce, free labor, advanced culture, and political liberty.

Smith remained in Glasgow until 1764, a successful and devoted teacher and an able academic administrator. His university duties brought him into frequent contact with the merchant elite of Glasgow, who elected him a burgess of the city in 1762.

Mid-eighteenth-century Glasgow, where Smith began to write his inquiry into the wealth of nations, was a provincial town of some 23,000 inhabitants. It was enjoying an economic boom based on the burgeoning trans-Atlantic economy and on protectionist legislation enacted by the British government. What had formerly been expensive luxuries, such as sugar, tea, and coffee, were now being grown by European entrepreneurs in the New World and in the East Indies and were being imported into Europe in ever-larger quantities. Another of these new imported pleasures was tobacco, grown in Britain's American colonies and exported by the merchants of the Chesapeake region. Under the provisions of the Navigation Acts, goods produced by British colonies could be transported only in British ships. Thus the tobacco grown in America and destined for Europe had to pass through a British port. In Smith's day, Glasgow's prosperity was based on its role as the major entrepot for American tobacco, one quarter of which was sold in Britain while the remainder was shipped on to ports in the North Sea, the Baltic, and the Mediterranean. The enterprising merchants of Glasgow used some of their profits to found industries which produced manu-factured goods for export to the British colonies—goods which mercantilist legislation made it impossible for the colonies to produce for themselves. It was through his acquaintance with the merchants of Glasgow that Smith learned at first hand of the distorting effects of protective, mercantilist legislation on the national and international economy.[11]

While living in Glasgow, Smith was a frequent visitor to nearby Edinburgh. With a population of less than 50,000 in a country of under a million and a half inhabitants, Edinburgh was the center of Scottish economic and cultural life. The reading public in Scotland was too small for authors to live on the sale of their books, and the only professional man of letters in the country was David Hume, who turned from philosophy to writing topical essays and history. Most distinguished Scottish intellectuals were lawyers, professors, or clergymen, closely tied to the leading institutions of their land. The intellectual and political life of Edinburgh revolved around clubs frequented by members of the economic, political, and cultural elite. In 1754, Smith and his friend Hume helped organize a club called the Select Society for men from well-born families, including im-proving landlords, lawyers, merchants, bankers, and clergymen. The club met regularly to debate questions of political, economic, and social policy and to provide its members with a forum in which to practice the art of public speaking. The Select Society symbolized the close link between speculative learning and social improvement that marked the Scottish Enlightenment, and it gave birth to a number of offshoots such as the "Edinburgh Society for Encouraging Arts, Sciences, Manufactures and Agriculture in Scotland." Many of its members went on to leading positions in Scottish government, courts, and universities, and even to Parliament and the House of Lords in London.[12]

Though Smith was born in Scotland and spent most of his life there, he did not deal primarily with the Scottish experience or write exclusively for a Scottish audience. He wrote for a British audience or—more broadly—for a trans-European and trans-continental audience. He shared this cosmopolitan orientation with David Hume, the other intellectual giant of the Scottish Enlightenment, and with other major figures of Scottish cultural, economic, and political life.

As a result of the Union of 1707, Scotland had relinquished its sovereignty and independence. In return, its landowning elite had gained access to the Houses of Parliament in London, and its merchants and manufacturers had gained access to the British market through a customs union. By Smith's day, the upper levels of the Scottish aristocracy had taken up residence in London and had become members of the British ruling class. One of them, the Third Earl of Bute, became the tutor and then first minister to George III when he ascended to the throne in 1760. Bute's career was an indication of how far a Scot might ascend, and during his ministry there were many opportunities for other well-connected Scots in London. As the merchants and improving landlords of Scotland were well aware, the growing economic prosperity of their country was due in good part to its customs union with England.

Scottish intellectuals generally followed this philo-English orientation. They tried to eliminate Scotticisms from their writings as well as from their speech. When Smith returned to Scotland after six years among Englishmen at Oxford and gave his public lectures in Edinburgh, he was complimented for "his pronunciation and his style [which] were much superior to what could . . . be acquired in Scotland only."[13] Some years thereafter, the Society for Promoting the Reading and Speaking of the English Language in Scotland was formed as an offshoot of the Select Society of Edinburgh. Its purpose was to import teachers from England to instruct gentlemen in the proper pronunciation of English, since the Scottish accent was a social handicap to their

advancement in London.[14] Smith's orientation toward London
and toward the culture and polity of the United Kingdom was
shared by members of the Scottish elite who described themselves not as Scotsmen but as "North Britons" and tried to
assimilate themselves and their compatriots to English culture.
At the same time, their distinctive perspective freed them from a
certain English intellectual provincialism which conceived of
British liberty as the unique historical legacy of the purported
"ancient constitution" of England or of the Glorious Revolution
of 1688.[15] They viewed British institutions without the pieties of
the British elite: they did not share the Anglican self-understanding of the regime according to which the legitimacy of the state
was closely linked to the established church, and were disposed
to value institutions such as the Parliament and the monarchy
more for their current functions than for their historical venera-
bility.[16] As we shall see, Smith thought that the English could
learn some important institutional lessons from Scottish models.

Although Smith did not write primarily for a Scottish
audience, his interests and orientations were deeply influenced
by the Scottish environment. Oriented by a Calvinist religious
heritage to the great universities of the Netherlands, by legal
development to the Roman law tradition of Continental Europe,
and by shared intellectual interests to the French Enlightenment,
Smith and the other great figures of the Scottish Enlightenment
tended to be more cosmopolitan than their English counterparts.
Their provincial cosmopolitanism drew them toward a comparative and historical inquiry into the origins and effects of institutions.

Within Scotland there were regions at very different stages
of social and economic development, creating what one scholar
has described as a "social museum at Edinburgh's back door."[17]
Through the early decades of the eighteenth century, the society
of the Gaelic-speaking Highlands, which had remained beyond
the reach of the central government, was still based on the clan.
In the absence of government control over violence, self-protection came from clan membership. The hereditary chieftain of the
clan was the highest political and military authority, with the
power of life and death over his subjects. In 1745, the Highland
clans had sided with the Jacobite revolt against the British throne
and had threatened the more economically developed, English-
speaking Lowlands. After the revolt was crushed, the Highlands

were "pacified" by the permanent stationing of government troops and the chieftains of the clans were exiled. Contributing further to the dissolution of the clan system was the gradual integration of the region into the market economy of the Lowlands. The role of central government and commerce in the development of civilization would figure prominently in Smith's writings.

Within the more advanced Lowlands, social relations based on the market and free labor existed alongside the remnants of older forms of social organization. Feudal relations, in which the landlord exercised political and judicial control over his tenants, were abolished in the countryside only in the 1740s, and until well into the second half of the century rural tenants were still obliged to provide feudal services. Landlords often served as justices empowered to control wage rates, a power they used to keep wages down. In the countryside, the "kirk session"—the Presbyterian assemblies of the Church of Scotland—disciplined the morals of its members by punishing failures of Sunday observance and the vices of drunkenness and sexual profligacy through censure and fines.[18] Beyond the more cosmopolitan and mercantile port cities of the south of Scotland lay this ethnological hinterland in which older and more direct forms of political and cultural control still predominated. It was by comparison with them that Smith judged the newer forms of human relationship that prevailed in the more politically and economically developed regions of Europe.

With such a multiplicity of political, economic, and social forms so close at hand, it is no wonder that Scottish intellectuals in Edinburgh and Glasgow were given to reflecting on the "stages" of society and the role of government and commerce in the movement from one stage to another.

The reasons for the intellectual superiority of the Scots at midcentury have been debated from their day to ours, but the dynamism of their intellectual life is beyond doubt. "Is it not strange," wrote David Hume in 1757, "that at a time when we have lost our Princes, our Parliaments, our independent Government, even the Presence of our chief Nobility, are unhappy in our accent and Pronunciation, speak a very corrupt Dialect of the Tongue which we make use of; is it not strange, I say, that in these Circumstances, we shou'd really be the People most distinguish'd for Literature in Europe?"[19] In an age when intellectual life at

Oxford and Cambridge was stagnant, the Scottish universities flourished. Beginning in Smith's day, and increasingly in the last decade of the eighteenth century, the flower of English aristocracy journeyed northward to "go to school with the Scots." It was to Smith himself that prominent British politicians entrusted the education of their sons.[20]

The concept of the political philosopher as the teacher of legislators reaches back to Plato and Aristotle.[21] Revived by the Italian humanists and their northern European successors,[22] it was adopted by many members of the Enlightenment, who sought to influence the holders of power or to occupy government posts themselves. Nowhere was this conception more plausible than among the top rank of Scottish intellectuals, with their close connections to the ruling elites of Scotland and England, their participation in the emerging bureaucracy, and their commitment to social improvement. Smith's pupil and first biographer, Dugald Stewart, placed his teacher in the company of such eighteenth-century intellectuals as Quesnay, Turgot, and Beccaria, who aimed at the improvement of society "not by delineating plans of new constitutions, but by enlightening the policy of actual legislators."[23] An awareness of Smith's milieu and career helps explain his stated intention in *The Wealth of Nations* to contribute to "the science of a statesman or legislator."[24]

The first book for which Smith is remembered, *The Theory of Moral Sentiments*, was published in 1759 to great acclaim in Scotland and England. Hume sent a copy of the book to Edmund Burke, who gave it an intelligent and enthusiastic review in the *Annual Register*, inaugurating a cordial if sporadic relationship with Smith based on mutual respect. Smith's book was well received not only in Edinburgh and London but on the Continent as well. By the time of Smith's death in 1790 *The Theory of Moral Sentiments* was in its sixth edition, and by the end of the century three French and two German translations had been published.

The book was also admired by Charles Townshend, a leading British member of Parliament, who in 1755 had married Lady Dalkeith, a dowager of fabulous means.[25] In 1763, Townshend lured Smith away from Glasgow to become tutor to his stepson, Henry Scott, the Duke of Buccleuch, by offering him a handsome sum and a generous lifetime pension. For two years, Smith accompanied the young Duke on his Grand Tour of the

Continent, using the opportunity to visit Voltaire in Geneva and to confer with many of the leaders of the French Enlightenment in Paris. Through the contacts of his friend Hume—then a secretary to the British ambassador in Paris—and the social standing of his young charge, Smith had entree to the upper ranks of Parisian salon society. He met one of the editors of the great *Encyclopédie*, d'Alembert; François Quesnay, the King's physician and a leader of the physiocratic school of political economy; and A. R. J. Turgot, who in 1757 had coined the term "laissez-faire" in his article for the *Encyclopédie* and would later become Louis XVI's Minister of Finance. Smith also used the opportunity to collect information on duties and taxation in Europe for the book he was writing on political economy. Returning to England late in 1766, Smith lived first in Kirkcaldy and then in London on the pension provided by the Buccleuch estates. There he set about completing *The Wealth of Nations*.

Even before the publication of *The Wealth of Nations*, leading political figures in London were seeking his advice. The esteem of his former employer, Charles Townshend, and the regard of his former charge, the Duke of Buccleuch, strengthened Smith's links to the highest levels of British politics. He was a frequent visitor at Dalkeith, the estate of the Duke of Buccleuch, who had become a representative Scottish peer in the House of Lords. When Townshend became Chancellor of the Exchequer he asked Smith to assist him on taxation projects. Concerned with the ever more rebellious American colonies, the Secretary of State, Lord Shelburne, asked Smith about the precedent offered by the colonies of the Roman empire. "They seem to have been very independent," Smith wrote prophetically. "They frequently rebelled and. . . . Being in some measure little independent republics they naturally followed the interests which their peculiar Situation pointed out to them."[26]

After the publication of *The Wealth of Nations* in 1776, Smith's star rose even higher. He was appointed a Commissioner of Customs for Scotland, in part through the patronage of the Duke but also because Lord North and leading figures at the Treasury were impressed by his writings.[27] When he visited London, his advice was solicited by members of Parliament and government ministers despite changes of administration. Late in life, during a visit to the house of Lord Dundas, the assembled leaders of British government—Pitt, Addington, Wilberforce, and Grenville—rose in respect until he was seated, because, as Pitt explained, they were all his scholars.[28] In what remains of Smith's correspondence with leading politicians on questions of trade, it is striking how often he sought to stiffen their backbone, urging them to buck the pressure from particular interests for the sake of the common good. On the issue of lifting trade restrictions on the subjugated province of Ireland, for example, he advised a leading politician that "to crush the Industry of so great and so fine a province of the empire, in order to favour the monopoly of some particular towns in Scotland or England, is equally unjust and unpolitic. . . . Nothing, in my opinion, would be more highly advantageous to both countries than this mutual freedom of trade. It would help to break down that absurd monopoly which we have most absurdly established against ourselves in favour of almost all the different classes of our own manufacturers."[29]

Smith spent his last decade in Edinburgh, devoting most of his time to his job as Commissioner of Customs. He began new projects, but completed none to his satisfaction. Though his days were filled with the concerns of trade and revenue, his mind seems to have turned back to the questions of ethics and the social formation of character central to *The Theory of Moral Sentiments*, which he substantially revised and expanded. He seems to have lived according to the dictates of benevolence which that book tried to evoke in its readers. He lived a modest style of life, despite his pension, his earnings as Commissioner of Customs, and the royalties from his books. Yet when he died in 1790 his estate was minimal, for over the years he had given away most of his income in acts of charity, which he took care to conceal.[30]

Smith's career, like that of his contemporary, Edmund Burke, exhibits the links created through the patronage of men of extraordinary intellectual talent by men of extraordinary power and wealth. Adam Smith was very much an Establishment intellectual. Born on the periphery of the British Establishment, he rose through the recognition of his intellectual achievements by those at the center of political power. The practical bent of his moral philosophy, combined with the knowledge gleaned from his close personal contacts with merchants and politicians, endow his books with a rare combination of the abstract and the tangible, the general and the particular.

   The Wealth of Nations was neither the first book of economics nor the first work to advocate a lifting of trade restrictions. In writing the book, Smith drew upon a large pamphlet literature going back almost a century, and upon theoretical works of more recent origin. The determination of price by the forces of supply and demand, productivity gains through the division of labor, the negative impact of tariffs on consumers, the advantages of freer trade—all had been argued before. The impact of Smith's book lay in its synthesis of ideas clearly articulated, conceptually linked, and forcefully impressed on the minds of readers. The book differed from earlier economic tracts because it was written by a professor of philosophy accustomed to analyzing and systematizing ideas for presentation to a student audience. His style, like that of a good lecturer, combined clear statements of theory with illustrative and often amusing examples.[31]

   These qualities enhanced Smith's readership among men of letters and men of affairs. It led to a fruitful marriage of insider knowledge and critical outsidership, a perspective fostered by his Scottish perspective on British affairs.

CHAPTER TWO

Gentlemen, Consumers, and the Fiscal–Military State

MOST PEOPLE IN THE GREAT Britain of Smith's day lived in what many of us would regard as poverty. Hundreds of thousands were willing to risk the possibility of death in transit and years of indentured servitude for the chance to migrate to the New World. Yet the population of Britain was probably better off economically than that of any other major nation on the globe. Conditions were improving, slowly but demonstrably, and many of those who emigrated had tasted material improvement and were motivated not by desperation but by the desire to better their fortune.[1] To put relative poverty and wealth in perspective, take the standards of apparel considered necessary by ordinary day laborers, the lowest of the working poor. In England, Smith reports, the poorest day laborer of either sex would be ashamed to appear in public without leather shoes. In Scotland, a rung lower on the ladder of national wealth, it was considered inappropriate for men of this class to appear without shoes, but not for women. In France, a rung lower still, custom held that both men and women laborers could appear shoeless in public.[2] And below France there were many rungs in Europe. And below Europe there were many more rungs.

In the course of the eighteenth century, Great Britain went through four economic revolutions: the revolution in agricultural production, the financial revolution, the consumer revolution, and a transformation of methods of production which set the stage for the industrial revolution. Though the factory and the steam engine make a brief and striking appearance in the early pages of *The Wealth of Nations,* neither the new form of industrial organization nor the new sources of power figure prominently in Smith's account of how Britain had become relatively wealthy or how it might become wealthier still. British industrial output trebled in the course of the eighteenth century, but in 1776 the "industrial revolution" lay in the future. In retrospect we recognize that the years in which Smith was writing *The Wealth of Nations* were a period of significant technological innovation: James Hargreave's spinning jenny and Richard Arkwright's waterframe were beginning to transform the production of cotton textiles, and James Watt was developing the radical improvements to the steam engine which would inaugurate the age of steam. But these innovations were to have their real impact in the decades *after* Smith's book was published. The improved steam engine was still in very limited use, and the factory system was still in embryo.[3]

The Wealth of Nations grew out of Smith's reflections on the economic growth that eighteenth-century Britain had already achieved. The gradual but unmistakable rise in the standard of living not only of the rich but of the working poor was hampered, in Smith's eyes, by some of the protectionist restrictions to which his countrymen attributed their growing riches; it could be speeded up by extending the greater market freedom already visible in parts of the economy to the economy as a whole. By the middle of the eighteenth century the old system of economic regulation was being abandoned in domestic trade but was being strengthened in foreign trade. Much of *The Wealth of Nations* was an argument for expanding the freer market regime already apparent in internal trade to the realm of international commerce.

Perhaps the most remarkable feature of the British economy from the late sixteenth through the early nineteenth century was the rise in agricultural production.[4] The economy remained agriculturally based throughout Smith's lifetime; in fact, the success of British agriculture was a precondition for the other three revolutions. By the mid-eighteenth century, British agriculture was almost entirely commercialized: farm production was no longer consumed by those who produced it but instead was sold either within the country or abroad. By mid-century Britain exported more agricultural products than it imported.

Because agricultural production was becoming more efficient as it grew, it was possible for the British population to increase (though at a rate of less than 1.5 percent per annum),[5] for the number of people employed in agriculture to remain roughly the same, and for the price of agricultural products to decline. The rapid increase in agricultural output occurred largely on land owned by the gentry and the aristocracy. Though many of the improvements were made by tenants, enterprising members of the gentry and aristocracy took the lead. They experimented with new crops and new techniques (such as liming the soil and making greater use of draught animals) and engaged in regional specialization to make the most efficient use of soil and climate conditions.

The traditional elites would also play a leading role in the growth of transportation, manufacturing, and finance as the century progressed.[6] It is misleading to think of eighteenth-century England and Scotland in terms of nobles and gentry versus middle-class merchants, or of landowners versus traders. In Scotland, the same families who had long owned the land took the initiative in making it more productive and in responding to the possibilities opened up by the expanding national and international markets. Some of those families went into trade and finance while maintaining their landed interests. And some families which had acquired their wealth through trade bought land while remaining active in merchant activities.[7] In Smith's day Britain was dominated by "gentlemanly capitalism."[8]

For over a century, Britain had been beyond the stage at which the margin between the need for food and the level of agricultural production was so narrow that the survival of a large part of society depended on the harvest. In earlier times, the slimness of that margin had justified government regulation of everything from how the land was worked to when and where grain could be sold.[9] During the seventeenth century, however, as food became more plentiful, government regulation had become less pervasive. The Act for the Encouragement of Trade (1663), for example, permitted merchants to buy grain for resale so long as prices did not rise above certain rather high levels; legal impediments to enclosure and investment in agricultural land were removed during the same decade.[10] By Smith's day,

Scotland too had advanced beyond the point where poor harvests meant starvation and death, thanks in good part to the economic stimulus provided by access to the English market as a result of the Act of Union. Scotland regularly produced more grain than it consumed.[11]

The decline in government regulation of the production and distribution of grain was followed by the abandonment of government regulation of wages. The traditional practice whereby county magistrates set wage rates was falling into disuse. The decline of the guilds, which had begun in the late seventeenth century, had affected manufacturing by the 1730s and 1740s and had extended to the service and construction industries by the 1760s. The "freedoms" of the guilds—the exclusive legal right to practice a trade or a craft within an incorporated town—were being challenged, ignored, or regarded as unenforceable. One potent restriction on freedom of trade remained, however—namely, cartel agreements in which the producers in a particular regional industry agreed among themselves to fix prices. Such practices were illegal, and Parliament, under pressure from organized groups whose interests were at risk, sought to curb them. The mine owners of Newcastle, for example, who had agreed among themselves to fix the price of coal, were opposed by coal merchants and coal shippers, who demanded parliamentary action to create a free market in coal.[12]

The relative freedom apparent in internal trade was absent from international trade. Trade with other European powers was generally viewed by policy makers as a form of undeclared warfare. Their objective was to maximize benefits to England while minimizing those to rival nations, and their prime weapon in this war was the imposition of duties on imported goods. Customs duties were originally levied to provide the national government with revenue—in the year in which *The Wealth of Nations* was published they still furnished almost a quarter of the nation's tax revenue.[13] But during the first half of the eighteenth century they came to be seen as a means of protecting British producers by adding to the market price of imported goods. In its efforts to protect domestic industries from foreign competition, Parliament went so far as to prohibit entirely the importation of certain goods. A 1721 prohibition against importing calicos stimulated the growth of the British cotton industry; a year later, the use of cotton buttons was prohibited in an attempt to

encourage the silk and mohair industries; and in 1748 the
wearing of fine French linens (cambrics) was prohibited on
similar grounds.[14] From 1763 through 1776 a new spate of
legislation prohibited the importation of foreign silk and leather
gloves, of stockings and velvet. Duties on linen and on some
types of paper were also raised.[15]

Even more elaborate were the restrictions on transcontinental trade, which was becoming an ever more important facet of
the British economy. By mid-century more than half of Britain's
foreign trade depended either directly or indirectly on transcontinental trade, and commodities from Europe's colonies were
reaching an ever wider market. Trade with the European continent had once dominated Britain's trade, but now goods shipped
to and from colonial markets were rising in volume. This shift
benefited ports like Glasgow, which thrived on the colonial
tobacco trade.[16] Under the Navigation Acts, trade between
England and its colonies was protected by tariffs and limited to
British shipping, and many Britons were convinced that colonial
trade was a source of great wealth. Writing in 1776, amid signs of
revolt in the American colonies, Smith disagreed emphatically
with the common wisdom. "The rulers of Great Britain," he
wrote, "have, for more than a century past, amused the people
with the imagination that they possessed a great empire on the
west side of the Atlantic. This empire, however, has hitherto
existed in imagination only. It has hitherto been, not an empire,
but the project of an empire; not a gold mine, but the project of a
gold mine; a project which has cost, which continues to cost, and
which, if pursued in the same way as it has been hitherto, is likely
to cost immense expence, without being likely to bring any profit;
for the effects of the monopoly of the colony trade . . . are, to the
great body of the people, mere loss instead of profit."[17] Recent
historians have confirmed Smith's assessment. On the whole, the
colonies were probably a net drain on the British economy, since
the costs of protecting and administering them were greater than
the profits that flowed back to the mother country. Colonial trade
was profitable to the owners of colonial plantations and farms,
who were well represented in Parliament, but it was British
taxpayers and consumers who bore the costs.[18]

Yet despite these barriers and prohibitions, the most important economic fact of Smith's day was that the nation was
becoming wealthier—not just its elite, but its working people as

well. For perhaps the first time in history, acquiring a basic minimum of food, shelter, and clothing was a nearly universal expectation.[19] Contemporary observers were struck by the relative ease with which an ordinary laborer could support himself and his family.[20] Wage rates increased gradually for most of the century, most rapidly in the 1760s and 1770s, when Smith was at work on *The Wealth of Nations*.[21] Moreover, new manufacturing technologies made it possible to employ women and even children—whose labor had usually been confined in the past to the farm or the home—in remunerative jobs. As a result, total family wages rose to the point where a substantial portion of the laboring classes could reasonably hope to purchase goods that were once beyond their reach.[22] As wages rose and as the costs of production fell in agriculture and in the manufacture of basic necessities such as textiles for clothing, the standard of living rose. What had once been regarded as "luxuries" came to be seen as mere "decencies." Then "decencies" became "necessities" and the very definition of "necessities" changed. Tea, a luxury beverage of the upper classes when the century began, was the daily drink of road workers by mid-century; the per capita consumption of tea increased fifteenfold in the course of the century.[23] Objects which had long been reserved for the rich came within the reach of a large part of society. Blankets, linens, pillows, rugs, curtains, pewter, glass, china, brass, copper, and ironware flowed into English homes. Many of the fortunes, small and large, of eighteenth-century entrepreneurs were made by producing more cheaply goods with mass-market appeal: nails, buttons, buckles, candlesticks, cutlery, crockery, and saucepans.

The consumer revolution which surged forward in the third quarter of the eighteenth century was both the stimulus and the beneficiary of the industrial revolution that was then in its earliest stages. Items that had formerly been purchased once in a lifetime could now be bought several times over, not because they were less durable but because they were so much less expensive. Goods once produced laboriously at home—clothes, beer, candles, cutlery, and furniture—could now be purchased. Marketing too was transformed. Goods which had formerly been available only at weekly markets or occasional fairs or from roving pedlars could be purchased any day of the week but Sunday. It was in the eighteenth century that England became what Smith called "a nation of shopkeepers"—to the convenience of their customers. Advertisements for new products and fashions made their first appearance and soon filled the pages of the newspapers. Fueling and channeling this new ability to buy was the desire to emulate those who were one rung up on the social ladder. The middling orders sought to simulate the manners, morals, and merchandise of the gentry, the maid those of her mistress. What was new was not of course the *desire* to consume: it was the unprecedented *ability* to consume, made possible by the increase in national wealth and the declining cost of goods.[24]

Elite writers responded in consternation to the rising living standard of the laboring classes. Economic arguments were added to the moralistic denunciation of "luxury" as promoting sin and undermining civic virtue. Higher wages, it was said, would undermine the will to work, because workers would work only long enough to meet their traditional requirements and then would choose more leisure over more income.[25] There is in fact some (not very reliable) evidence that this may have happened in England in the first half of the eighteenth century, but by the second half of the century wage earners were willing to work longer and harder to earn more, perhaps because of the increasing availability of new commodities at prices they could afford.[26] Some writers also warned that high wages would boost the price of British manufactured goods, making them less competitive in international trade.[27]

Smith took the opposite position. While he was not the first to challenge the utility-of-poverty theory, in *The Wealth of Nations* he clinched the argument against it.[28] He pointed out that real wages had risen consistently during the century as a result of falling food prices and the improved quality and variety of subsistence goods. The increase in real wages—what Smith called "the liberal reward of labour"—was to be welcomed. "To complain of it is to lament the necessary effect and cause of the greatest public prosperity," he wrote.[29]

POLITICS AND ECONOMICS IN BRITAIN

By Smith's time Britain was ruled not by a king and a narrow, oligarchic aristocracy but by a large propertied class made up predominantly of landholders but increasingly of merchants as well. The greatest of these landholders were indeed aristocrats, but their influence rested on their wealth and property rather than on their rank and lineage.[30] In an age when real governmental power was centered in the House of Commons,[31] property produced the wealth which allowed powerful men to buy boroughs and appoint members of Parliament. The economic role of the state was growing rapidly, creating ever more incentive for economic interest groups to see to it that their concerns were represented in Parliament. Consequently, the links between various propertied groups and government were intimate and intense.

It was the policy of national aggrandizement in foreign affairs which led to the growth of government. The expansion of British power was motivated by the demands of its propertied classes for dominance in international commerce, and during the century preceding *The Wealth of Nations* Britain defeated its leading competitors, the Dutch and the French, for control of international trade from North America to India. By the middle of the eighteenth century, Britain had become "the supreme example in the western world of a state organized for effective war-making."[32] The domination of trade routes and the protection of overseas bases and colonies required a sizeable navy and the ability to deploy ground troops in time of war. But rather than maintaining a large permanent standing army and navy, which might have bankrupted the Treasury, the British followed a different scheme. In peacetime they kept their armed forces— and their military spending—at relatively modest levels. In time of war, the Treasury would buy soldiers and sailors on the open market. The substantial deficits occasioned by the cost of this wartime expansion were covered by large-scale borrowing. By far the largest portion of government spending (amounting to 75 or 85 percent of the annual budget) went either to current military spending or to debt service for past military spending incurred during war.[33]

The ability of the government to borrow money at low rates was an important factor in the rise of Britain's naval power and its economic growth in the eighteenth century. In earlier times, before nations had access to the capital market, wars were often won by whichever government was the last to run out of money to pay and supply its troops. The Bank of England was chartered in 1694 because the government of William III needed money to continue its war against the French in Flanders. As with most European governments of the day, England's expenditures usually exceeded its revenues. Throughout most of the seventeenth century, the government had raised its revenues in the same manner as its rival, France. In both countries, private money-lenders lent money to the Crown to cover government expenses. The government sold the right to collect some form of tax (such as excise taxes on sweet wine) to a "tax farmer," who paid a stipulated amount to the government and kept for himself whatever additional sum he could extract from the populace. Such tax farmers also acted as "financiers" and lent money to the government to cover its short-term deficits. This was an expensive practice, for the government paid the same rate of interest as did private individuals.[34]

When the English government chartered its national bank in 1694, it was following the lead of the Italians and the Dutch. The newly chartered Bank of England lent the government £1,200,000, in return for the government's promise to pay an annual sum of £100,000 in perpetuity, and to permit the Bank to receive deposits, make loans, and issue notes. Among the Bank's stockholders were investors from the City of London, the King and Queen, and Dutch investors. The Bank soon functioned as the leading purchaser of the interest-bearing bonds which covered the national debt.

Shares of the Bank of England were traded on the London Stock Exchange along with those of the great chartered trading corporations, the East India Company and the South Sea Company. Also traded on the Exchange were bonds and other financial instruments through which the government borrowed from the private money market, instruments such as Army debentures, Navy bills, and Exchequer (i.e., Treasury) bills.[35] In each case the government promised to pay the face amount at some future date and a fixed annual interest until the bill became due. The emergence of this stable, public market for servicing the national debt was the most politically significant economic innovation of the age. It enabled the British government to borrow funds at a far lower rate than could the French government, which continued to rely on moneylenders and tax farmers. Moreover, the expansion of credit and the freer circulation of capital caused interest rates in London to fall rapidly, providing a further stimulus to commerce. The advantages to English power and English commerce brought by this "financial revolution" are now widely acknowledged by historians, but at the time the public reacted to the new institutions with suspicion and even hostility.[36]

The ability of the government to borrow money at low rates depended on the confidence of investors that the government would be able to raise the requisite revenue through taxes. The government was able to do so because it had the support of the propertied classes (on whom most of the taxes fell) and because its tax-collecting bureaucracy was among the most extensive and efficient in Europe. Britain became what one historian has termed a "fiscal-military state": its war-making activities reflected the wishes of its propertied classes, which in turn accepted the burden of taxation.[37]

Indirect taxes, such as customs and excise duties, were of growing importance in state finance, however. Unlike older forms of taxes collected by amateurs, these new taxes required the services of professional revenue officers, the precursors of the government bureaucracy of the nineteenth century. By the time Smith was appointed Collector of Customs, professional revenue officers already outnumbered clergymen.

Several factors in addition to the increased taxing power of the state led economic interests to organize in order to influence Parliament. The Bubble Act of 1720 decreed that a joint-stock company could be formed only if Parliament authorized it with a specific act. Since without such legislation it was difficult and legally risky to raise the capital needed to build turnpikes and other large-scale projects, the organizers of such projects needed Parliamentary support. Landlords seeking to enclose village commons or gain legal title to "open fields" previously held in common also required the permission of Parliament.

"Projectors" in search of parliamentary authorization for joint-stock companies, improving landlords seeking enclosure, merchants and manufacturers in quest of exemptions or modifications of existing tariffs, shareholders of the great monied companies like the East India Company—all turned to Parliament for authorization and protection. As a result, by Smith's day parliamentary activity had come to revolve around endorsing, enforcing, or curbing economic interests. Lobbying by commercial interest groups had become a highly organized affair: such groups raised funds, set up committees, tried to get their representatives elected to the House of Commons, and sought to influence members of Parliament. Any attempt to alter tariffs ran up against a wall of parliamentary opposition. Far from acting in concert, however, the interest groups competed with one another, since measures that benefited one set of producers, merchants, or localities were likely to injure the interests of some other set. There was in fact no coherent mercantile policy because there was no coherent mercantile interest. Instead, warring factions competed in their efforts to influence the government to preserve existing privileges or to grant new ones.[38]

In the 1760s and 1770s, one of the most divisive issues in Parliament was legislation affecting the price of grain. The existing legislation reflected the domination of Parliament by landed interests. Heavy duties made it expensive to import grain, and under a system of "bounties" exporters of grain were paid a subsidy out of government funds. Following a series of cold, wet seasons which led to poor harvests and rising grain prices, riots broke out against farmers who were alleged to be holding back supplies and against grain merchants who were accused of hoarding grain to drive up prices. Petitions to Parliament demanding that import duties and export bounties be lowered received the strong support of urban manufacturers, who sensed that lower food prices might justify lower wages and bring higher profits. In 1772 the existing scale of bounties and duties was revised to keep more grain in Britain when prices were high. During the parliamentary debate on this law Edmund Burke suggested that the most effective long-term means of matching the supply of grain to the demands of the poorest section of society was through a market unhindered by legislation.[39] Four years later, Smith would suggest a much more comprehensive plan for raising the real standard of living of the poor, a plan which would confirm the wisdom of eliminating restrictions on the grain trade. Indeed, Smith would show that the moral values traditionally invoked to regulate economic activity could be more fully realized by easing or eliminating regulations.

CHAPTER THREE

Self-Love and Self-Command: The Intellectual Origins of Smith's Civilizing Project

To put Adam Smith's evaluation of a market society into perspective, we must recall the characteristic attitudes of the great traditions of European thought toward the pursuit of gain through trade. For these traditions comprised the backdrop of formal arguments and typical associations against which eighteenth-century intellectuals would write.[1] Even when they were no longer advanced explicitly, these arguments and associations lingered on as residues influencing popular perceptions as well as more articulate discussions of commerce.

There was no room—or very little—for commerce and the pursuit of gain in the conceptions of the good society conveyed by the classical Greek and Christian traditions, which continued to influence intellectual life through the eighteenth century and beyond. Civil law, a tradition with its origins in the Roman empire, emphasized the protection of property and served as a reservoir of more favorable attitudes toward the accumulation of wealth. The wars of religion waged during the early modern period marked a turning point in the relations between these traditions. For as people came to recognize the high cost of imposing a unified vision of the common good on everyone, they turned to the Roman tradition of civil law, which focused upon giving each his own rather than subordinating all to some vision of the common good. In search of shared standards of law and

conduct which did not depend upon revelation, they reformulated the ancient tradition of stoicism, which emphasized the
development of self-command.

INTELLECTUAL TRADITIONS

The following passage, written by Father Thomassin, a Catholic
cleric, in his *Traité de Négoce et de l'Usure* of 1697, expresses the
predominant view of commerce in the Christian tradition:

> Those who accumulate possessions without end and
> without measure, those who are constantly adding new
> fields and new houses to their heritage; those who
> hoard huge quantities of wheat in order to sell at what
> to them is the opportune moment; those who lend at
> interest to poor and rich alike, think they are doing
> nothing against reason, against equity, and finally
> against divine law, because, as they imagine they do no
> harm to anyone and indeed benefit those who would
> otherwise fall into great necessity. . . . [Yet] if no one
> acquired or possessed more than he needed for his
> maintenance and that of his family, there would be no
> destitute in the world at all. It is thus this urge to
> acquire more and more which brings so many poor
> people to penury. Can this immense greed for acquisi-
> tion be innocent, or only slightly criminal?[2]

Another passage, this one from the "Essay upon the Probable Methods of Making a People Gainers in the Balance of
Trade," published by the English political economist Charles
Davenent in 1699, expresses the position of civic republicanism,
which derived from classical Greek origins:

> Trade, without doubt, is in its nature a pernicious thing;
> it brings in that wealth which introduces luxury; it gives
> rise to fraud and avarice, and extinguishes virtue and
> simplicity of manners; it depraves a people, and makes
> way for that corruption which never fails to end in
> slavery, foreign or domestic. Lycurgus, in the most
> perfect model of government that was ever framed, did
> banish it from his commonwealth.[3]

Both the Christian and civic republican traditions were suspicious of commerce, regarding it as inimical to the pursuit of virtue. Both drew upon and modified ancient Greek thought. Aristotle regarded commerce—the "trafficking in goods" in which money was both the means and the goal of exchange—as hazardous to the moral well-being of the individual and inimical to political virtue. His ethical theory stressed moderation, the mean between the extremes of excess and defect. Unlike more moral pursuits, he maintained, the pursuit of wealth lacked any natural, intrinsic limit and so was prone to excess. Thus, in the ideal regime, a regime that was ruled by the best citizens and that rewarded virtue, those who engaged in trade would play no political role. "In the city that is most finely governed," he wrote, "the citizens should not live a vulgar or a merchant's way of life, for this sort of way of life is ignoble and contrary to virtue."[4] By Aristotle's time the Athenian populace was being fed with grain purchased abroad, but in the ideal *polis* there was no room for internal commerce or external trade.[5] Aristotle expressed the Greek view of freedom, which held that government should be shared among free men, each of whom was the head of an economically self-sufficient household. Worldly needs would be taken care of by household slaves or by independent craftsmen, neither of whom were deemed worthy of citizenship.[6]

Most classical writers saw no justification for the merchant's deriving income from buying and selling. They assumed that the material wealth of humanity was more or less fixed, which meant that the gain of some was a loss to others. Profits from trade were regarded as morally illegitimate.

The suspicion of the classical Greeks was succeeded by the intense hostility of the Church Fathers.[7] The Gospels warned repeatedly that riches were a threat to salvation. "Do not lay up for yourselves treasures on earth," Jesus is reported to have preached in his Sermon on the Mount. "For where your treasure is, there will your heart be also." "You cannot serve God and mammon," he warned (Matthew 6:19–24). And, most famously, "It is easier for a camel to go through the eye of a needle than for a rich man to enter the kingdom of God" (Mark 10:24). Paul added that "the love of money is the root of all evils" (Timothy 6:10).

Accompanying this disparagement of wealth was a denigration of merchants and the pursuit of profit. "Jesus entered the temple of God and drove out all who sold and bought in the temple, and he overturned the tables of the moneychangers and the seats of those who sold pigeons. He said to them, 'It is written, "My house shall be called a house of prayers"; but you make it a den of robbers'" (Matthew 21:12–13). Referring to these verses, the early canon *Ejiciens Dominus* declared that the profession of the merchant was scarcely ever agreeable to God.[8] That declaration was later incorporated into the *Decretum*, the great collection of canon law compiled by Gratian in the middle of the twelfth century. Gratian condemned trade and its profits absolutely, a view reflected in medieval Christian liturgy. In the prayers for the Thursday before Easter, Judas Iscariot was referred to as "that most vile of merchants."[9]

The Church Fathers preserved the classical assumption that since the material wealth of humanity was more or less fixed, the gain of some could only come at a loss to others. In the words of St. Jerome, "It is not without reason that the Gospel calls the riches of this earth 'unjust riches,' for they have no other source than the injustice of men, and no one can possess them except by the loss and ruin of others." St. Augustine was more pithy: "Si unus non perdit, alter non acquirit," he claimed. ("If one does not lose, the other does not gain.")[10]

A contradictory view held that commerce was part of a providential design to permit men to enjoy the widely scattered fruits of the earth. First suggested by the pagan teacher Libanius of Antioch in the fourth century, this view was echoed by his pupils, the early Church Fathers St. Basil and St. John Chrysostom. But it appears to have faded away thereafter.[11]

From about 1100 through 1300, the economy of Europe began to expand. Cities grew larger, and new financial instruments were invented, including joint liability, deposit and exchange banking, letters of credit, bills of exchange, and insurance. The scholastic theologians of the period developed a more nuanced and less hostile attitude toward trade, distinguishing profits arising from sales or the employment of others from the stigmatized category of usury.[12] Thomas Aquinas, the greatest of the scholastics, revived and expanded Aristotle's arguments in favor of the social utility of private property. He and his successors distinguished the evils of dishonesty and fraud in trade from commerce itself. Aquinas, John Duns Scotus (1274–1308), and San Bernardino of Siena (1380–1444) all recognized that merchants provided a service in supplying their customers with distant wares and were entitled to remuneration for that service.[13]

Yet this more positive view of trade remained highly qualified.[14] Although trade was accepted as a necessary part of society, commerce for the sake of profit was generally disdained as unworthy of those who pursued a virtuous life, and the motivations of those who engaged in trade still met with mistrust.

Divine grace made it possible for man to love God, and that love, known as charity, was to be reflected in the relationship of Christians to one another. From Augustine through Aquinas and beyond, the Christian tradition viewed pride as a fundamental human vice.[15] Humility and meekness were the prerequisites for responding to the divine grace which made salvation possible, and those virtues were difficult to reconcile with mercantile life. Echoing Aristotle, Aquinas asserted that the just distribution of goods required that people receive in proportion to their status, office, and function within the institutions of a structured community.[16] Hence he decried as covetousness the accumulation of wealth to improve one's place in the social order.[17] The pursuit of profit remained linked in Christian theology to the cardinal sins of *avaritia* (avarice) and *luxuria* (lechery).[18] Aquinas, like Aristotle, held that "trade, insofar as it aims at making profits, is most reprehensible, since the desire for gain knows no bounds but reaches into the infinite."[19]

The Catholic hostility to profit-seeking survived in the sermonizing of Dutch Calvinists and English Puritans at least through the early seventeenth century.[20] In the Christian tradition, to pursue profit was to endanger salvation; the search for gain in this world was likely to lead to the loss of the next.

Civic republicanism also looked to Aristotle for its assumptions regarding virtue and commerce. Aristotle had viewed man as an essentially political being who could achieve his fullest development only through participation in the community. The civic republican tradition assumed that political participation was the highest form of activity, and that the needs of the community took precedence over other moral demands. Only a shared vision of the public good would hold society together, it asserted.[21]

Machiavelli reformulated and reinvigorated this pre-Christian tradition. Christian thinkers had shared Aristotle's view that the polity should fulfill some shared purpose (*telos*). But whereas Aristotle saw the ultimate purpose of the polity as a this-worldly one of civic participation, Christian theologians (at least since Augustine) regarded the polity as a way-station which prepared the soul for salvation and eternal life with God.[22] Machiavelli revived the classical ideal of citizenship, stressing the need for self-sacrifice for the common good, a virtue essential in war and best promoted by preparation for war. In general, the civic republican tradition identified "virtue" with devotion to the public good, and "liberty" with participation in political life. Republican liberty was the freedom to take part in what advanced the common good, above all the protection of the commonwealth against foreign domination. Virtue and liberty so construed required that the citizen possess enough property to provide him with independence and the leisure to pursue political activity. The possession of property—by which most civic republican theorists meant land—was a prerequisite of citizenship, because by freeing men from the need to engage in productive activity it allowed them to devote themselves to the fate of the commonwealth. To devote oneself to acquiring property, however, was unworthy of the citizen. From Aristotle through the defenders of slaveholding in the antebellum South, theorists of the civic republican tradition assumed that citizenship would be limited to those who were unencumbered by the need to engage in economically productive activity.[23]

The civic republican tradition, then, stressed collective liberty in the sense of freedom from foreign domination, and individual liberty in the sense of the freedom of citizens to participate in political activity. The specter haunting those steeped in the civic republican tradition was corruption and self-interest. Corruption arose when those who should devote themselves to public virtue either chose or were forced by circumstance to pursue private, material interests. The deflection of citizens from concern for the common good led to the decay of political institutions, and ultimately to the dissolution of the commonwealth through internal disintegration or foreign conquest.

Moralists in the civic republican tradition believed that luxury led to national decline. In seventeenth and eighteenth century England, the most admired model of civic republicanism was Sparta, the ancient Greek city-state whose social institutions had fostered a way of life devoted to self-sacrifice in war. The image of Sparta (which did not quite accord with historical reality) was of a communal and military community with an economy based on the equal division of land, a political culture which eschewed commerce, and an educational system designed to foster the virtues of obedience and courage. Sparta's constitution, attributed to Lycurgus, a lawgiver of the ninth century B.C., banished luxury, moneymaking, and the use of coins.[24] Sparta stood as the mythical model of a polity in which devotion to the defense of the city was combined with equality, austerity, and hostility to commerce and money-making. In France, moralists pointed to the ancient Roman republic as the exemplar of civic republican virtues. They regarded Polybius' account of the decline of Rome as a warning against the corrupting influence of luxury. The richer the commonwealth became, the more determined would be the pursuit of material satisfactions by individuals at the expense of the common good. Material comfort, it was alleged, made men soft and effeminate: nations which pursued luxury would be defeated by the armies of more austere, virtuous, and warlike nations.

Alongside the Christian and civic republican traditions, and sometimes intertwined with them, was the tradition of civil jurisprudence. Also classical in origin, this tradition was embodied in the *Corpus iurus civilis*, a digest of civil law compiled by Justinian in the sixth century. This code reflected a Roman empire which was highly commercial, with a legal system that permitted free bargaining.[25] Rediscovered during the revival of learning in the twelfth century, it became the basis of civil law on the European continent. The tradition of civil jurisprudence stressed the rule of law and regarded the protection of property from arbitrary confiscation by government as a central freedom.[26] Its focus was not on virtue—in either the sense of Christian righteousness or civic devotion to the public good—but on specified *rights*, which were intended to protect the individual from coercion by the holders of political power and to protect his possessions from confiscation.

Whereas Christian theology and civic rhetoric were essentially *normative*, with their visions of the holy or virtuous life, civil law was concerned primarily with what belonged to each individual.[27] Within the civil law, with its concern for the rights of subjects and for their possessions, was a latent individualism, perhaps a "possessive individualism."[28] Rather than valuing the liberty to participate *in* government, it valued freedom *from* government, a freedom guaranteed by law.

The upheavals of the early modern era elevated the tradition of civil law into a significant competitor to the Christian and civic republican traditions. When the unity of western Christendom was shattered in the sixteenth century, a period of religiously motivated civil and international war set in which was to last for well over a century. The great historical fact which served as the moral backdrop for thinking about capitalism was not the factory or the mill, but war between men with rival views of salvation, men who were so sure of their own view of salvation that they were prepared to shed the blood of their fellow man in order to save his soul.[29]

It was in this setting that intellectuals began to devise a model of political life that would enable those with radically different visions of the good and holy to live together, and that would incidentally rescue intellectual humanists steeped in multiple religious and national cultures from the attacks of religious fanatics. In search for a more restricted core of politically imposed obligations upon which men of differing ultimate commitments might agree, they transformed the tradition of civil law into what became known as "natural jurisprudence."[30] Their defense of cultural pluralism is expressed in the words of the Dutch jurist and statesman, Hugo Grotius, who, in *The Rights of War and Peace* (1625), asserted that "there are several Ways of Living, some better than others, and every one may choose what he pleases of all those Sorts."[31] A central figure in the development of natural jurisprudence, Grotius abandoned the notion that the purpose of a just polity was to create a society of virtuous men. Instead, he stressed the right of individuals to use the world for their private purposes, and the duty of the state to protect that right.[32] Through the influence of Grotius and the other great theorists of natural jurisprudence, Samuel Pufendorf and John Locke, the characteristic concerns of the tradition of civil law came to overshadow those of the Christian and civic republican traditions.

Though primarily a continental tradition, civil jurisprudence played a central role in Scottish intellectual life. The culture of educated Scots had for centuries been peculiarly concerned with legal matters, ever since James I of Scotland had decreed that all barons and freeholders must have their oldest sons instructed in the law. Municipal law in Scotland, unlike that of England, was based on Roman law, and by the seventeenth century many Scottish jurists were attending Dutch universities, which taught Roman law. The study of Roman law, by the seventeenth century known as "natural jurisprudence," linked legal studies with moral philosophy and political science, and with a humanistic rationalism which put it at odds with the Calvinism of the Scottish Kirk, the dominant cultural force in Scottish life.[33] Natural jurisprudence was transformed into social science by Scottish intellectuals who attempted to modernize it by giving it an empirical basis in the observed principles of human nature and by linking it to historical development.[34]

Another powerful influence on European thought during the seventeenth and eighteenth centuries was neo-stoicism. Justus Lipsius, a Flemish humanist instrumental in recovering the thought of the Roman Stoics and applying it to contemporary affairs, preserved their emphasis on the development of moderation and self-control. But whereas the Romans had often associated self-discipline with an attitude of passivity in the face of an ultimately benign though inscrutable universe, neo-stoicism valued self-discipline for its active worldly effects.[35]

The influence of neo-stoicism proceeded in two directions. In one direction it helped provide absolutism with intellectual legitimation. It encouraged the state to take the lead in disciplining society by developing an army and a bureaucracy which would inculcate the values of work and discipline. This influence was most apparent in Prussia.[36] In the other direction, neo-stoicism was more influential in the Netherlands, where moderation and self-control were emphasized by the theologian Dirck Coornhert and the jurist Hugo Grotius, who took from the Stoics the notion of the natural sociability of man.[37] These Dutch influences were in turn conveyed to eighteenth-century Scotland by Scottish scholars schooled in the Dutch universities. The struggle between the two models of national development forms one of the great plots of modern history, stretching beyond the early modern era and beyond Europe itself. At issue was whether the neo-stoic virtues of self-discipline should be inculcated through government edicts specifying individual behavior and backed by the power of an absolutist state, or whether man's natural sociability could become the basis of self-discipline without extensive state supervision.

From Humanism to Social Science

In 1687, Isaac Newton had demonstrated with the law of universal gravitation the ability of natural science to reveal universal laws of remarkable explanatory power. Adam Smith shared the hope of most Enlightenment thinkers of creating a science that would illuminate the social world as Newton had begun to illuminate the natural world. The science of man, like the science of nature, was regarded as part of "natural theology," which was devoted to uncovering God's creation through the use of methods more reliable than revelation.[38] Like David Hume, Smith believed that since theological and metaphysical questions were not subject to definitive answers, the philosopher should devote himself to more worldly matters.

> The administration of the great system of the universe
> . . . the care of the universal happiness of all rational
> and sensible beings, is the business of God and not of
> man. To man is allotted a much humbler department,
> but one much more suitable to the weakness of his
> powers, and to the narrowness of his comprehension;
> the care of his own happiness, of that of his family, his
> friends, his country. . . . The most sublime speculation
> of the contemplative philosopher can scarce compen-
> sate the neglect of the smallest active duty.[39]

As a moral philosopher, Smith was concerned about the nature of moral excellence. But like many other Enlightenment intellectuals, he tried to begin by describing man as he really *is*. His conception of man was not as an intrinsically good creature corrupted by society, nor as an irredeemably evil creature except for the grace of God. His project was to take man as he is and to make him more like what he is capable of becoming, not by exerting government power and not primarily by preaching, but by discovering the institutions that make men tolerably decent and may make them more so.

Though Smith wrote brilliantly about the psychological basis of scientific investigation in an early essay on the history of astronomy, and though he discussed the psychology of theoretical exposition in his lectures on rhetoric, he never explicitly formulated his own method of investigating social life. But its elements are clear enough. It called for identifying widely shared psychological propensities—such as the propensity to seek the attention and approval of others—and for attempting to explain the regularities of human action in terms of those propensities. Moreover, it entailed an inductive attempt to discover regularities in social life through observation and comparison, for which history provided much of the raw data. Finally, it called for an examination of the ways in which human propensities were shaped and molded into particular character types by historically changing social, political, cultural, and economic structures.

In conducting this investigation, Smith drew on more than a century of scholarly reflection on the role of the passions. A widespread though diffuse intellectual trend had sought to analyze the passions in order to channel them into morally beneficial directions through social institutions. This tradition of reflection, which we will call "the institutional direction of the passions" (or, in the interest of conciseness, "psychological institutionalism"), formed a bridge between the recovery of classical philosophy by the humanists and the rise of modern social science.

The tradition of psychological institutionalism grew out of a project undertaken by Erasmus and other sixteenth-century humanists to civilize society through the systematic cultivation of control over human emotions and impulses.[40] The original version of this project drew on the ancient Stoics and focused on the pedagogic development of virtue and reason in order to control and inhibit the passions.[41] By the mid-seventeenth century, following a century of civil and religious war, the feasibility of the project was widely questioned by writers who spoke of the futility of trying to subordinate the passions to reason or to virtue. Their skepticism was voiced by the French moralist La Rochefoucauld, who began his *Maxims* with the statement, "Our virtues are most often but disguised vices."

The humanist project took an unexpected turn with the rise of neo-Augustinianism, an effort by both Catholic and Protestant theologians to return to Augustine's doctrine of natural depravity, from which man could find salvation only through God's grace. Paradoxically, the roots of psychological institutionalism, which blossomed in the French and Scottish Enlightenments of the eighteenth century and was largely optimistic about the prospects for human betterment, lay in this pessimistic view of man. The Catholic version of neo-Augustianism was espoused mainly by the Jansenists, who stressed that as a consequence of Original Sin all real virtue (such as charity) depended not on man's natural self but on the possibility of transcending his natural self through grace. From this assumption, neo-Augustinian moralists deduced the doctrine of "moral rigorism," the belief that no action undertaken on the basis of natural dispositions is truly virtuous. Yet these moralists could not deny that men often *appeared* to act virtuously, and that society itself subsisted in no small part on acts of *apparent virtue.* So they set about unmasking acts of apparent virtue by revealing the hidden, disreputable motives that lay behind them. In their attempt to buttress that contention, they moved from moral rigorism to a heightened social and psychological sensitivity.[42]

Foremost among the unworthy motives they identified was self-love. True charity had its origin in the love of God, the Jansenists maintained, but some acknowledged that self-love was frequently the motive behind actions which gave the appearance of charity. In the introduction to his influential treatise on civil law (published in 1689 and in English translation in 1722), the Jansenist Jean Domat declared that self-love was "the incomprehensible remedy" which God had created to preserve society despite man's fallen state.

> The fall of man not having freed him from his wants, and having on the contrary multiplied them, it has also augmented the necessity of labor and commerce, and of ties; for no man being sufficient of himself to procure the necessaries and conveniences of life, the diversity of wants engages men in an infinite number of ties, without which they could not live.
>
> This state of mankind induces those who are governed only by a principle of self-love, to subject themselves to labor, to commerce, and to ties which their wants render necessary. And that they may reap advantage from them, and preserve in them both their honor and their interest, they observe in all those intercourses, integrity, fidelity, sincerity: so that self-love accommodates itself to everything, that it may reap advantage from all things. And it knows so well how to adapt its different steps to all its views, that it complies with all duties, and even counterfeits all virtues. . . .

We see, then, in self-love, that this principle of all the evils is, in the present state of society, a cause from whence it derives an infinite number of good effects, which in their nature being true and real goods, ought to have a better principle. And thus we may consider this venom of society as a remedy which God makes use of for supporting it, seeing that although it produces in those persons whom it animates only corrupted fruits yet it imparts all these advantages to society.[43]

A similar treatment of the paradox that benevolent actions may result from unvirtuous passions appears in "On Charity and Self-Love," an essay written in the late seventeenth century by another Jansenist, Pierre Nicole:

Although nothing is more opposed to charity which relates everything to God than self-love which revolves entirely around the self, yet there is nothing more similar to the effects of charity than those of self-love. So closely does it follow the same paths that one could hardly do better in marking those to which charity should lead us, than to discover those actually taken by enlightened self-love.

Nicole admitted that the sin of cupidity lay behind much of commerce but pointed out that it was through "this commerce that all the needs are in some fashion fulfilled, without charity playing any role whatsoever." Consequently "in states where it has no place because the true Religion is banished from them, one lives in no less peace, security, and comfort, than if one were in a republic of Saints." Only God's grace can bring ultimate salvation, but enlightened self-love can create this-worldly "human decency" (l'honnêteté humain).[44]

The search for knowledge of the passionate, egoistic origins of virtuous behavior spread to French, British, and Dutch analysts who sought to improve man's worldly behavior through harnessing this knowledge rather than warning of its inadequacy as a means to salvation.[45]

Most of the passions, it was claimed, could be reduced to one or another form of pride, the non-rational and deep-seated desire to be admired.[46] Pride was the basis of man's desire for approbation and his fear of disapprobation, and it was to these motives that much of his behavior could be traced. Yet, it was also argued, the desire for approbation—though not in itself virtuous—could produce the next best thing to virtue, and could serve much the same purpose, by prompting men to conform to socially approved standards of behavior. This view was in keeping with the growing sense among seventeenth-century moralists that, though human reason could discover the nature of the good and the virtuous, *reason on its own was not sufficiently strong to control human behavior, which was motivated by the passions.* Depending on the leanings of the analyst, this claim could be given either a cynical or a religious interpretation.

The religious interpretation was expressed by Jacques Abbadie, a French Protestant who was forced into exile in England, where his works were widely read in translation. As a theologian of the "Arminian" school, Abbadie disputed the claims of Jansenism and Calvinism that salvation was reserved for the predestined few and that it depended on irresistible grace over which men had no control. He held that the passions are implanted by God in all men. In his *The Art of Self-Knowledge* of 1692, he maintained that God implanted the desire for praise to counteract the fact that men are motivated by the passions rather than by reason:

> It pleased the wisdom of the Creator to give us, for judge of our actions, not only our reason, which allows itself to be corrupted by pleasure, but also the reason of other men, which is not so easily seduced, . . . [since] they are not so partial to us as we are to ourselves. It is this desire of being esteemed that makes us courteous and considerate, obliging and decent, makes us wish for decorum and gentle manners in social relations.

The urge to be well regarded by our fellow man, according to Abbadie, is a providential tool for the perfection of society.[47]

Bernard Mandeville, in his widely read, widely decried, and highly influential *Fable of the Bees* of 1714, made a similar point in a more cynical tone, conveyed by his subtitle, "Private Vices, Public Benefits." Mandeville's ironic, indeed scandalous suggestion was that civilization would come to a halt if men and women actually acted according to the moral standards they professed.

He held that attempts to promote virtuous behavior were futile and even counterproductive, and suggested that public good was the product of egoistic motives. He suggested a more efficacious approach to the promotion of virtuous behavior: "Whoever would civilize Men, and establish them into a Body Politick must be thoroughly acquainted with all the Passions and Appetites, Strength and Weaknesses of their Frame, and understand how to turn their greatest Frailties to the Advantage of the Publick."[48] The task of the legislator, Mandeville argued, was not to repress man's egoistic impulses but to provide institutional channels through which they could be asserted for the ultimate benefit of the public. A properly contrived social framework would perform that function more or less automatically, without the direct intervention of the legislator.[49]

By the time Smith addressed himself to questions of moral philosophy and public policy, he could draw on over a century of reflection on the possible social benefits of the passions and how they might be channeled through social institutions.[50] Mandeville had suggested that "The Power and Sagacity as well as Labour and Care of the Politician in civilizing the Society, has been no where more conspicuous, than in the happy Contrivance of playing our Passions against one another."[51] Writing in 1746, the *philosophe* Vauvenargues agreed: "If it is true that one cannot eliminate vice, the science of those who govern consists in making it contribute to the common good."[52] Josiah Tucker, an Anglican divine who was the foremost British advocate of free trade before Adam Smith, echoed the sentiment a decade later: "The main point to be aimed at, is neither to extinguish nor enfeeble self-love, but to give it such a direction, that it may promote the public interest by pursuing its own."[53]

Two broad strategies had been suggested for harnessing man's natural passions through institutional means to serve the common good. The first was to preserve or create institutions which would pit otherwise malicious motives against one another. This strategy of counterbalancing competing egoistic motives is evident in Smith's treatment of market competition in *The Wealth of Nations*. According to the second strategy, some modes of self-love, if channeled through social institutions, can be made to contribute to morally desirable conduct.[54] It was this strategy which lay behind Smith's *Theory of Moral Sentiments*, in which he showed subtly and convincingly that social institutions could channel self-love into decent and sometimes virtuous behavior.

From "Luxury" to "Universal Opulence"

As we will see, though Smith was skeptical of the wisdom and motives of legislators, he regarded it as the duty of the philosopher to encourage them to pursue the common interest. The role of the science of politics was to furnish maxims and criteria for judging the fitness of laws and institutions for the guidance of lawmakers. For over half a century before the publication of *The Wealth of Nations,* it had been recognized that modern political science must ascribe a central role to economic policy. At the end of the seventeenth century, Charles Davenant, while praising the ancient Spartan virtues, judged them inadequate in the modern world. For given the military competition between nations and the rising costs of warfare, an expanding economy was a necessary condition of national defense and national glory. Thus the nation's governors must be carefully schooled in the laws of commerce.[55] A book by the influential Dutch statesman Pieter de la Court, *The True Interest and Political Maxims, of the Republic of Holland,* first published in Dutch in 1662 and in English in 1746, linked civic republican themes to free trade by arguing that Holland's ability to defend itself depended on free-trade policies. (Smith owned a copy of the book.) De la Court cautioned against attempts "to curb or restrain our citizens and natives, any more than strangers, from their natural liberty of seeking their livelihoods in their native country, by select and authoriz'd companies and guilds."[56] In an essay of 1741, David Hume noted that trade and commerce had been ignored by writers on politics from the time of the ancients through Machiavelli: only the recent "great opulence, grandeur, and military achievements" of Holland and England had made commerce a central concern of ministers of state and of "speculative reasoners."[57] What Smith called "the science of a legislator" must therefore concern itself with political economy as well as with such traditional topics as law and national defense.

The design and the rhetoric of Smith's works reflect his intention not only to *instruct* legislators by enunciating general principles but to *motivate* them to pursue the common interest.

The most effective means of communicating general principles, he believed, was through the presentation of a well-articulated system of thought, and the most effective means of motivating legislators to take action was through the use of the rhetorical strategy of exaggeration.

Smith lectured for years on rhetoric, the ancient art by which those in public life sought to influence their fellows. The rhetorical mode that dominated *The Wealth of Nations* was didactic discourse, which sought to instruct through the strength of the argument presented. On matters of great urgency, Smith resorted to rhetorical discourse, which, he explained to his students, "endeavours by all means to persuade us, and for this purpose it magnifies all the arguments on the one side, and diminishes or conceals those that might be brought on the side contrary to that which it is designed that we should favour."[58]

Smith was well aware of the aesthetic elements of argument. He described to his students the pleasure derived from conceiving "the phenomena which we reckoned the most unaccountable, all deduced from some principle (commonly, a well-known one) and all united in one chain."[59] In a passage in *The Theory of Moral Sentiments* dealing with the relationship between our perceptions of beauty and of utility, Smith argued that people are often motivated to promote the public welfare by the aesthetic satisfaction they derive from contemplating the workings of a coherent system:

> When a patriot exerts himself for the improvement of any part of the public police [policy], his conduct does not always arise from pure sympathy with the happiness of those who are to reap the benefit of it. . . . [We may] be eager to promote the happiness of our fellow-creatures, rather from a view to perfect and improve a certain beautiful and orderly system, than from any immediate sense or feeling of what they either suffer or enjoy. . . . If you would implant public virtue in the breast of him who seems heedless of the interest of his country, it will often be to no purpose to tell him, what superior advantages the subjects of a well-governed state enjoy; that they are better lodged, that they are better clothed, that they are better fed. These considerations will commonly make no great impression. You

> will be more likely to persuade, if you describe the great
> system of public police [policy] which procures these
> advantages, if you explain the connexions and depen-
> dencies of its several parts, their mutual subordination
> to one another, and their general subserviency to the
> happiness of the society; if you show how this system
> might be introduced into his own country, what it is
> that hinders it from taking place there at present, how
> those obstructions might be removed, and all the
> several wheels of the machine of government be made
> to move with more harmony and smoothness, without
> grating upon one another, or mutually retarding one
> another's motions. It is scarce possible that a man
> should listen to a discourse of this kind, and not feel
> himself animated to some degree of public spirit. . . .
> Upon this account political disquisitions, if just, and
> reasonable, and practicable, are of all the works of
> speculation the most useful. They serve . . . to animate
> the public passions of men, and rouse them to seek out
> the means of promoting the happiness of the society.[60]

This passage, published in 1759, reveals Smith's rationale for *The Wealth of Nations.*

It was by no means taken for granted in the eighteenth century that legislators should seek to improve the lot of common people. That material well-being was morally desirable was disputable; that it ought to extend beyond the elite was almost subversive. Moralists often treated material prosperity under the rubric "luxury."[61] This was not a morally neutral word; it was a term of opprobrium, connoting not comfort but excess, the possession of non-necessities. As goods regarded as "luxuries" came to play a central role in international trade, debate about the moral ramifications of the burgeoning capitalist economy centered on the concept of "luxury."

Both the civic republican and the Christian traditions con-demned the pursuit of material wealth, though for different reasons. According to the civic tradition, the pursuit of wealth corrupted the virtuous citizen, who should sacrifice his private concerns for those of the commonwealth, defending it in war and seeking glory. According to the Christian tradition, the pursuit of wealth distracted people from the pursuit of salvation. Augustine in *The City of God* had cautioned that prosperity begets luxury and then avarice. Subsequent Christian moralists warned that luxury binds the flesh to the world and to the devil.[62] The Christian tradition often described virtue in ascetic terms: abstinence, privation, and humility were the qualities to be cultivated. It saw wealth as a temptation to sin, diverting people from the imitation of Christ and his virtues of abstinence, humility, and love. Although the two traditions were essentially incompatible, moralists amalgamated them in their condemnation of luxury as an invitation to both sin and corruption.[63]

During the early Enlightenment intellectuals in England and France sought to legitimate the pursuit of material prosperity as a worthy political goal. The moral rehabilitation of luxury evident in Mandeville's *Fable of the Bees* of 1714, was taken up by Jean-François Melon in his *Political Essay on Commerce* of 1734, by Voltaire in the poems "The Worldling" and "Defence of the Worldling" of the mid-1730s, and by Hume in his essay "On Luxury," first published in 1742. These writers rejected both a political culture based on martial virtues and warfare and a religious culture based on piety. They endorsed instead a culture that valued sociability and that looked for guidance to philosophy, science, literature, and the arts. By the mid-eighteenth century this new congeries of values had come to be known in England as "refinement" and in France as "civilization."[64] In *An Enquiry Concerning the Principles of Morals* of 1751, David Hume scorned what he called "the monkish virtues" of ascetic self-denial as contributing nothing to social cooperation. And Voltaire, in his *Philosophical Dictionary*, declared, "We live in society; therefore nothing is truly good for us that isn't good for society."[65]

Voltaire attempted to reverse the terms of the Christian and civic traditions by making poverty seem sordid. "Abundance is the mother of the arts," he wrote in "The Worldling."[66] Henceforth the argument that material prosperity was the prerequisite for civilization would be repeated by virtually every proponent of economic growth. Hume changed the title of one of his essays from "Of Luxury" to "Of Refinement in the Arts." Because modern urban society was richer than older societies, it was argued, it could be more civilized. Voltaire defended luxury against its detractors by pointing out that many of what his contemporaries considered basic necessities had once seemed quite extraordinary items. "If one went back to a time when men wore no shirts, if someone had told them that they ought to wear light, fine, shirts of the most elegant material, and white as snow, they would have cried, 'What luxury! What effeminacy! Such magnificence is scarcely suitable for kings! You want to corrupt our morals and destroy the state!' "[67] He developed the notion further in his *Philosophical Dictionary:*

> When scissors, which surely do not date from remote antiquity, were invented, what wasn't said against the first people who clipped their nails, and who cut some of the hair that fell down over their noses? They were doubtless called dandies and squanderers, who bought an expensive instrument of vanity to mar the work of the Creator.[68]

Voltaire also restated several of the *economic* arguments for luxury that Mandeville and Melon had developed at length. Material consumption by the rich—traditionally denounced as a vice—creates a demand for the labor of the poor, who profit from the creation of greater wealth. Spending by the rich thus enables the poor to become somewhat richer, Voltaire argued, pointing to the growing taste for luxury goods among the lower rungs of society in England and France.[69] Moreover, it was the desire for luxuries which had led to transoceanic commerce, a development which increasingly linked the inhabitants of the earth.[70] By improving the lot of the poor, by enriching the state, and by fostering international contacts, argued the defenders of material well-being, the desire for luxuries could lead to public benefits.

While Adam Smith would adopt many of these arguments, he substituted "universal opulence" for "luxury" to emphasize that commercial society was to be judged according to the benefits it bestowed on society in general rather than according to the benefits it bestowed on the elite. He shared Voltaire's view that it was better to be rich than to be poor, but he measured national wealth by the extent to which subjects were decently lodged, clothed, and fed. In a lecture of 1762 which foreshadowed *The Wealth of Nations* he said, "the wealth of a state consists in the cheapness of provision and all other necessaries and conveniences of life."[71] His main concern was to promote the availability of goods which made a decent life possible for all.

Smith's intellectual starting-point was the tradition of natural jurisprudence then dominant in the Scottish universities. The governing assumption of the seventeenth-century proponents of that tradition was that society *could not be* and *need not be* governed by some shared faith or purpose which dictated the proper distribution of property. Thinkers in this tradition sought instead to discover some universal or near-universal core of rules which would allow men of differing convictions to live together in relative peace. They distinguished between justice and virtue. Justice was the minimum of rules which we have a right to demand that others observe, which are enforceable by law, and without which society cannot survive. Justice could only guarantee "to each his own." It could not and should not try to create a virtuous society. It should protect property and exchange, but it should not try to provide "distributive justice" by allocating possessions according to some universally shared criteria, since there are no such criteria.[72] Smith's friend David Hume made this point in his *Enquiry Concerning the Principles of Morals* (1751):

> We shall suppose that a creature possessed of reason but unacquainted with human nature deliberates with himself what rules of justice or property would best promote public interest, and establish peace and security among mankind. His most obvious thought would be to assign the largest possessions to the most extensive virtue, and give every one the power of doing good, proportioned to his inclination [to do good]. In a perfect theocracy, where a being, infinitely intelligent, governs by particular volitions, this rule would certainly have place, and might serve to the wisest purposes. But were mankind to execute such a law, so great is the uncertainty of merit, both from its natural obscurity and from the self-conceit of the individual, that no determinate rule of conduct would ever result from it; and the total dissolution of society must be the immediate consequence.[73]

The definition of justice as the protection of property and exchange seemed to ignore one of the central issues of the tradition of natural law, namely the claims of the poor on the rich in times of extreme dearth when famine threatened the very lives of the poor. The argument most often invoked to justify government regulation of the market was the moral and political need to provide grain to the poor. Pufendorf and Locke adumbrated a solution to the problem of reconciling property rights with the needs of the poor: they sought to eliminate absolute, life-threatening scarcity through economic growth. Smith would try to show that the moral values invoked to regulate economic activity could be more fully realized by a less regulated market.[74] Indeed he went further, making the well-being of the poor the touchstone of his policy recommendations. To those who decried the spread of "luxury," Smith argued that the aim of economic policy should be to increase the real purchasing power of the working majority by keeping the price of commodities low and wages high.[75]

The traditional view, which saw the wealth of the rich as purchased at the expense of the poor, assumed a stagnant economy, so that for one man to gain wealth another must lose. This was the view expressed by Father Thomassin in his *Traité de Négoce et de l'Usure*. It was also the view expressed by Jean-Jacques Rousseau at the conclusion of his *Discourse on Inequality* (1755) when he wrote that in commercial society "the privileged few . . . gorge themselves with superfluities, while the starving multitude lack the bare necessities of life."

Smith took up Rousseau's challenge and showed that it was possible to direct the passions through the marketplace in a way that would lead to "universal opulence" and help make life more decent for all.

PART II

DESIGNING THE DECENT SOCIETY

CHAPTER FOUR

The Market: From Self-Love to Universal Opulence

POLITICAL ECONOMY, "CONSIDERED AS A branch of the science of a statesman or legislator" had two objectives, Smith wrote: to provide plentiful revenue and subsistence to the people, and to provide the state with sufficient revenue to cover the cost of public services—services which, as we shall see, Smith wanted to expand.[1] The first four books of *The Wealth of Nations* are devoted to the first objective, the last book to the second.

In formulating his science of the legislator, Smith took from the civic republican tradition the need for the virtuous man to concern himself with the common good. But he found other aspects of that tradition unsatisfactory. As Smith's student Dugald Stewart noted, Smith rejected the emphasis of the ancient philosophers on forms of government and the means by which they could perpetuate themselves and extend the "glory of the state." "It was reserved for modern times," Stewart wrote, "to investigate those universal principles of justice and of expediency, which ought, under every form of government, to regulate the social order; and of which the object is, to make as equitable a distribution as possible, among all the different members of a community, of the advantages arising from the political union."[2]

Here was a critique of the civic tradition on several counts. It had been wrong to attempt to regulate the entire social order by

virtue, rather than by "justice" and "expediency." In its focus on
the virtue of participation in government, it had confined its
concern to a narrow elite, neglecting the effect of the political
system on "all the different members of the community." In its
focus on forms of government, it had neglected the needs of most
of the members of the community. Smith's own concern was to
ensure that the political process contribute to the well-being of
the nation as a whole.[3]

This well-being extended beyond the political elite. And it
was defined not primarily in terms of political participation but in
terms of improving the quality of life in the private realms of the
family and of production and consumption. Smith's emphasis
reflected a moral elevation of the importance of "ordinary life,"
as well as the transformation of the Christian virtue of charity
into the Enlightenment virtue of practical benevolence. Thus
while Smith continued the civic republican concern for the
common good, his definition of that good placed greater weight
on the moral and material well-being of men and women in their
day-to-day lives.

It was to this end that he devoted his remarkable powers of
observation and analysis. Take, for example, his musings on
whether wheat, oatmeal, or potatoes was the most nutritional
food:

> In some parts of Lancashire it is pretended, I have been
> told, that bread of oatmeal is a heartier food for
> labouring people than wheaten bread, and I have
> frequently heard the same doctrine held in Scotland. I
> am, however, somewhat doubtful of the truth of it. The
> common people in Scotland, who are fed with oatmeal,
> are in general neither so strong, nor so handsome as the
> same rank of people in England, who are fed with
> wheaten bread. They neither work so well nor look so
> well; and as there is not the same difference between
> the people of fashion in the two countries, experience
> would seem to show, that the food of the common
> people of Scotland is not so suitable to the human
> constitution as that of their neighbours of the same
> rank in England. But it seems to be otherwise with
> potatoes. The chairmen [men who carry chairs], por-
> ters, and coalheavers in London, and those unfortunate

women who live by prostitution, the strongest men and the most beautiful women perhaps in the British dominions, are said to be, the greater part of them, from the lowest rank of the people in Ireland, who are generally fed with this root. No food can afford a more decisive proof of its nourishing quality, or of its being peculiarly suitable to the health of the human constitution.[4]

The "absent-mindedness" of which Smith has sometimes been accused may have been the result of his habit of storing and analyzing the data at hand in search of larger patterns of human existence.

People are more likely to accept a new theory, Smith believed, when they are confronted with facts that cause them to wonder and that disturb their mental tranquillity. When the new theory suggests a way of resolving the puzzling facts, tranquillity is restored and people experience a sense of aesthetic satisfaction which makes them more receptive to the theory. The original draft of *The Wealth of Nations* opened with such a puzzle, and the final version is an extended commentary on it.

Smith began with a paradigmatic paradox first suggested by John Locke and subsequently taken up by a host of eighteenth-century writers on political economy. In his *Essay Concerning Civil Government* of 1689, Locke had written that in America, where there were few people and an abundance of natural resources, "A King of a large and fruitful Territory there feeds, lodges, and is clad worse than a day Labourer in England."[5] Locke had used this paradox to support his belief that labor was the real source of economic value, and that government, by assuring the individual of the fruits of his labor, advanced the prosperity of society.

Smith worked and reworked Locke's paradox, changing its characters, refining its formulations, elaborating its examples, and altering its implications. Here is a version from the early 1760s:

The unassisted labour of a solitary individual, it is evident, is altogether unable to provide for him such food, such cloaths, and such lodging, as not only the luxury of the great but as the natural appetites of the

meanest peasant are, in every civilized society, supposed to require. Observe in what manner a common
day labourer in Britain or in Holland is accommodated
with all these, and you will be sensible that his luxury is
much superior to that of many an Indian prince, the
absolute master of the lives and liberties of a thousand
naked savages. . . . Compared, indeed, with the yet
more extravagant luxury of the great, his accommodation must no doubt appear extremely simple and easy;
and yet, perhaps, it may be true that the accommodation of a European prince does not so much exceed that
of an industrious and frugal peasant, as the accommodation of this last exceeds that of the chief of a savage
nation in North America.[6]

The point is still that a man of low status in a rich society might
be better off materially than the wealthiest and most powerful
man in a poor society. Here is the final version in *The Wealth of
Nations:*

Observe the accommodation of the most common
artificer or day labourer in a civilized and thriving
country. . . . Compared, indeed, with the more extravagant luxury of the great, his accommodation must no
doubt appear extremely simple and easy; and yet it may
be true, perhaps, that the accommodation of an European prince does not always so much exceed that of an
industrious and frugal peasant, as the accommodation
of the latter exceeds that of many an African king, the
absolute master of the lives and liberties of ten thousand naked savages.

The solution to the riddle, Smith suggests, lies in the fact
that even the common laborer in a wealthy country like Britain or
Holland has thousands of people working to provide his material
needs or "accommodations":

The number of people of whose industry a part, though
but a small part, has been employed in procuring him
this accommodation, exceeds all computation. The
woollen coat, for example, which covers the day labourer, as coarse and rough as it may appear, is the
produce of the joint labour of a great multitude of

workmen. The shepherd, the sorter of the wool, the wool-comber or carder, the dyer, the scribbler, the spinner, the weaver, the fuller, the dresser, with many others, must all join their different arts in order to complete even this homely production. How many merchants and carriers, besides, must have been employed in transporting the materials from some of those workmen to others who often live in a very distant part of the country! How much commerce and navigation in particular, how many ship-builders, sailors, sail-makers, rope-makers, must have been employed in order to bring together the different drugs made use of by the dyer, which often come from the remotest corners of the world!. . . . If we examine, I say, all these things, and consider what a variety of labour is employed about each of them, we shall be sensible that without the assistance and co-operation of many thousands, the very meanest person in a civilized country could not be provided, even according to, what we very falsely imagine, the easy and simple manner in which he is commonly accommodated.[7]

Several lessons are implicit in Smith's example. First, in a rich country people tend to underestimate the advantages they derive from the economic system because they compare themselves to the wealthy and powerful in their own society instead of asking "How did we get this rich?" Second, power does not guarantee material comfort, while inequality of income and power may be quite compatible with material comfort. True, there were inequalities of wealth and power in contemporary Britain, but despite those inequalities the common laborer enjoyed an impressive degree of material well-being.

Here was an application of Smith's suggestion in his lectures on rhetoric regarding the persuasive effect of demonstrating that "the phenomena that we reckoned most unaccountable" could be "deduced from some principle (commonly a well-known one) and united in one chain." The material advantages enjoyed by the lowly laborer compared to the powerful chief was the unaccountable phenomenon which The Wealth of Nations set out to explain. The first principle in Smith's systematic chain of explanation was the uniquely human propensity to exchange goods in search of self-interest. The second principle was the division of labor. Smith tried to demonstrate to legislators that with properly structured institutions these two common and well-known principles could be used to channel the nation toward "universal opulence."

The division of labor, Smith maintained, was the great mechanism which increased human productivity and made universal opulence a possibility.[8] He described a pin-making factory in which an assembly line of ten workers, each specialized in a particular function, could produce 48,000 pins per day. Working individually, he reckoned, they might each produce 20 pins a day at most, for a total of 200 pins. In this case the division of labor would increase output by 240 times. In using a pin factory to make his point (an example often cited in the eighteenth century), Smith was not extolling the advantages of the factory system in which the entire production process took place under one roof. The factory was merely the setting in which the division of labor was most *visible*, and Smith was using it to represent a larger process in which the division of labor was more widespread. Still, Smith believed that the gains in productivity from the division of labor applied to farming as well, though the seasonal nature of agriculture made it likely that the greatest gains would come in industrial production.[9]

The first link in Smith's chain of explanation was that *the division of labor produces greater wealth, which makes possible "universal opulence."*

The division of labor, he explains, makes workers more proficient in performing specialized tasks. It saves time that would otherwise be lost in switching from one task to another. And it favors "the invention of a great number of machines which facilitate and abridge labour, and enable one man to do the work of many."[10] As an example of such machines he cites the "fire-engine," known to us as the steam engine, the most important prime mover of the industrial revolution.

The division of labor, Smith continues, applies not only to physical labor but to mental labor as well. There too specialization leads to greater dexterity, a saving of time, and an expansion of knowledge.[11] An important role in the advance of technology is played by "those who are called philosophers or men of speculation, whose trade it is, not to do any thing, but to observe every thing, and who, upon that account, are often capable of combining together the powers of the most distant and dissimilar objects." By "philosophers" Smith seems to have meant both social scientists and natural scientists.[12] This insight may have arisen from Smith's own experience. James Watt achieved a decisive breakthrough in improving the Newcomen steam engine while serving as "Mathematical Instrument Maker" to the University of Glasgow in the years when Smith was teaching there. And Watt made that breakthrough by applying the discoveries of Joseph Black, a professor of "philosophical chemistry" at Glasgow with whom Watt worked closely and who eventually became Smith's literary executor.[13]

The second link in Smith's chain of explanation was that *the division of labor leads to specialization, expertise, dexterity, and machinery, thereby producing greater wealth.*

The division of labor is made possible by the ability of men to *exchange* their labor or the products of their labor, Smith explains. And the greater the range of exchange, the more extensive the division of labor becomes. The systematic exchange of labor and the products of labor are what Smith termed collectively as "the market." Thus the greater the size of the market, the greater the possible gains in production.[14] In short, *market exchange fosters a greater division of labor, which leads in turn to specialization, expertise, dexterity, and improved machinery, thereby creating greater wealth.*

What sets the market in motion and keeps it going is the propensity to satisfy self-interest through exchange. This propensity, Smith points out, is uniquely human and is the ultimate reason why humans are the only species that can progress over time. Smith links that propensity to the wealth of nations: *self-interest leads to market exchange, which fosters the division of labor, which leads in turn to specialization, expertise, dexterity, and improved machinery and ultimately creates greater wealth.*

"The propensity to truck, barter, and exchange one thing for another," to bargain, to contract—all are synonyms. They all say, "Give me that which I want, and you shall have this which you want."[15] Smith believed that, though this propensity was innate in human nature, its influence on economic relations had come about slowly, gradually, unintentionally, and as yet imperfectly. As market exchange became the basis of economic life, society reached the stage where "Every man . . . lives by exchanging, or becomes in some measure a merchant, and the society itself grows to be what is properly a commercial society."[16]

If we recall the stigmatization of the merchant in the traditions of civic republicanism and Christian thought, we can appreciate the re-evaluation of values which Smith proclaimed. Civic republicanism had regarded the occupation of buying and selling as grounds for disqualifying one from citizenship. The Christian tradition had viewed the pursuit of self-interest as a passion and hence part of man's animal nature. For Smith, it was the pursuit of self-interest through the exchange of the fruits of labor that set man off from the animals and gave him his specifically human dignity. "Nobody ever saw a dog make a fair and deliberate exchange of one bone for another with another dog," Smith remarked. "Nobody ever saw one animal by its gestures and natural cries signify to another, this is mine, that is yours; I am willing to give this for that."

This capacity for exchange is what makes human beings uniquely capable of progress, Smith believed. It "encourages every man to apply himself to a particular occupation, and to cultivate and bring to perfection whatever talent or genius he may possess for that particular species of business." Without the opportunity for exchange, men have no way of recognizing or making use of their natural talents. It is the possibility of exchange which makes the *differences* between individuals *useful* to one another and which distinguishes human beings from animals:

> Each animal is still obligated to support and defend itself, separately and independently, and derives no sort of advantage from that variety of talents with which nature has distinguished its fellows. Among men, on the contrary, the most dissimilar geniuses are of use to one another; the different produces of their respective talents, by the general disposition to truck, barter, and exchange, being brought, as it were, into a common stock, where every man may purchase whatever part of the produce of other men's talents he has occasion for.[17]

Man is by his very nature dependent on others, and in a "civilized," "commercial" society he depends on a vast array of anonymous others to produce most of what he needs. "In civilized society he stands at all times in need of the cooperation of assistance of great multitudes, while his whole life is scarce sufficient to gain the friendship of a few persons." He is unlikely to satisfy his needs, however, if he relies solely on the altruism of the people upon whom he depends:

> It is not from the benevolence of the butcher, the brewer, or the baker, that we expect our dinner, but from their regard to their own interest. We address ourselves, not to their humanity but to their self-love, and never talk to them of our own necessities but of their advantages. Nobody but a beggar chuses to depend chiefly upon the benevolence of his fellow-citizens.[18]

In this passage, perhaps the most quoted in *The Wealth of Nations,* Smith is not denigrating benevolence or the altruistic concern for others ("humanity"). Nor is he antipathetic toward friendship—on the contrary, for him friendship implied an intimacy that was rarely achieved in human relations. His claim is that an economic system cannot be based on benevolence, which is a limited sentiment not easily extended to those with whom one is not familiar.[19] An economic system with an extensive division of labor, in which millions of individuals depend upon the production of others to meet their needs, cannot be founded upon sentiments which are morally admirable but necessarily limited.

For Smith, it was morally degrading not to *be* benevolent, but to choose to depend on the benevolence of other people with whom one has no close emotional connection. Without the possibility of appealing to the self-interest of others, one is forced to elicit their good will in morally demeaning ways:

> When an animal wants to obtain something either of a man or of another animal, it has no other means of persuasion but to gain the favour of those whose services it requires. A puppy fawns upon its dam, and a spaniel endeavours by a thousand attractions to engage the attention of its master who is at dinner, when it wants to be fed by him. Man sometimes uses the same arts with his brethren, and when he has no other means of engaging them to act according to his inclina-

tions, endeavours by every servile and fawning attention to obtain their good will.[20]

To the extent that every man becomes a merchant rather than a
slave, retainer, serf, or servant, the relations of direct dependence
upon a master which foster servile behavior are replaced by
relations of greater personal freedom. The ability of legally free
individuals to appeal to the self-interest of others through
exchange creates greater social interdependence along with
personal independence from the will of an individual master.
The fact that commercial society provides a greater degree of
freedom than earlier social systems was for Smith an important
moral argument in its behalf.

    The ability of commercial society to provide greater wealth
was also an important moral argument in its behalf. Smith
advanced this argument implicity, with his many references to
the morally demeaning nature of life in a poor society. On the
very first page of *The Wealth of Nations* he contrasts commercial
nations with primitive nations that lack commerce and the
division of labor and that "are so miserably poor, that, from mere
want, they are frequently reduced, or, at least, think themselves
reduced, to the necessity sometimes of directly destroying, and
sometimes of abandoning their infants, their old people, and
those afflicted with lingering diseases, to perish with hunger, or
to be devoured by wild beasts."[21] Elsewhere, Smith cites the
legitimization of infanticide as evidence of the moral degradation
caused by the lack of material means.[22] While wealth may
corrupt, Smith implied, absolute poverty corrupts absolutely.

    Self-interest, then, channeled by the market, leads to the
division of labor and makes possible a society of universal
opulence. This process, wrote Smith, "is not originally the effect
of any human wisdom, which foresees and intends that general
opulence to which it gives occasion."[23] Here Smith is introducing
another leitmotiv of *The Wealth of Nations*, the notion of the
unanticipated consequences of purposive social action.[24] Time
and again Smith points out that many of the most influential
institutional improvements in human history were unplanned.
He also insists that the *effects* of deliberate actions are often quite
different from the *intentions* of the actors. The self-interested
behavior of the individual that leads to a socially beneficent
outcome, for example, is both unplanned and unintended.

This emphasis on the divergence between intention and effect constituted another implicit criticism of the Christian and civic republican traditions, and it continues to make moralists queasy. Both traditions had stressed that benevolent intentions were responsible for the creation and maintainance of a polity. By divorcing effects from intentions, Smith made it unnecessary to transform self-interested economic behavior by means of preaching and propaganda, strategies which had not worked in the past and were unlikely to work in the future.

Yet on another level Smith preserved the concern of civic republicanism for the common good. Those who could be motivated to promote the public interest are in need of that "superior reason and understanding, by which we are capable of discerning the remote consequences of all our actions, and of foreseeing the advantage or detriment which is likely to result from them."[25] The legislators for whom Smith wrote *The Wealth of Nations* were politicians who could be motivated to promote the public interest. By observing the science of the legislator which Smith provided, they would improve their ability to foresee the consequences, both positive and negative, of their legislative actions.

The keystone of *The Wealth of Nations* was Smith's exposition of how the market should be structured to maximize universal opulence, Smith tried to show that without restrictions on labor, prices, and supply, the natural human propensity of self-interest would bring about the sale of commodities at the lowest price possible at any given level of economic development. Since it was in the interests of everyone in their capacity as consumers to be able to buy the most with their money, this arrangement would redound to the benefit of all. None of those who took part in the production of those commodities—the laborers who did the physical work, the landlords who leased the land, the "undertakers" who invested the capital—provided their services out of a concern for the welfare of consumers. All acted out of self-interest, motivated by the desire to better their own condition.[26] But by pursuing their self-interest through the market, they ended up benefiting the consumer. Smith's social science could explain the logic of the mechanism which transformed the quest for self-interest into universal opulence. Once the logic of the mechanism was understood, it could be put in place by legislators now in a position to anticipate the beneficent social effect of the market mechanism, fueled though it might be by self-interest.

At each level of economic development, Smith reasoned, the price of commodities reflected the average cost of labor, the average level of profits, and the average rent of land prevailing in the economy. Smith called this the "natural price"—the lowest price at which a given commodity could be produced without loss and hence the lowest price at which it could be made available for any extended period of time.[27] As is so often the case in Smith's writings, the term "natural" is not descriptive but normative: it refers to the situation that *ought* to exist. The natural price is the price that is most beneficial to consumers—and in a commercial society, all men and women were consumers, whatever else they might be.

The *actual* price at which a commodity is sold Smith called the "market price." That price is determined by the relationship between the quantity *offered* by producers and the amount *desired* by those with the ability to pay for it—that is, between the supply and the effectual demand for the commodity. At any given time, the market price may be higher or lower than the natural price. But when the market price falls *below* the natural price, self-interest will motivate the producers to move their capital or labor to some other activity that will bring them a larger profit or a higher wage. That will cause a decrease in the supply of the original commodity, and, so long as effectual demand remains the same, the market price will rise. When the market price of a commodity rises *above* the natural price, producers engaged in the production of other commodities will be motivated to move their resources into the production of this one, in pursuit of a higher-than-average profit or wage. In time that will cause an increase in the supply of the original commodity, and, so long as effectual demand remains the same, the market price will fall. The market price acts as a signal that keeps producers informed of the relationship between supply and demand.[28]

If the market could be structured to operate along the lines of Smith's model, the market price of all commodities would continually gravitate toward their natural price—that is, the lowest price at which they could be produced given the availability of labor, land, and capital. The market would then be providing the greatest possible benefit to all consumers.[29] Moreover, by directing capital to the source of highest profit, the market would be channeling resources toward the production of those commodities for which demand exceeded supply. The market, therefore, is the most efficient mechanism for using self-interest to augment the wealth of the nation and for promoting the well-being of the populace.

Smith was aware that most members of society are not landlords or merchants but "servants, laborers, and workmen of different kinds" whose income consists of the wages they earn. Their welfare is the prime concern of economic policy, as Smith conceived it. "No society can surely be flourishing and happy, of which the far greater part of the members are poor and miserable," he wrote. "It is but equity, besides, that they who feed, clothe and lodge the whole body of the people, should have such a share of the produce of their own labour as to be themselves tolerably well fed, clothed and lodged."[30] The chief economic concern of the legislator, in Smith's view, should be the purchasing power of wages, since purchasing power is the measure of material well-being.

In the absence of reliable statistics, Smith was obliged to draw on impressionistic evidence about commodity prices to demonstrate that real wages had risen considerably in England since the last century and had recently begun to rise in Scotland as well.[31] That was in good part because the market-induced efficiences of the division of labor had driven down the price of manufactured goods.[32] The market process had thus benefited the laborer, though he might be unaware of the link between the long-term increase in national wealth and his own interests. "His condition leaves him no time to receive the necessary information, and his education and habits are commonly such as to render him unfit to judge even though he was fully informed," Smith observed.[33] As national wealth continued to grow, real wages might continue to rise,[34] Smith maintained, as long as the demand for labor grew faster than the supply of laborers. But for that to happen employers would have to earn a profit high enough to provide the capital they needed to hire more employees and to invest in new technologies to make labor more productive.[35] The task of the legislator concerned with the general interest, therefore, was to maintain society in this "progressive state," in which the accumulation of capital continued to promote the growth of wealth.[36]

The most influential members of Parliament were landowners, who tended to hold to the traditional view that low wages were a necessary spur to workers and who regarded urban wage rates as irrelevant to their own economic interests. For Smith to succeed in getting his policy recommendations enacted, he would have to convince the landowners that their interests were not at odds with those of wage earners. In *The Wealth of Nations* Smith attempted to demonstrate that the declining price of manufactured goods also benefited landowners, a fact, he noted, they had often failed to recognize. He explained that as the wealth of society increases and as more capital is invested in making land more productive, the real rent of land also rises. Moreover, as the price of manufactured goods declines, the purchasing power of the income derived from the sale of agricultural products increases. If they really understood their interests, Smith wrote, landowners would recognize that their own interests were "strictly and inseparably connected with the general interest of the society. Whatever either promotes or obstructs the one, necessarily promotes or obstructs the other."[37] Smith thus demonstrated that they would serve their own interests by implementing the free-market structures that would benefit the mass of consumers. As an intellectual concerned to promote the general good, Smith appealed not only to the benevolence of the holders of political power but to their self-interest as well.

CHAPTER FIVE

The Legislator and the Merchant

FOR THE MARKET TO FUNCTION most effectively, every man must be able to sell his labor, invest his capital, or rent his land in a manner that best promoted his self-interest. The market would produce the best possible outcome for consumers under conditions of what Smith called "free competition" or "perfect liberty." But, as Smith showed, much of European society and government was still structured to impede the free movement of labor, capital, land, and goods. Though these barriers to free competition were due in part to antiquated institutions, they were due primarily to the effects of self-interest. Smith did not believe that there was a natural harmony of interests in society. He believed that the public interest would be best served if every man channeled his self-interest *through the market*. But he realized that from the point of view of the individual producer or group of producers it was most beneficial to *circumvent the competitive market* with its attendant risks, and use all available means to prevent competition, in order to obtain the highest possible price for their wares. In short, the pursuit of self-interest meant short-circuiting the market.

Smith took certain aspects of the contemporary market order and generalized them into a model of how the economy might function under conditions of free competition. The task, as he saw it, was to leave the individual producer no alternative but to pursue his economic interests in a way that would advance the public good.[1] It was the force of market competition, he insisted, that led producers, merchants, and laborers to "an unremitting exertion of vigilance and attention."[2] The Sisyphian task of the legislator dedicated to the public interest was to prevent them from bypassing the market and to keep it humming at full speed despite the efforts of organized economic interests to protect themselves from market competition.[3]

Both workers and employers, for example, tried to circumvent the labor market—workers in an effort to raise their wages beyond what free competition would allow, employers in an effort to keep wages low. Each group tried to organize to pursue its self-interest, but under existing conditions the contest was unequal. The law prohibited workers from combining in order to raise wages, but it did not prohibit employers from combining in order to keep wages low. And the employers had more political influence than the workers. "Whenever the legislature attempts to regulate the differences between masters and their workmen, its counsellors are always the masters," Smith noted. This differential in political power was due in part to the fact that most of the "masters" had the vote while few of the "workmen" did.[4] The employers had other advantages: in case of a strike they could hold out longer than the workers, who depended on wages for their daily sustenance. Because employers were fewer in number, it was easier for them to connive without calling attention to themselves.[5] The best corrective, Smith thought, was to maintain a "progressive state" in which the increasing demand for labor would make it difficult for employers to hold wages down.

The most effective means of circumventing the competition of the market was through legal restrictions on the freedom to sell commodities or labor. Legal monopolies gave an individual or a trading company the sole right to sell certain products. That right gave the monopolists the power to keep supply below demand, thus keeping the market price above the natural price.[6] Similarly, guilds and related organizations had a legal right to limit the supply of labor in specific occupations, thus keeping wages above the competitive level. They also had the right to limit output, thus keeping the profits of producers above the natural price.[7]

The task of the legislator concerned to increase the wealth of the nation by promoting free trade was made difficult by the fact that "the private interests of many individuals irresistibly oppose it."[8]

The Wealth of Nations is a compendium of the attempts of individuals and groups to promote their own interests at the expense of the public interest. They had varying success. The citizens of the towns, Smith noted, contrived to keep up the price of urban-made goods, at the expense of the inhabitants of the countryside.[10] "People of the same trade seldom meet together, even for merriment and diversion, but the conversation ends in a conspiracy against the publick, or in some contrivance to raise prices," he observed.[11] Domestic manufacturers and merchants profited from the imposition of high duties on imported goods, at the expense of landlords, farmers, and laborers.

The merchants and manufacturers had the greatest success in persuading legislators that their particular interests were identical to the general interest. Few in number, concentrated in large cities, and with ample funds at their disposal, their "sophistry and clamour" was more effective than that of rival groups.[12] Their determination to limit competition was at odds with the public interest, which demanded maximum competition.[13] The merchants had been long accustomed to limiting competition in domestic trade, and recently they had learned to limit competition in international trade as well.[14] They lobbied for the absolute prohibition of certain imports and for the imposition of heavy duties on others.[15] Smith showed that such restrictions were inimical to the public interest. Not only did they raise the price of consumer goods, but they channeled capital and labor away from industries where real demand was greatest into industries where legal restrictions kept profits artificially high.[16]

Most of Book IV of *The Wealth of Nations* is devoted to an attack on the international trade policies then dominant in Europe. Smith referred to those policies as "the mercantile system" (a phrase first used by the Count de Mirabeau in 1763). He used this polemical term to encapsulate his critique of existing policies, which, incidentally, were less coherent and less of a system than Smith made out. They were based on the view that international economic relations constitute a "zero-sum game" in which one nation's gain must be another's loss. International trade was perceived as a tacit struggle against rival nations, a view congenial to the civic republican conception. That struggle often led to outright warfare and violence as nations tried to secure trade privileges, trade routes, and colonies.[17] Smith endeavored to redirect international relations along more cosmopolitan and pacific lines. The rising prosperity and proficiency of other nations, he argued, "are all proper objects of national emulation, not of national prejudice or envy. . . . Mankind are benefited, human nature is ennobled by them. In such improvements each nation ought, not only to endeavour itself to excel, but from the love of mankind, to promote, instead of obstructing the excellence of its neighbours."[18] The function of the intellectual was to counteract national prejudices and the idea that national welfare necessarily came at the expense of other nations — a premise that inevitably led to international conflict.

Smith coined the term "mercantile system" to describe the dominant economic doctrine because he believed that it reflected both the *interests* and the *mentality* of merchants and manufacturers, whose quest for monopoly had been extended to a view of international commerce in which each nation's interest "consisted in beggaring all their neighbours." "Each nation has been made to look with an invidious eye upon the prosperity of all the nations with which it trades, and to consider their gain as its own loss. Commerce, which ought naturally to be, among nations, as among individuals, a bond of union and friendship, has become the most fertile source of discord and animosity," Smith lamented. That view reflected "the impertinent jealousy of merchants and manufacturers."

Smith argued for recognition that "a nation that would enrich itself by foreign trade is certainly most likely to do so when its neighbours are all rich, industrious, and commercial nations."[19] Free trade would transform international commerce from a source of war into the basis of peaceful relations and mutual benefit. The market would serve both national and international interests once legislators were guided by the science of political economy developed by Smith and other intellectuals devoted to the common weal, rather than by the partisan advice of merchants.

In regard to colonies, Smith believed that they were good for the nation insofar as they extended the market and made possible a more productive division of labor. But to grant British merchants a monopoly over trade with the colonies benefited merchants at the expense of the nation, an expense which was aggravated by the military costs of maintaining the monopolies.[20]

The conduct of international commerce by privileged companies with a monopoly on trade with foreign regions was even more destructive. The growth of European trade with China, India, Japan, and the East Indies, Smith reasoned, ought to have been of great benefit to European consumers. But the benefit was limited because the trade was conducted by monopolies such as the East India Companies of Holland, England, and France.[21] Such companies, which established military control over foreign regions in order to carry on their trade monopoly, were detrimental to the home country and ruinous to the subject nations, Smith maintained. Domestic consumers were at the mercy of suppliers unrestrained by competition and free to limit supply in order to keep prices high.

If mercantilist policies had kept Europe from gaining the full potential benefits of transcontinental trade, their effect on non-European peoples had been far more negative, Smith showed. The British East India Company, for example, restricted the export of Indian goods to Europe and had wastefully destroyed any excess supply in order to limit production and keep prices high. The problem, Smith believed, lay not in the corruption of particular officers but in the very structure of the situation in which a profit-making company exercised sovereign power. A true sovereign, Smith argued, would recognize that his revenue depended on the wealth of the nation, which he would try to promote through freer trade. Were the East India Company to act as a sovereign, it would seek to import European goods into India as cheaply as possible and to pay as much as possible for Indian goods exported to Europe. But since the Company was made up of merchants seeking to use their monopoly on Indian trade to maximize their profits, the company's interest lay in charging as much as possible for the European goods it sold to the people of India, while paying the Indians as little as possible for Indian-made goods exported to Europe. Here was a case in which the structures of institutional power channeled private self-interest against the public interest of the Indian populace. "As sovereigns," Smith wrote of the officers of the East India Company, "their interest is exactly the same with that of the country which they govern. As merchants their interest is directly opposite to that interest." The effect of Company rule, he concluded, was to stunt the growth of the Indian economy.[22] In the East and West Indies the effect of centuries of European colonialism on the native population had been similarly detrimental.

And yet, Smith predicted, the long-term consequences were likely to be beneficent for these non-European regions as well. The superiority of European power allowed the Europeans to commit injustices with impunity. But as a result of commerce initiated by the Europeans, Smith conjectured, the colonial peoples might ultimately acquire the knowledge and technology which would allow them to build up their own instruments of power. Thus "the inhabitants of all the different quarters of the world may arrive at that equality of courage and force which, by inspiring mutual fear, can alone overawe the injustice of independent nations into some sort of respect for the rights of one another."[23] This somber but optimistic vision of the future is yet another example of Smith's cosmopolitan but pragmatic moralism.

Smith's overarching aim in *The Wealth of Nations* was to refine existing institutions in such a way that man's selfish passions would be harnessed to the general good, leaving producers no alternative but to pursue their economic interests in a manner conducive to the welfare of society.[24] In the second edition of the book, Smith summed up his argument:

> Consumption is the sole end and purpose of all production; and the interest of the producer ought to be attended to, only so far as it may be necessary for promoting that of the consumer. The maxim is so perfectly self-evident, that it would be absurd to attempt to prove it. But in the mercantile system, the interest of the consumer is almost constantly sacrificed to that of the producer; and it seems to consider production, and not consumption, as the ultimate end and object of all industry and commerce.[25]

Maxims described as "self-evident," however, often require extensive explanation before the reader comes to accept the author's premises. And it is the paramount interest of the consumer that occupies Smith in the first four books of *The Wealth of Nations*.

It was to man's other roles and other needs that Smith devoted his lectures on jurisprudence, most of *The Theory of Moral Sentiments,* and the final book of *The Wealth of Nations.* In those works, whether he was analyzing markets, religious sects, or universities, he pointed out the unintended consequences of individual action and of government policy.

CHAPTER SIX

Social Science as the Anticipation of the Unanticipated

MODERN SOCIAL SCIENCE WAS BORN during the Enlightenment out of attempts to develop systematic knowledge on an empirical basis. Its goal was to improve man's earthly lot by reforming his institutions. The favored political strategy of moderate enlightenment thinkers was for intellectuals versed in the new science to advise legislators either directly, or indirectly through the organs of "public opinion," such as the newspapers and books which were reaching an ever-wider audience.[1] In Scotland the theme of the unintended and unanticipated consequences of social action became a focus of Enlightenment thought and indeed marked the transition from moral philosophy to social science.

The theme of the unanticipated consequences of social action had been highlighted by Bernard Mandeville in his *Fable of the Bees* and was more faintly evident in Montesquieu's *Spirit of the Laws*, both of which had a strong influence on Scottish intellectuals. In the third book of *A Treatise of Human Nature*, which had impressed Smith when he was still a student, Hume had emphasized that moral actions flowed less from rational conviction than from the passions. The idea of the unanticipated consequences of human action suggested an alternative to the venerable but ineffective strategy of trying to convince men rationally to be more virtuous. For Smith, as for Hume, the most effective way to make men more moral was to channel their passions through institutions to produce beneficent outcomes.[2] Understanding the gap between intentions and results was therefore central to Smith's civilizing project.

This theme pervades *The Wealth of Nations*. Indeed the book is almost an encyclopedia of the effects of unintended consequences in human affairs, a phenomenon (or an analytic perspective) which fascinated Smith. In calling attention to the gap between intentions and results, Smith was not saying that deliberate attempts to better the human condition are futile. In *The Theory of Moral Sentiments*, he had praised that "superior reason and understanding, by which we are capable of discerning the remote consequences of all our actions, and of foreseeing the advantage or detriment which is likely to result from them."[3] Smith's science of a legislator was intended to improve the legislator's ability to anticipate the previously unanticipated consequences of his actions. The reform of human institutions demanded an awareness that the *consequences* of actions are often different from the *intentions* which motivate the actors.

This was no recipe for the revolutionary replacement of existing institutions by new ones designed by the social scientist. On the contrary, Smith believed that many existing institutions were already highly functional, that others could be made to function better, and that yet others provided models for innovation. Many of the institutions which provided the greatest benefit to society had developed in an unplanned fashion, without deliberate human foresight.[4] But Smith did not intend this as a call to quietism: the purpose of social science was to aid the legislator in preserving, reforming, or designing institutions that channel the motives of men toward socially beneficent ends.

The theme of the unanticipated consequences of human action appears with many variations in *The Wealth of Nations*, and in *The Theory of Moral Sentiments*. Smith demonstrates that the consequences are sometimes positive and sometimes negative, or positive from the perspective of society but negative from the perspective of the actor. In a well-known passage he speaks of unintended consequences which are beneficial for both the actor and for society at large:

> Every individual is continually exerting himself to find out the most advantageous employment for whatever capital he can command. It is his own advantage,

indeed, and not that of the society, which he has in
view. But the study of his own advantage naturally, or
rather necessarily leads him to prefer that employment
which is the most advantageous to the society.[5]

Smith notes that most people prefer to invest in domestic
industries so that they can supervise their investments, and in
industries that return the highest profits. He concludes:

As every individual, therefore, endeavours as much as
he can both to employ his capital in the support of
domestic industry, and so to direct that industry that its
produce may be of the greatest value; every individual
necessarily labours to render the annual revenue of the
society as great as he can. He generally, indeed, neither
intends to promote the publick interest, nor knows how
much he is promoting it. By preferring the support of
domestick to that of foreign industry, he intends only
his own security; and by directing that industry in such
a manner as its produce may be of the greatest value, he
intends only his own gain, and he is in this, as in many
other cases, led by an invisible hand to promote an end
which was no part of his intention. Nor is it always the
worse for the society that it was no part of it. By
pursuing his own interest he frequently promotes that
of the society more effectually than when he really
intends to promote it.[6]

The image of the "invisible hand" in this passage (the only
place in the *Wealth of Nations* in which it appears) is a metaphor
for the socially positive unintended consequences of the market,
which through the profit motive and the price mechanism
channels self-interest into collective benefits. There is nothing
mysterious about the "invisible hand,"—at least once its functions have been made manifest by social science. And yet the
notion that the market bestows positive benefits on society seems
contrary to common sense. The consumer knows that the
merchant charges him more for a commodity than he paid for it.
Moreover, after trying to purchase it as cheaply as possible, the
merchant is trying to sell it for all he can get! The consumer finds
it hard to understand how he can benefit from a system made up
of such merchants. The legislator knows that merchants, manu-

facturers, and laborers are typically self-seeking, at least in their economic roles. Smith's claim that the outcome of all this self-seeking is a contribution to the common good is at first puzzling. In the very next paragraph Smith explains that the superiority of the market in allocating resources is based upon its superiority in coordinating information.

> What is the species of domestick industry which his capital can employ, and of which the produce is likely to be of the greatest value, every individual, it is evident, can, in his local situation, judge much better than any statesman or lawgiver can do for him. The statesman who should attempt to direct private people in what manner they ought to employ their capitals, would not only load himself with a most unnecessary attention, but assume an authority which could safely be trusted, not only to no single person, but to no council or senate whatever, and which would nowhere be so dangerous as in the hands of a man who had folly and presumption enough to fancy himself fit to exercise it.[7]

The legislator, then, cannot be aware of the myriad interactions that occur in a sophisticated economy. Nor can anyone else. But the individual, motivated by the desire for economic gain, is quite capable of assembling information about the supply and demand for a single commodity in a particular market. Thus the legislator should usually refrain from trying to control prices and production. That should be left to the "invisible hand" of the market. As we shall see, however, creating the preconditions for the market and compensating for its negative effects will sometimes require the visible hand of government.

Smith believed that people are better judges of local economic opportunities than distant legislators are, and he began from the premise that people are motivated to engage in economic activity by self-interest. But he did not believe that people correctly perceive their true self-interest, much less that they act "rationally." In The Wealth of Nations, Smith explored at length the propensity to overestimate the likelihood of gain and to underestimate the likelihood of loss in a variety of activities, from soldiering to smuggling.[8]

In the Theory of Moral Sentiments, he used "the invisible

hand" as a metaphor for unintended outcomes which are *negative* from the perspective of the actor but *positive* from the perspective of society.

Smith's contention that the pursuit of wealth often leads to negative outcomes from the perspective of the actor is a key element in Smith's civilizing project. His parable of the Ambitious Poor Man's Son is his most striking statement of that view:

> The poor man's son, whom heaven in its anger has visited with ambition, when he begins to look around him, admires the condition of the rich. He finds the cottage of his father too small for his accommodation, and fancies he should be lodged more at ease in a palace. . . . He feels himself naturally indolent, and willing to serve himself with his own hands as little as possible; and judges that a numerous retinue of servants would save him from a great deal of trouble. He thinks if he had attained all these, he would sit still contentedly, and be quiet, enjoying himself in the thought of the happiness and tranquillity of his situation. He is enchanted with the distant idea of this felicity. It appears in his fancy like the life of some superior rank of beings, and, in order to arrive at it, he devotes himself for ever to the pursuit of wealth and greatness.

To attain his goals of ease and social esteem, the Ambitious Poor Man's Son drives his body to fatigue and his mind to exhaustion. To outdo his rivals, he "serves those he hates, and is obsequious to those whom he despises."

> Through the whole of his life he pursues the idea of a certain artificial and elegant repose which he may never arrive at, for which he sacrifices a real tranquillity that is at all time in his power, and which, if in the extremity of old age he should at last attain to it, he will find to be in no respect preferable to that humble security and contentment which he had abandoned for it. It is then, in the last dregs of life, his body wasted with toil and diseases, his mind galled and ruffled by the memory of a thousand injuries and disappointments which he imagines he has met with from the injustice of his enemies, or from the perfidy and

ingratitude of his friends, that he begins at last to find that wealth and greatness are mere trinkets of frivolous utility. . . . Power and riches appear then to be, what they are, enormous and operose [elaborate] machines contrived to produce a few trifling conveniencies to the body, consisting of springs the most nice and delicate, which must be kept in order with the most anxious attention, and which in spite of all our care are ready every moment to burst into pieces, and to crush in their ruins their unfortunate possessor. . . . [They] leave him always as much, and sometimes more exposed than before, to anxiety, to fear, and to sorrow; to diseases, to danger, and to death.[9]

Were this the end of the parable, its lesson would be a stoic reiteration of the worthlessness of worldly wealth and power. But Smith gives the parable a gloss which reveals his debt to the tradition of the institutional direction of the passions. Although the real benefits of power and riches may not be commensurate with what we imagine them to be, he asserts that "it is well that nature imposes upon us in this manner."

It is this deception which rouses and keeps in continual motion the industry of mankind. It is this which first prompted them to cultivate the ground, to build houses, to found cities and commonwealths, and to invent and improve all the sciences and arts, which ennoble and embellish human life; which have entirely changed the whole face of the globe, have turned the rude forests of nature into agreeable and fertile plains, and made the trackless and barren ocean a new fund of subsistence, and the great high road of communication to the different nations of the earth. The earth by these labors of mankind has been obliged to redouble her natural fertility, and to maintain a greater multitude of inhabitants.

The pursuit of ease, riches, and social status, though motivated by a misapprehension of their real worth, redounds to the benefit of society by making possible the accumulation of the wealth and productive power that generates the higher satisfactions of culture. It provides an incentive for nations to come to know one another, thus contributing to cosmopolitanism. And it enables more people to live decently, to acquire the "necessaries of life" which allow them to escape the moral degradation of absolute poverty.

Immediately following this parable Smith introduces the image of the invisible hand to demonstrate the unanticipated and unintended consequences of individual action which benefit both the individual and society at large. Here Smith repeats what was by 1759 already an old argument among proponents of economic growth, namely that the pursuit of luxury by the wealthy provides support for the non-wealthy whom the rich hire and pay.[10] "The proud and unfeeling landlord . . . without a thought for the wants of his brethren," Smith wrote, is prompted to increase the productivity of the land and to employ others to work it by his desire to consume. Though his desire to consume is far out of proportion to his ability to consume, it makes it possible for his employees to live decently.

> The rich only select from the heap what is most precious and agreeable. They consume little more than the poor, and in spite of their natural selfishness and rapacity, though they mean only their own convenien- cy, though the sole end which they propose from the labours of all the thousands whom they employ be the gratification of their own vain and insatiable desires, they divide with the poor the produce of all their improvements. They are led *by an invisible hand* to make nearly the same distribution of the necessaries of life, which would have been made had the earth been divided into portions among all its inhabitants, and thus without intending it, without knowing it, advance the interest of the society, and afford the means to the multiplication of the species.[11]

Smith offers an example of the unanticipated consequences of human intentions in his discussion in *The Theory of Moral Sentiments* of the emotional sources and political function of deference. Moralists, Smith notes, "warn us against the fascina- tion of greatness"—a sentiment so strong that the rich and powerful are often more respected than the wise and virtuous. Here too an invisible hand is at work which transforms seeming- ly unvirtuous propensities into benefits for society. For, says Smith, "Nature has wisely judged that the distinction of ranks, the peace and order of society, would rest more securely upon the plain and palpable difference of birth and fortune, than upon the invisible and often uncertain difference of wisdom and virtue. The undistinguishing eyes of the great mob of mankind can well enough perceive the former: it is with difficulty that the nice discernment of the wise and virtuous can sometimes distinguish the latter."[12] Here, as he so often does in his social theory, Smith chooses to accept the moral imperfections of the bulk of mankind and to tailor institutions to suit those imperfections.

As we will see when we turn to Smith's account of the historical origins of commercial society, Smith returns, in *The Wealth of Nations*, to the "proud and unfeeling landlord." There he argues that the most beneficial qualities of modern commercial society came about as the unintended result of historical processes in which the key actors mistook their own interests. Even the malign policies of European governments have sometimes had a happy outcome:

> The English puritans, restrained at home, fled for freedom to America, and established there the four governments of New England; the English Catholics, treated with much greater injustice, established that of Maryland; the Quakers, that of Pennsylvania. The Portuguese Jews, persecuted by the inquisition, stript of their fortunes, and banished to Brazil, introduced, by their example, some sort of order and industry among the transported felons and strumpets, by whom that colony was originally peopled, and taught them the culture of the sugar-cane. Upon all these different occasions it was, not the wisdom and policy, but the disorder and injustice of the European governments which peopled and cultivated America.[13]

But Smith also provides numerous instances of unanticipated outcomes which are *negative* from the perspective of both the actor and society at large. He demonstrates, for example, that the quality of education at Oxford and Cambridge was eroded by the unanticipated effects of philanthropy. The philanthropists who endowed professorships had intended to improve the quality of learning. The assured income from these endowments, however, had freed the professors from the need to depend on student fees and had destroyed their incentive to devote themselves to teaching.[14] Similarly, pious donors motivated to strengthen the established church had provided endowments for the higher education of its ministers. Yet that education had rendered the ministers unsuited to deal with the common man and had prepared the ground for evangelical sects.[15] In economic policy, Smith showed that time and again legislation intended to boost the production or the price of some commodity through government bounties had failed, or had produced the opposite of the intended effect, because its framers had misjudged its impact.[16] Government attempts to promote domestic agriculture by placing restrictions on manufacture and foreign trade had actually retarded agricultural growth, Smith argued, because by decreasing the availability of goods which landlords and farmers wanted to buy, they destroyed the incentives to boost agricultural production.[17] Legislation intended to increase government revenues by raising customs duties could have the opposite of the intended effect, Smith showed, by discouraging consumption of the commodity in question or by encouraging smuggling. He suggested to legislators that government might have a better chance of increasing revenue if it lowered such duties.[18] By familiarizing themselves with past errors, legislators would be more likely to achieve the desired effect.

Smith's emphasis on unintended consequences gives portions of The Wealth of Nations an ironic tone. Moralists find that tone disturbing, because it seems to call into question the relationship between motivation and result. Those who pride themselves on their worldliness, however, find it congenial. This tone may have been intentional. It may have been part of Smith's rhetorical strategy for appealing to men of affairs who in the cynical world of Georgian politics were unlikely to heed overtly moral appeals. "Men are fond of paradoxes," he noted, "and of appearing to understand what surpasses the comprehension of ordinary people."[19] By calling attention to the unanticipated consequences of human actions, Smith reveals hidden connections in the social world and gives his readers a sense of intellectual superiority and perspicacity which makes his analysis all the more acceptable.[20]

CHAPTER SEVEN

Commercial Humanism: Smith's Civilizing Project

THE RHETORIC OF *The Wealth of Nations* and of *The Theory of Moral Sentiments* reflect their different purposes and intended audiences. *The Wealth of Nations* was written primarily to persuade legislators to pursue economic policies which would lead to "universal opulence." Its rhetoric expresses Smith's desire to provide a methodical account of political economy which by the force of its arguments and the beauty of its system would motivate legislators to pursue the public good and would provide them with information and models of how to do so on matters relating to wealth.

The Theory of Moral Sentiments was written primarily for intellectuals concerned with the philosophical definition of virtue and the social scientific explanation of how men become moral. But its intended audience was much larger, encompassing the educated public. Its purpose was to make its readers more virtuous by examining the nature of morality and by reinforcing their sense that acting virtuously is worthwhile. In part, the book is a guide to manners and rules of conduct, a genre stretching back to the humanists.[1] In part it is a treatise on social psychology, offering a phenomenological description of how conscience is formed. In part it is a disquisition on moral philosophy, scrutinizing the nature and comparative value of the virtues. And in part it is a sermon, subtly reminding the reader that virtue is the ultimate source of happiness, satisfaction, and peace of mind. *The Theory of Moral Sentiments*, then, is not only a work of analysis addressed to the intellect: it is also a hortatory book filled with illustrations of moral quandaries and characters, intended to evoke the passions of its readers in the interest of making them more moral.[2] To modern readers, the author might seem a composite of John Rawls, Jean Piaget, and Miss Manners.

Adam Smith began as a moral philosopher, was led by his moral concerns to political economy, and after completing his great work of political economy returned to moral philosophy. While every man in commercial society "becomes in some measure a merchant," Smith never imagined that he acts as a merchant in every part of his life, and even when he is acting as a merchant it is for reasons which are ultimately non-economic. He viewed human beings as eminently social creatures whose pleasures, conception of self-interest, and conscience originate in their reactions to the sentiments and opinions of others. The conceptual common denominator of Smith's major works is the analysis of the ways in which social institutions tend to pattern character through their appeal to human passions. Some of the passions he viewed as dangerous and in need of suppression, some as benign, and some as capable of leading beyond the benign to the morally noble. Depending upon the incentives provided by institutions, passions can be channeled to morally laudable and socially beneficent forms of behavior.

For Smith, the promotion of national wealth through the market was a goal worthy of the attention of moral philosophers because of its place in his larger moral vision—his civilizing project. Smith valued the market most because it promoted the development of cooperative modes of behavior and because it made men more self-controlled and more likely to subordinate their asocial passions to the needs of others. In short, it made men more "respectable" in their behavior.

Both the civic republican and the Christian traditions had assumed that society was held together by some shared vision and purpose. In the civic tradition, that purpose was the preservation of collective liberty, which required the cultivation of military virtue; in the Christian tradition, it was the shared devotion to Christ which made virtue possible and which united the lower and upper orders of society. Smith's vision, while allowing for military virtue and for religious institutions, envisaged a society held together in part by market relations of mutual self-interest, in part by deference, and in part by a culture of respectability which would extend to all social orders, encouraging men to treat one another with decency and increasing the respect of the upper classes for the lower classes. To a remarkable though often unrecognized degree, this was the path taken by Victorian England.[3]

In this project, Smith was a legatee of earlier attempts by intellectuals to bring their learning to bear on the moral improvement of society, attempts which went back to the humanists. In its tendering of advice to the legislator, *The Wealth of Nations* recalled the earlier tracts of Renaissance humanists. But Smith's books are as striking for their departures from Renaissance humanism as for their continuities. For while Smith's work, like that of the humanists, focused on the promotion of virtue, it differed on *how* virtue was to be promoted, *which* virtues were to be promoted, and *whose* virtue was to be promoted. The humanists had focused on improving the virtues of the sovereign.[4] This was one of Smith's tasks as well, but he was far more concerned with improving the character of the majority in a society in which men were increasingly interconnected through networks of buying and selling rather than through legal subordination to one another. While the humanists had focused on changing the heart as a means to improve institutions, Smith emphasized the role of institutions in promoting virtuous behavior.

Taken together, Smith's works articulate a vision of "commercial humanism."[5] For Smith, basic moral sentiments are universal, but the degree to which they are developed and the balance between them vary in response to the demands of social institutions, which change over the course of history. "In general, the style of manners which takes place in any nation, may commonly upon the whole be said to be that which is most suitable to its situation," he noted. "Hardiness is the character most suitable to the circumstances of a savage; sensibility to those of one who lives in a very civilized society."[6]

Smith was not the first to suggest that commerce promoted the development of more "civilized" behavior—that was almost a commonplace of eighteenth-century enlightened thought.[7] But perhaps no other thinker devoted as much attention to describing how the market and commercial society could be structured to develop that constellation of self-control, industry, and gentleness which moralists from the humanists through David Hume had valued. The framework of Smith's work is perhaps best understood as the institutionalization of neo-stoicism, in which the ethic of self-command is universalized and transformed from a moral injunction addressed to an intellectual and political elite into a policy objective for the entire society.[8] It was a stoicism transformed by early-modern psychological institutionalism. In the seventeenth century, French moralists such as La Bruyère and La Rochefoucauld had derided the possibility that passionate man could ever achieve the stoic virtues of self-command.[9] Smith set out to show how—in a moderated and indirect form—such virtues could become widespread.

The Theory of Moral Sentiments, which he first published in 1759 and revised heavily in the year before his death, was Adam Smith's first book and his last book. It was about the nature and origins of virtue, defined as "the temper of mind which constitutes the excellent and praiseworthy character."[10] It dealt not with virtue in the singular, but with virtues in the plural. Smith was critical of the tendency of philosophers to display their ingenuity by trying "to account for all appearances from as few principles as possible."[11] Since life is socially and morally complicated, he assumed, it requires a wide range of character traits; moreover, the character of some people is inevitably less excellent than that of others. Far from believing that virtue was somehow being made irrelevant by the rise of commercial society, Smith thought that commercial society made the performance of some virtues more likely and the performance of other virtues more necessary.

In explaining how his theory of the virtues related to earlier theories, Smith identified three conceptions of virtue which his own work was intended to renew by placing them on the intellectually firmer basis of psychological institutionalism. The first conception stressed propriety, the direction of the passions to their proper goals, and the moderation of the passions to a level compatible with the interests and emotions of others.[12] The second conception stressed prudence, the judicious pursuit of happiness, which stems in part from conduct which arouses the respect and approval of those around us.[13] The third conception emphasized the importance of disinterested benevolence, altruistic action on behalf of others.

Smith's position was that all these qualities are admirable: the problem was to get people to live up to any of them. The traditional solutions of "precept and exhortation" were inadequate for this purpose.[14] Drawing on the tradition of the institutional direction of the passions, Smith looked to the structure of emotional incentives provided by social institutions to channel, cultivate, and dampen passions, and thereby to improve character. The quality of character which is necessary for the realization of any virtue, Smith emphasized, is the ability to control oneself. "Self-command is not only itself a great virtue," Smith asserted, "but from it all the other virtues seem to derive their principal lustre."[15] Without self-command, the virtues of prudence, propriety, or benevolence cannot be exercised.

Man's psychological make-up includes "malevolent and unsocial passions," such as anger and resentment, which Smith sought to subdue through self-control, using the other passions. The superior virtues grow out of our "benevolent and social affections," passions which he sought to develop and cultivate through proper social institutions and through moral philosophy.[16] His complaint against earlier philosophers and moralists was that they had devoted too little attention to a third category of affections—the selfish passions, such as the desire for attention and praise. These passions are not intrinsically antisocial, Smith argued. Indeed they can even be admirable when pursued according to the rules of justice so that they do not cause injury to others.[17] It was these passions which Smith felt it necessary to legitimate, as long as they were properly channeled. God may act from benevolence alone, but imperfect man acts from many motives aside from benevolence.[18] Because our beneficent passions are "very limited," they form an insufficient basis to motivate decent conduct toward the many people outside the range of our benevolent feelings.[19]

A recurring motif in Smith's thought is that man is a "weak and imperfect creature" and that most of us are far from perfection.[20] We can require people to conform to certain standards without admiring them for doing so. And when they go beyond those standards, we ought to esteem them. But to *expect* such behavior of most people is to chase a chimera. This notion of two levels of morality—one common and attainable by many, the other admirable but rare—was a stoic theme reiterated with many variations in the eighteenth century.[21] Cicero, whose *Of Duties* provide a digest of stoic moral ideas, remarked that "we do not live with men who are perfect and clearly wise, but with those who are doing splendidly if they have in them mere images of virtue."[22] He distinguished between true "honorableness" which "is found in wise men only and can never be severed from virtue" and those "middle" or "second-rate" duties which produce "semblances of the honorable." The duties in this latter category, which Cicero called "ordinary virtues" (*commune officium*) and which Seneca had termed "*convenientia,*" rather than being restricted to the wise were open to all.[23] In his discussion of stoic doctrines in *The Theory of Moral Sentiments,* Smith refers to these as the "imperfect, but attainable virtues" open to "those who had not advanced to perfect virtue and happiness." These attainable virtues produce "proprieties, fitnesses, decent and becoming actions."[24]

Smith took the ancient stoic notion that "images" or "semblances" of perfect virtue are attainable by the many through adherence to moral conventions and wedded it to the early-modern discoveries that self-love enlightened by the passion for approbation might produce human decency, and that self-interest could be channeled to produce socially beneficent behavior. A good deal of virtuous behavior, Smith wrote, is actually prompted by self-interest, including the worthy habits of "economy, industry, discretion, attention, and application of thought," along with such "inferior virtues" as "prudence, vigilance, circumspection, temperance, constancy, firmness."[25] In Smith's judgment, these were the virtues which commercial society was better suited than previous social arrangements to promote. He devoted *The Wealth of Nations* primarily to showing that self-interest, when properly channeled by social institutions, can produce socially beneficent effects and behavior. In *The Theory of Moral Sentiments,* he focused on the role the desire for approbation plays in producing propriety and virtue. In both works, as well as in his lectures on jurisprudence, he explored the institutional direction of the passions toward morally and socially beneficent ends. Though persuaded by writers of the seventeenth and eighteenth centuries that self-love and self-interest *may* lead to socially positive effects, he was aware that whether or not they *actually* do have such effects depends on the institutions through which they are channeled and directed.

Edmund Burke, a great admirer of *The Theory of Moral Sentiments,* struck a very Smithian note when he wrote:

> Men are qualified for civil liberty in exact proportion to
> their disposition to put moral chains upon their own
> appetites. . . . Society cannot exist unless a controlling
> power upon will and appetite be placed somewhere,
> and the less of it there is within, the more there must be
> without. It is ordained in the eternal constitution of
> things, that men of intemperate minds cannot be free.
> Their passions forge their fetters.[26]

Writing to a royalist member of the French national assembly in
1791, Burke expressed his belief that only the power of foreign
forces could restore order to revolutionary France. Smith shared
Burke's assumptions about the relationship between political
liberty and the control of the passions, but he drew rather
different implications from those assumptions. For Smith, the
necessary complement to political liberty lay in social institutions
which were so structured that men were drawn by their appetites
and passions to place limits on those very appetites and passions.
He believed that under proper institutional conditions men *are*
qualified for civil liberty. They can escape political subordination
to the lord and the bishop to the extent that social institutions
lead them to subordinate their immediate passions into decent,
prudent, and benevolent behavior toward others. "Natural liberty" is possible because man's natural "sociability"—his desire
for the sympathy, attention, and approval of others—makes him
capable of subordinating his egoistic desires to the demands of
shared social rules.

The main focus of *The Theory of Moral Sentiments* therefore is
on the social processes by which the egoistic passions are
channeled, moderated, and redirected, making it possible for
men to live peaceably with others, pursue their happiness with
foresight, and act altruistically. The psychological precondition
for the practice of any of these virtues is self-command, the
ability to control one's passions. In itself, self-command is not
sufficient to rank as moral, since it can be put to immoral uses.
But it is the psychological prerequisite for any sort of positive
moral achievement. As we will see, Smith approved of commercial society because it fosters self-control. But he believed that
commercial society requires a degree of self-control that the
market by itself cannot provide and that it may even threaten.

CHAPTER EIGHT

"The Impartial Spectator"

THOUGH *The Wealth of Nations* is rightly regarded as the work that served as the foundation of the discipline of economics, the seminal role of *The Theory of Moral Sentiments* in the development of sociology and social psychology is rarely appreciated. Readers familiar with the development of sociological theory will find that in that book Smith presents a conception of what Charles Horton Cooley was to call the "looking-glass self," and that Smith's discussion of the "impartial spectator" led to George Herbert Mead's distinction between the "Me" that reflects my perception of how others see me and the "I" that is capable of judging the "Me." Indeed, behind what may seem the archaic language of the *The Theory of Moral Sentiments* lies a theory of the development of conscience through the internalization of social norms, as well as a theory of how the morally developed individual is able to ascend from moral conformity to moral autonomy.

Before Smith's day, the source of conscience was held to lie in human reason, or in the love of God, or in some "moral sense" irreducible to other passions. Smith, building on the work of David Hume, saw conscience as rooted in and developing out of self-love and self-concern. The key to *The Theory of Moral Sentiments* is Smith's account of the unanticipated origins of conscience, of our willingness to act justly, prudently, and benevolently. Smith traces the development of conscience to the interaction of two psychological factors: our egoistic desire for approval, and our ability to imagine ourselves in the place of others. It is the combination of these two factors which allows social institutions to guide us toward self-control and even altruistic action.

Every man, Smith assumes, has a natural preference for his own happiness above that of other people. Within limits, this natural desire is morally laudable, indeed evidence of providential creation. Man is "by nature first and principally recommended to his own care; and as he is fitter to take care of himself than of any other person, it is fit and right that it should be so. Every man, therefore, is much more deeply interested in whatever immediately concerns himself, than in what concerns any other man."[1] If the pursuit of self-interest prompted us to violate the person and property of others, however, this natural egoism would bring about the dissolution of society.[2] A central theme of Smith's works is to show how our natural passions provide a psychological basis for social institutions which, if properly structured, prevent a descent into that Hobbesian state of nature in which each man is the enemy of every other.

Even those who assume that man is by nature selfish, Smith says, must acknowledge that there is an element in human nature that leads us to be concerned with the happiness and misery of other people. Why does their happiness lead us to be happy, and their misery lead us to feel compassion? Since we have no immediate experience of what others feel, Smith reasons, the answer must lie in our ability to imagine what we ourselves would feel if we were in their situation.[3] This process of imaginative projection into the circumstances of others is the first stage of what Smith calls "sympathy." But why should an egoistic creature pay attention to others? The human mind is so constituted, Smith argues, that we gain pleasure from observing in others "a fellow-feeling" with our own emotions.[4] This sense of shared emotions is sympathy, the sense that others share and hence *approve of* our level of emotions. Sympathy heightens our pleasure; it "enlivens joy and alleviates grief."

But because we have concerns of our own, we do not feel the same emotions in the same degree as the other person. That person, in turn, knows that we cannot feel his emotions in the same degree. But because he too wants to be in a situation of shared sympathy, he will moderate his sentiments to approach what he thinks our sentiments are. The desire for shared sympathy serves as a passionate motive for us to try to know and accommodate ourselves to the emotions of others. Because of this desire to share the sentiments of others, we learn to become the spectators of our own sentiments and actions. We project ourselves into the position of the other person, and try to see ourselves as he sees us, in order to bring our sentiments closer to his. Thus an acquaintance who is in obvious pain over the loss of a loved one tends to excite the emotion of grief in us as well, thus bringing our emotions closer to his. The acquaintance, on the other hand, knows that we cannot share the intensity of his grief, and he in turn is led to moderate it, for the time being, out of the sympathetic desire to share our emotions.[5]

For Smith, the origin of our ability to control our passions lies in this self-reflective capacity to view our situation through the eyes of others who are intrinsically less interested in it.[6] Our essential sociability—our desire to be in sympathetic harmony with the emotions of others who observe our conduct—leads us to moderate our behavior by bringing our emotions of joy or disappointment, triumph or resentment, down to the level which we imagine that others are able to sustain. To a situation in which we feel wronged, our immediate reaction is likely to be intense anger. But we may moderate the expression of that anger by considering how our grievance appears to others; in our search for their sympathetic approval, we may moderate our anger to the level with which we believe they can sympathize. By observing their response of approval or disapproval, we learn over time what degree of anger they regard as being within the bounds of propriety.

Our desire for the sympathy of others leads by steps to the restraint of our self-love.[7] Though we are naturally inclined to prefer our own interests to the interests of others, our egoism is restrained to the extent that we learn to judge our actions as they must appear to outsiders who do not share our egoistic partiality toward ourselves. Moral consciousness, for Smith, is a process of internal conversation, of talking to ourselves. In that process, our natural egoism is partially restrained by our awareness of an external standard, the standard which we would use to judge our actions if we were a *spectator* who was biased neither toward ourselves nor toward those affected by our actions. This is the standard of what Smith calls "the impartial spectator." Our consciousness of this standard leads us to "humble the arrogance of [our] self-love, and bring it down to something which other men can go along with."[8] Our imaginative identification with "the sentiments of the impartial spectator" provides the motivation which leads us to temper "our mutinous and turbulent passions."[9]

Christianity recommends that we "love our neighbour as ourselves," Smith writes, but the natural process by which we become moral is through social experiences which teach us "to love ourselves only as we love our neighbour."[10] This is Smith's reformulation of the strategy of using one passion to counteract another, a favorite theme of early-modern thought. In this case our natural desire for the fellow-feeling of others counteracts our natural egoism, creating "that great discipline which Nature has established for the acquisition of this [self-command] and every other virtue."[11] *The Theory of Moral Sentiments*, then, is not primarily a book about "sympathy"—it is a book about self-control which tries to *explain* how self-control comes about even as it moralistically *urges* self-control upon its readers.[12]

It was axiomatic to Smith, as to Hume, that *knowledge* of what is right is not enough to motivate men to *do* right. Smith criticized overly rationalist accounts of moral behavior which implied that merely *convincing* the agent of the rightness of moral actions would lead him to *act* morally. Rational conviction, Smith maintained, is not a sufficient motive for action. For while reason might help to decide the criteria of moral action, to explain moral behavior meant to show the non-rational or "sentimental" basis of the decision to act morally. The passions, traditionally regarded as the source of moral weakness, are for Smith a part of human nature implanted by an ultimately benevolent Creator. To overrate the role of reason in moral action is therefore to underrate the role of God:

> When by natural principles we are led to advance those ends, which a refined and enlightened reason would recommend to us, we are very apt to impute to that reason, as to their efficient cause, the sentiments and

actions by which we advance those ends, and to imagine that to be the wisdom of man, which in reality is the wisdom of God. Upon a superficial view, this cause [man's reason] seems sufficient to produce the effects which are ascribed to it; and the system of human nature seems to be more simple and agreeable when all its different operations are in this manner deduced from a single principle.[13]

But every part of nature, when attentively surveyed, equally demonstrates the providential care of its Author, and we may admire the wisdom and goodness of God even in the weakness and folly of man.[14]

Smith adopts, with modifications, the position of Jacques Abbadie and later Protestant moralists who attributed a providential role to man's passions. For Smith, the human desire for approbation, for the approval of others—what seventeenth-century moralists had called "pride"—is the first rung on the ladder leading to non-egoistic behavior. According to Smith it is our natural, God-given love of praise that makes us take into account the judgments of those around us, judgments which serve to restrain our natural egoism. It is the instinctive human desire for the approval of others which leads the individual to measure his behavior by the standards of others. From the reactions of others to our actions, we learn to see ourselves as they see us.

It is through social interaction, then, that we achieve any degree of morality. Social interaction provides a "mirror" in which we first observe our own behavior and become self-reflective.[15] In our desire to merit the approval of others, we judge our own actions as we think others would judge them. By observing the response of those around us to various forms of conduct, we learn "general rules concerning what is fit and proper either to be done or to be avoided."[16] We experience admiration for those whose proper, prudent, and benevolent conduct we approve, and this in turn makes us want to emulate them.[17] We learn to judge our own conduct, according to Smith, by applying to ourselves the standards that we use in judging the conduct of others.[18] To use a modern term, we "internalize" social norms. We take into our own mind the judgments of those around us as to the sorts of behavior that are prohibited, permitted, and praised.

Our regard for these general rules of morality is felt as "a sense of duty, a principle of the greatest consequence in human life, and the only principle by which the bulk of mankind are capable of directing their actions."[19] It is through this often unarticulated sense of *duty* that men acquire the reliable and stable characters on which society depends.

> The course clay of which the bulk of mankind are formed, cannot be wrought up to . . . perfection. There is scarce any man, however, who by discipline, education, and example, may not be so impressed with a regard to general rules, as to act upon almost every occasion with tolerable decency, and through the whole of his life to avoid any considerable degree of blame.
>
> [I]f without regard to these general rules, even the duties of politeness, which are so easily observed, and which one can scarce have any serious motive to violate, would yet be so frequently violated, what would become of the duties of justice, of truth, of chastity, of fidelity, which it is often so difficult to observe, and which there may be so many strong motives to violate? But upon the tolerable observance of these duties, depends the very existence of human society, which would crumble into nothing if mankind were not generally impressed with a reverence for those important rules of conduct.[20]

If our only innate desires were self-love and the desire for the sympathetic approval of others, we might act in such a way as to obtain the praise of others without really having earned it. Those who are morally weak are satisfied to deceive others in their search for praise, and they never get beyond this first rung on the moral ladder. But, according to Smith, man naturally desires not only to be praised, but to be truly *deserving* of praise, for to be mistakenly praised for something we ourselves know we have not done is to receive praise not directed at who we really are. A higher and more effective source of happiness, then, comes from acting in a way which merits the self-approval which comes from knowing that we have acted according to the standards of the impartial spectator. It is this moral sentiment of self-approbation which provides the motive for acting sincerely, for trying to be the sort of praiseworthy character we seem to be to others.[21]

Among the most remarkable aspects of Smith's psychology of morality is his account of the individual's movement from moral conformity to moral autonomy, which allows him to challenge the prevalent behavior around him. The individual's love of praise makes him dependent on the reactions of those around him. The love of praiseworthiness, by contrast, can be satisfied whether or not the individual actually receives the praise of those around him when he acts in a way that he knows would be deserving of praise by an impartial spectator who was truly knowledgeable about the motives that prompt his actions. The natural love of praise, writes Smith, leads "to the affectation of virtue, and to the concealment of vice." The natural love of praiseworthiness makes possible "the real love of virtue, and the real abhorrence of vice." The morally weak man is motivated only by the desire for praise; the "wise man" is motivated by the desire for praiseworthiness as well.[22]

The morally weak man may never ascend beyond the first rung of morality. To the extent that he acts virtuously, it is usually because his desire for praise allows him to govern his actions to conform to public opinion. The wise man, however—or perhaps all of us, to the extent that we are wise—who is motivated not by the desire for praise but by the desire to be praiseworthy, is not governed by public opinion. He is able to appeal to a "much higher tribunal": that of his own conscience, a synonym for what Smith calls the "impartial and well-informed spectator . . . within the breast."[23] Altruistic actions, according to Smith, are motivated less by the benevolent love of our neighbor or of mankind than by the passion to act in a manner that we know to be praiseworthy.[24]

Smith drew on the tradition which held that the passions are a source of socially beneficial behavior, but *The Theory of Moral Sentiments* is a refinement and critique of that tradition. Smith's major innovation was to assert that God had implanted in man not only a desire for the approbation of others but a desire for self-approbation: not only the desire to be seen by others as doing good but the desire to see ourselves as doing good; not only the desire to be loved but the desire to be worthy of love.[25] It is Smith's belief that the greatest dread comes from knowing ourselves to have violated moral law, while the greatest happiness comes from acting in a manner we know to be virtuous.[26]

Smith believed, in other words, that the human psyche was so created by God that man achieves pleasure in knowing that he has acted virtuously, and displeasure from the recognition that he has acted unvirtuously. Violation of moral law leads to "the torments of inward shame and self-condemnation," while obedience to moral law leads to "tranquility of mind, . . . contentment, and self-satisfaction."[27] Reward and punishment are a reality: virtuous behavior is rewarded with self-approbation, the greatest and most secure source of happiness, while violation of moral rules leads to self-condemnation. Because of God's providential design of human nature, the self achieves a higher pleasure in the self-approbation that comes from doing from what is good. From opposite perspectives, later Christian and atheistic commentators may find it difficult to credit the religious premises behind Smith's moral psychology. Both tend to dismiss this deistic conception of man's place in creation as "half-hearted unbelief." But for Smith and many others in the eighteenth century (and beyond), this conception of creation was more plausible than either the Christian conception of man's dependence on divine grace, or the atheistic denial either of the experience of self-approbation or of its link to a providential design.[28]

The happiness that comes from real friendship is also linked to virtue. "Vice is always capricious: virtue only is regular and orderly," according to the most important apothegm in *The Theory of Moral Sentiments*. Since it is virtue that makes men orderly, it is virtue that makes them dependable and trustworthy. Truly secure and permanent friendship, therefore, is shared only by the virtuous.[29]

In this manner, Smith restated in psychological institutionalist terms the Socratic contention that the greatest gain is the gain a good man obtains through the practice of the virtues.[30] For Smith, this is a result of the constitution of the human mind, which—like the propensity to truck, trade, and barter to improve one's fortunes—can be inferred from human experience. Much of the gap between Smith, Judeo-Christian, and Greek thought on the one hand, and Mandeville and much of modern social thought on the other, hinges on differing evaluations of this element of moral experience. Morality, according to Smith, is not a mere "rationalization." To see more deeply into the wellsprings of moral action, he maintained, is not to find the self-deluding mask of egoism. On the contrary, rational comprehension of the non-rational motives of virtuous action in the desire for self-approbation leads to the conclusion that for the man who obeys the dictates of conscience virtue can be its own reward. By contrast, social thought which merely encourages the prudent management of egoistic desires and discounts the reality of self-approval as the reward for moral action tends to conclude that the virtuous are those who have not caught on.

According to Smith, though this desire for self-approval is not equally developed in all, some people come to desire virtue for its own sake. In another variation on the theme of two levels of moral perfection, Smith argues that in judging our own behavior we may orient ourselves to either of two standards of proper action. The lower standard is the one actually attained by most of those around us. The higher standard is that of moral perfection, insofar as each of us is capable of understanding that ideal. This ability varies with our capacity to perfect our sense of what is morally just and proper by reasoning about our observations of the character and conduct of those around us. The wise and virtuous man aspires to this higher standard and tries to understand its implications.[31] Such men are able to challenge public opinion and to ignore the approval of the actual people around them who are less well informed or less noble in their judgments:

> [The man] who desires virtue for its own sake, and is most indifferent about what *actually* are the opinions of mankind with regard to him, is still, however, delighted with the thoughts of what they *should* be, and with the consciousness that though he may neither be honoured nor applauded, he is still the proper object of honour and applause, and that if mankind were cool and candid and consistent with themselves, and properly informed of the motives and circumstances of his conduct, they would not fail to honour and applaud him. Though he despises the opinions which are *actually* entertained of him, he has the highest value for those which *ought* to be entertained of him.[32]

Smith's innovation to the psychological institutionalism of his predecessors was in this insistence that there was a higher moral rung than action based on desire for the approval of others. Yet even those who ascend to the higher rung of acting in a manner they know to be virtuous, and consequently worthy of their own approval, first ascend to the lower rung.

Together, Smith's works lay out a theory of *social control*, not in the invidious sense of a system by which the elites of society control the lower orders for their own benefit, but in the sense of a system which *diminishes the need for government to create social order by force.*[33] In such a system society exercises control indirectly, as the individual learns to exercise self-control through his interaction with others in his efforts to live up to social conventions regarding what is acceptable and admirable.

> The all-wise Author of Nature has, in this manner, taught man to respect the sentiments and judgements of his brethren; to be more or less pleased when they approve of his conduct, and to be more or less hurt when they disapprove of it. He has made Man, if I may say so, the immediate judge of mankind; and has, in this respect, as in many others, created him after his own image, and appointed him his vicegerent [deputy] upon earth, to superintend the behavior of his brethren. . . .

At first the individual does so because he desires external approval, and later because he wants to be worthy of his own approval, which comes from knowing that he has tried to act virtuously:

> But though man has, in this manner, been rendered the immediate judge of mankind, he has been rendered so only in the first instance; and an appeal lies from his sentence to a much higher tribunal, to the tribunal of their own consciences, to that of the supposed impartial and well-informed spectator, to that of the man within the breast, the great judge and arbiter of their conduct.[34]

Though these standards of behavior and character arise from society, the individual observes them, not against his will, but with his willing cooperation, because he has come to value them.

*   *   *

For Smith, there is a close link between our moral duty to act benevolently and our emotional inclination to do so. Thanks to God's design of human nature, we are emotionally inclined to be most beneficent to those who most require our beneficence and to whom it can be most useful.[35] We tend to be most concerned with the welfare to those who are closest to us, emotionally, spatially, and culturally.

Benevolence begins at home and moves outward in concentric social spheres. "Every man . . . is first and principally recommended to his own care; and every man is certainly, in every respect, fitter and abler to take care of himself than of any other person."[36] This is one basis of Smith's argument for economic freedom in *The Wealth of Nations*. The extent of our benevolence is determined by the degree of our sympathy, and our ability to project ourselves emotionally into the position of others develops through our continuing relationship with them. Affection, Smith writes, "is in reality nothing but habitual sympathy." This habitual sympathy develops in response to situations which make mutual understanding necessary to happiness.

The people with whom we are most able to sympathize and to whom we feel the greatest affection are those with whom we are "habituated to sympathize" by frequent and intimate contacts, beginning with the members of our own family. It is the experience of living together "long and familiarly" which makes possible "delicious sympathy, confidential openness and ease" with close family members.[37] This sympathetic link to family members with whom one has lived in close contact is the basis of the strong sense of benevolence which most men and women feel toward their closest kin.

Benevolence, according to Smith, may also arise from nonfamilial situations in which propinquity, frequency of contact, and some degree of shared need foster the development of mutual concern. Professional colleagues and business partners, for example, sometimes develop true affection and benevolence for one another. Even neighbors, with whom contact is frequent if far less intimate, become objects of greater benevolence than do the anonymous others with whom contact is less frequent.[38] The largest circle to which we owe some active degree of benevolence is the state, which provides us and our family and friends with culture and protection; it is the largest social unit upon which our conduct can have significant influence.[39] Thus, Smith believed, benevolent feelings begin at home and extend with diminishing intensity to those at greater and greater social distances. There is a natural correlation between the objects of our benevolence and the possibility that our benevolence will have any effect on them.

The two levels of virtue reappear in Smith's important distinction between beneficence and justice. *Beneficence*, which prompts us to *promote* the happiness of others, is a superior virtue. Precisely for that reason, we cannot depend upon it or expect it of most men. We should applaud it when it occurs, but we should not use force to punish those who do not act as beneficently as we would wish.[40] *Justice* is the sense of fairness which forbids us from injuring others for our own advantage. Our internal conversation with the impartial spectator is the basis of our sense of justice, which depends on our ability to put the happiness of those we might harm on a par with our own happiness. The impartial spectator reminds the individual that "in the race for wealth, and honours, and preferments, he may run as hard as he can, and strain every nerve and every muscle, in order to outstrip all his competitors. But if he should justle, or throw down any of them, the indulgence of the spectators is entirely at an end. It is a violation of fair play, which they cannot admit of."[41] Smith's concept of justice as fair play corresponds to the definition of justice in the tradition of civil jurisprudence, in which justice is the right of each to his own. Without justice, conceived as the socially enforced protection of the individual's life and property, society cannot exist. Justice represents a minimal level of virtue which any society has a right to command of the individual through the use of force.[42]

We achieve moral perfection, according to Smith, when we restrain our selfishness and engage our benevolent sentiments, when we "feel much for others and little for ourselves."[43] Natural sympathy is the psychological basis of whatever degree of concern for others we are able to achieve. How much sympathy we actually feel and how much self-control we exercise in altering our actions depend on the degree to which we have developed, through the agency of social institutions, our capacities for self-mastery and benevolence.

Just as government plays a role in promoting the wealth of

the nation, so it plays a role in encouraging moral behavior.[44] Government performs its economic role by providing the framework in which the market can coordinate economic behavior for the public benefit. Similarly, government performs its moralizing role by providing the framework in which nongovernmental institutions can perform their socializing functions. Smith called for relatively little direct government control of individual behavior not because he regarded man as naturally good but because he believed that the passions should be disciplined by a variety of nongovernmental institutions. One of these institutions is the market, which, as we will see, Smith valued in part for the way in which it performs this disciplining function.

CHAPTER NINE

The Historical and Institutional Foundations of Commercial Society

INTELLECTUAL CONTINUITY AND INTELLECTUAL INNOVATION are often closely intertwined. Innovation is motivated by an author's dissatisfaction with a theory which he regards highly enough to warrant a rigorous examination of its weaknesses and limitations. Such was Smith's relationship to Thomas Hobbes and to the seventeenth-century theorists of civil jurisprudence. Smith criticized Hobbes for maintaining that the orderliness of social life depended on government control, a view which made obeying the sovereign's laws the essence of virtue.[1] Although Smith believed that government does play an essential role in maintaining a decent society, he insisted that it is a more limited and indirect role than Hobbes suggested.

The great seventeenth-century theorists of civil jurisprudence—Grotius, Pufendorf, and Locke—had identified a core of rights derived from nature which it was the duty of government to ensure. Foremost among those rights were personal liberty, the right to property, and the right to form contracts. The problem with the natural rights theorists, according to Hume and Smith (as formulated by Smith's student Dugald Stewart) was their inadequate account of the social and political institutions which were the necessary preconditions for securing such rights.[2] Following the lead of Hume and another

Scottish intellectual, Lord Kames, Smith demonstrated that the rights claimed by the natural-rights theorists were based on the development of social and historical institutions.[3] Whether or not men were endowed by God with inalienable rights to life, liberty, and property, it was evident that in most times and in most places they had not enjoyed those rights. *The question Smith set out to answer in his lectures on jurisprudence was how in western Europe in general and Britain in particular historical institutions had evolved to provide some approximation of those rights.* In this attempt to give a social, institutional, and historical basis to rights once deemed "natural" (by Locke) or primarily dependent on state power (by Hobbes), Smith made an important contribution to the development of what might be termed a morally informed social science and an empirically based moral philosophy.

In contrast to Hobbes, Smith maintained that government force and direction were not the prime sources of orderly social life. That is what his frequent references to "natural liberty" were meant to convey. But he did not mean that merely limiting the coercive power of government would bring about a beneficial social order. Rather, he believed that social institutions and their shared standards would make possible a high degree of justice and order without direct government intervention. The process of character-formation was "natural" in that it was a product of the many informal sets of rules and expectations which arose from socializing with others rather than from the threat of political coercion. *The Theory of Moral Sentiments* is—among much else—an explanation of how social institutions channel the passions and shape men who are capable of concern for others and of respecting their rights. Rather than beginning with a delineation of "natural rights," Smith starts by analyzing how men develop a sense of duty, and hence of the expectations which others could have of their conduct. The awareness of duty, and the ability to make one's conduct conform to one's duties toward others, are what Smith meant by "character." Indeed, when the fourth edition of *The Theory of Moral Sentiments* was published in 1774, Smith gave it this subtitle: "An Essay towards an Analysis of the Principles by which Men Naturally Judge Concerning the Conduct and Character, First of their Neighbours, and Afterwards of Themselves."

HISTORY AND LAW

In *The Theory of Moral Sentiments,* Smith showed how the desire for sympathy transforms self-love into character and generates the shared social standards that would be held by an impartial spectator. While Smith explored the more or less constant passions of the individual, he was more concerned with the degree to which historically developed institutions channel those passions in directions which are morally desirable and adapted for social survival. In his lectures on jurisprudence he examined the way in which shared standards are formalized into law, and the way in which the structure of government power influences the degree to which law is just, in the sense of meeting the standards of impartiality.

Smith's lectures on jurisprudence were intended to provide universal guidelines to aid legislators in reforming the existing, positive law of their states.[4] Smith explored the history of law in an attempt to discern the legal, political, and social institutions which make possible a high degree of liberty and prosperity without direct government domination of social life. He reworked, expanded, and published certain portions of the lectures as *The Wealth of Nations,* but he never managed to perfect to his own satisfaction the sections dealing with forms of government, family law, and property law. Still, those sections offer a description and an analysis of the institutions necessary for a decent society which complement the institutional arguments of *The Theory of Moral Sentiments* and *The Wealth of Nations.*

In *The Theory of Moral Sentiments,* Smith showed how the operation of mutual sympathy, without any deliberate human intention or planning, gives rise to shared social standards that are common enough to make orderly social life possible. The implicit reasoning behind Smith's approach is that rules and institutions gain social approval because of their functional efficacy: in the long run, those that provide a modicum of security, comfort, and decency will be approved, while those that do not will be disapproved.[5] The historical record therefore makes it unnecessary for each generation to reinvent the wheel of human institutions. By studying the institutional record of past societies, the moral philosopher turned social scientist can derive lessons for the present. In his lectures on jurisprudence, which are grounded in the moral psychology of *The Theory of Moral*

Sentiments, Smith explained why some institutions are superior to others in directing the passions to socially beneficent ends. In his attempt "to give an account of the general principles of law and government," he made use of historical materials for normative purposes. His reading of the past through the lens of psychological institutionalism would show the most workable and beneficial structure of laws and government, thus providing the basis of the science of a legislator.[6]

Smith's frequent references to "natural liberty" should not obscure the crucial role he assigned to government and law. Both *The Theory of Moral Sentiments* and *The Wealth of Nations* reveal the importance of these institutions in Smith's overall conception, but it is in the unpublished lectures on jurisprudence that they take center stage. The purpose of the law is twofold. First, it ought to ensure justice by preventing the expression of passions and interests at the expense of others. Second, it ought to sanction and enforce the institutional arrangements which channel the passions in the direction of moral decency, physical survival, and material well-being.

Social order, for Smith, is not "spontaneous" or automatic. It is founded on institutions, and one task of the legislator is to recognize the superiority of social institutions which have been tested by historical experience and to embody them in law. Law should reflect the way in which an impartial spectator would judge the justice of a situation. Smith shows how changing political and economic structures create standards and expectations which an impartial observer would hold.[7]

Smith saw the history of law as a storehouse of information about how shared standards have emerged over time. In his historical account of property rights he shows how impartial spectators in historically developed institutions come to respect property rights and to regard the keeping of contractual promises as "reasonable expectations."[8] He saw the growth of contract law as a reflection of the changing expectations created by the spread of commerce.[9] As commerce increased, there was a greater social need for honoring contractual promises, and a greater sense of disappointment felt by those subjected to broken promises. Contract law was a response to that need. As we will see, in tracing the history of law related to the family, Smith showed how the changing institutional structure of the family at different stages of history led to changing standards and expectations regarding women.

To be sure, law embodies shared social standards very imperfectly, because positive law reflects the differential power of those who make the laws.[10] The degree to which impartial standards are institutionalized in law depends on relations of power, material and spiritual. One of Smith's main historical themes is how changes in the balance of power in society— between men and women, between religious sects, between kings and nobles—have occasionally led to the emergence and legal codification of impartial standards that can serve as guides to legislators.

The reality of "rights," Smith stressed, depends on their enforceability, which in turn depends on shared expectations and on the power of government. Even universally recognized "natural rights" that ensure protection from murder and injury depend for their enforceability on the power of government.[11] Laws concerning property and contracts, the family, and the relationship between state and citizen, Smith maintained, all deal with "acquired rights." The *recognition* of acquired rights, as well as their effective *enforcement*, varies with the institutional structure of society.[12] To explain the evolution and interrelationship of those rights, Smith laid out a theory of historical development.

THE STAGES OF HISTORY

In his lectures on jurisprudence and in *The Wealth of Nations*, Smith employed a four-stage theory of history based on a taxonomy suggested by Lord Kames. Those four stages were the stage of hunters, the stage of shepherds, the stage of agriculture, and the stage of commercial society. Smith did not intend to offer an exhaustive, comprehensive theory of history or to suggest that history progresses in linear fashion. Rather, he meant his stages of historical development to be taken as heuristic models to illuminate the relationship between forms of property, marriage, government, collective defense, and economic production. Although each stage develops out of earlier stages, it is by no means inevitable that a given society will progress from one stage to the next. In fact, as history shows, some societies have regressed from higher to lower stages. The direction in which a society moved had depended on historical contingency and unanticipated consequences. A social scientific understanding of the relationship of governmental, legal, military, social, and economic institutions, Smith hoped, would help legislators to exploit the possibilities which commercial society offered for improving the physical and moral well-being of its members and to prevent a regression to a lower and morally inferior stage of institutional development.

In his account of the stages of history Smith combined the views of human nature presented in *The Theory of Moral Sentiments* with a vast range of historical and anthropological evidence about earlier and contemporary societies. He drew on the history of civil, common, and ecclesiastical law and on the literature of classical Greece and Rome, the Bible, and travelers' accounts of the societies of the New World, Africa, and Asia. He also drew on David Hume's historical essays and on Montesquieu's recently published *Spirit of the Laws*.

In the stage of hunters, as Smith described it, men are nomadic and support themselves by hunting, gathering, and fishing. Their division of labor is rudimentary, and their technology primitive. Since society at this stage is materially poor, population is sparse and scattered. There can be little accumulation of wealth, and consequently there is a high degree of material equality and little conception of property. Thus there is little demand for government authority or for legal institutions to adjudicate property disputes. Since government is too weak to interfere in the familial realm, there is no domestic law. Thus the husband and father is the absolute master of his wife and children.[13] This was the condition that prevailed among the native tribes of North America in his own day, Smith believed.

Although all societies at one time had been at the hunting stage, some of them had proceeded from the hunting of animals to their domestication, thus inaugurating the stage of nomadic shepherds. The domestication of animals marks a great institutional transition. Since domestic animals can now be accumulated, the notion of private property emerges and with it the need for formalized rules governing the protection and transmission of property. Over time, as some people accumulate more animals than others, inequality of wealth arises, and with it the dependence of the poor on the rich. In this stage of society, the rich have few objects on which to spend their accumulated wealth other than on subordinates who become their dependent retainers. The man with the greatest number of retainers becomes the chief.[14] At this stage of society the great inequalities of wealth create the widest gap in power and influence between the rich and the poor, since the few wealthy men have many poor subordinates who are directly dependent on them.[15]

With the emergence of the concept of property, which Smith called "the grand fund all dispute," laws and government arise to protect the property of the rich from violent seizure by the poor. "Property and civil government very much depend on one another," Smith wrote. "The preservation of property and the inequality of possession first formed it, and the state of property must always vary with the form of government."[16] Smith's emphasis on the role of government in protecting property was not intended as a condemnation of the wealthy or of government. On the contrary, without that protection the desire to better one's fortune could not be channeled into pacific economic activity.

Compared with hunting societies, shepherd societies are able to support larger populations and devise a more complex structure of property. The functions of government are not yet differentiated, however. The chief combines in his own person both executive power—the power to employ force against outsiders—and a degree of judicial power. History is full of examples of more settled societies that were overrun and conquered by nomadic shepherds, including the overthrow of the Roman empire by the nomadic shepherd societies of the north. In Smith's day, shepherd societies were still prevalent in Asia and Africa, and in the Scottish Highlands as well.[17]

In regions combining rich soil with a geography making for easy defense, societies based on agriculture arose. Smith's analysis of the stage of agricultural society comes largely *after* his analysis of the stage of commercial society—a reminder that history does not follow a unilinear development from stage to stage. It was in ancient Greece and Rome that commercial societies developed out of the stage of agriculture. Smith traced this development once again to geography: the ancient city-states grew up where the soil was rich, where the topography was favorable to defense, and where easy access to the sea favored exchange with other societies. Commerce fostered the development of the arts and manufacture, making these societies relatively rich and civilized. Smith linked the emergence of democracy in ancient Athens with the growth of commerce. Commerce contributed to social mobility and blurred the rigid distinction between the rich and powerful nobility and the commoners. By the time of Pericles, the beginnings of democratic government had appeared.[18]

Ancient Athens and Rome were commercial societies only in a limited sense, however. Despite the grandeur of their cultural attainments, they were fundamentally flawed, for Smith, by the fact that their economies were based on slavery. These ancient examples of commercial society and republican government were also reminders of the great flaw which haunted the civic republican tradition: both had succumbed to external attack, for reasons which Smith believed were inherent in their structure. As freemen came to support themselves by manufacturing for the market rather than by agriculture, they became less fitted for the rigors of military service and less inclined to go to war. Military glory brought no material profit, and men oriented to profit were less willing to take part in life on the battlefield.[19] Both Athens and Rome eventually fell to societies which were less developed economically and less civilized. Athens fell to the Macedonians,[20] and Rome fell to tribal societies from the north. In short, the spread of commerce in the ancient world led to military defeat, the end of self-government, and a decline in the level of arts and culture.[21]

Smith saw the destruction of the Roman empire as a great regression in the history of Europe. Communications and transportation were disrupted, and commerce and manufacture fell into decay. On the ruins of the commercial empire sprang up agricultural societies without centralized government.

Smith's most detailed analysis of the stage of agriculture appears in Book Three of *The Wealth of Nations*, where he traces the gradual emergence of modern commercial society from the feudal age of agriculture which preceded it.

After the fall of the western Roman empire, the chiefs of the victorious barbarian nations seized control of the land by force of arms. Large tracts controlled by a small number of barons formed the basis of military and political power. Land came to be regarded not as a source of economic well-being but as a power base. Under Roman law, land could be divided up as it passed from generation to generation. But under the feudal laws of primogeniture and entail, land could no longer be broken into small parcels. For a time these laws served a valid purpose, because the power of the baronial landlord and his ability to defend his holdings depended on his owning an estate of substantial size.[22] But with the decline of the protective function of the barons, primogeniture and entail had become anachronistic barriers to economic progress. "Laws frequently continue in force long after the circumstances which first gave occasion to them, and which could alone render them reasonable, are no more," Smith wrote.[23] In Smith's day, between a fifth and a third of the land of Scotland remained encumbered by legal restrictions which prevented its sale under the laws of entail.[24]

The hereditary feudal landowners, Smith observed, had little incentive to improve the productivity of their land. Nor did the serfs who worked the land, since they were obliged to turn over much of their produce to their legal superiors.[25] Any gain would accrue to the lord, either in the form of feudal dues or through direct seizure. Thus the security of property and person which were preconditions of economic growth were lacking in feudal society.

Economic stagnation was coupled with the degradation that goes with personal dependency. The noble landlord was the virtual ruler of his tenants, their judge and legislator in time of peace, their leader in time of war, and their protector. With both political control and economic control in the same hands, most men were dependent on and subject to the arbitrary control of their lord.[26] Even so, they enjoyed little security, because the feudal lords were often in latent or open battle with one another. The weakness of the central power (the king) created insecurity of person and property and left the majority of the population under the arbitrary control of the lords.[27]

Smith attributed the dissolution of this feudal, agricultural stage to the unintended consequences of the landowners' response to the economic stimuli arising in the towns. The kings saw the towns as handy sources of revenue with which to strengthen their power over the barons. And so they protected the towns and granted them the privilege of framing and enforcing their own laws. Here Smith finds the origin of "order and good government, and along with them the liberty and security of individuals."[28]

Smith returned in The Wealth of Nations to the "proud and unfeeling landlord" he had introduced in The Theory of Moral

Sentiments. In place of a parable, he used a detailed argument to show that the most valuable qualities of modern commercial society were the unintended consequences of historical processes in which the key actors mistook their interests.

In the absence of foreign trade and the manufacture of luxuries, Smith observed, the feudal landlord had nothing to buy with the economic surplus provided by his land. He spent it on "a multitude of retainers and dependants, who having no equivalent to give in return for their maintenance, but being fed entirely by his bounty, must obey him."[29] It was the availability of luxury goods from the towns that triggered the process of change. The lord's desire for more income to buy more luxuries gave him an incentive to raise his rents. But his tenants insisted that he grant them in return greater property rights, beginning with longer leases, to make it worth their while to invest in improving the productivity of the land. The relationship evolved from serfdom, to tenancy, to rental tenancy with long leases. Each step encouraged the tenant to invest more heavily in improving the land, and each step made the tenant's relationship to the landlord more contractual and less arbitrary. Over time, the lords lost both physical and judicial control over those who lived on their land. Smith's summary of this process is deliciously ironic:

> [W]hat all the violence of the feudal institutions could never have effected, the silent and insensible operation of foreign commerce and manufactures gradually brought about. These gradually furnished the great proprietors with something for which they could exchange the whole surplus produce of their lands, and which they could consume themselves without sharing it either with tenants or retainers. All for ourselves, and nothing for other people, seems, in every age of the world, to have been the vile maxim of the masters of mankind. As soon, therefore, as they could find a method of consuming the whole value of their rents themselves, they had no disposition to share them with any other persons. For a pair of belt buckles perhaps, or for something as frivolous and useless, they exchanged the maintenance, or what is the same thing, the price of the maintenance of a thousand men for a year, and

with it the whole weight and authority which it could give them. . . . and thus, for the gratification of the most childish, the meanest and the most sordid of all vanities, they gradually bartered their whole power and authority.[30]

Having sold their birth-right, not like Esau for a mess of pottage in time of hunger and necessity, but in the wantonness of plenty, for trinkets and baubles, fitter to be the play-things of children than the serious pursuits of men, [the barons] became as insignificant as any substantial burgher or tradesman in a city. A regular government was established in the country as well as in the city, nobody having sufficient power to disturb its operations in the one, any more than in the other.[31]

Smith was of course exaggerating for rhetorical effect: it would take many more buckles than any lord might covet to equal the cost of maintaining a thousand men. But his mention of the belt buckle highlights the failure of the lords to recognize their self-interest—to the ultimate benefit of society.

Smith regarded this decline in the power of the nobility, and the concomitant rise in the power of the central government, as prerequisites for the liberty that characterizes modern commercial society.[32] In the great transformation brought about by commerce between town and countryside, "order and good government, and with them, the liberty and security of individuals" were introduced "among the inhabitants of the country, who had before lived almost in a continual state of war with their neighbours, and of servile dependency upon their superiors. This, though it has been the least observed, is by far the most important of all their effects."[33]

At the conclusion of this historical sketch Smith offers one of his clearest statements of the role of unanticipated consequences in human history:

A revolution of the greatest importance to the public happiness was in this manner brought about by two different orders of people who had not the least intention to serve the public. To gratify the most childish vanity was the sole motive of the great proprietors. The merchants and artificers, much less ridiculous, acted merely from a view to their own interest, and in pursuit of their own pedlar principle of turning a penny wherever a penny was to be got. Neither of them had either knowledge or foresight of that great revolution which the folly of the one, and the industry of the other, was gradually bringing about.[34]

For Smith, the restrictions on the sale of land imposed by the laws of primogeniture and entail were products of historical developments with negative consequences since they limited the movement of investment capital into agriculture. Those laws reflected "manners and customs" which had made sense under an older system of government and agriculture but had remained in effect after that system had dissolved.[35] The implication for the legislator was that such institutional lags should be remedied by eliminating the outdated laws.[36]

The rise of a sovereign state able to protect the life, liberty, and property of its citizens was an unanticipated consequence of the diminished political power of the secular feudal lords on one hand and of their religious counterparts on the other. To explain the decline of the political power of the Church, Smith used essentially the same scheme he had employed to explain the decline of the political power of the feudal landlords. Smith described the political power and legalized privilege of the medieval Church as "the most formidable combination that ever was formed against the authority and security of civil government, as well as against the liberty, reason, and happiness of mankind, which can flourish only where civil government is able to protect them." The Church and its various orders commanded substantial economic power by virtue of their huge landholdings and the tithes to which they were entitled. Since tithes and land rents were usually paid in kind, the clergy had at their disposal huge amounts of grain, wine, and meat which they were unable to consume. So they used it to support the poor, who in turn venerated and respected the Church. The economic power of the Church thus enhanced both its spiritual role and its political influence. "In that constitution," wrote Smith with deistic distaste, "the grossest delusions of superstition were supported in such a manner by the private interests of so great a number of people as put them out of all danger from any assault of human reason: because though human reason might perhaps have been able to unveil, even to the eyes of the common people, some of the delusions of superstition, it could never have dissolved the ties of private interest."[37]

Once again, it was the spread of "arts, manufactures, and commerce" which led to a shift in power, by providing those with surplus income the chance to spend more of it on themselves. The clergy, like the feudal barons, increased their rents and granted longer leases and greater legal independence to their tenants. Now that they were able to spend more on their own comforts, they devoted less to charity. As time passed, the ties of material interest which bound the common people to the clergy grew weaker, leaving the Church with its spiritual authority but with diminished political power. Finally its spiritual authority too suffered erosion as the clergy displayed a growing appetite for material goods. By the sixteenth century, the lower orders of the people "were provoked and disgusted by the vanity, luxury, and expence of the richer clergy, who appeared to spend upon their own pleasures what had always before been regarded as the patrimony of the poor." The declining influence of the Church over the populace enabled the monarchs of Europe to increase their influence over the clergy at the expense of Rome, even before the Reformation.[38]

Thus *the emergence of central government with a monopoly of political control, at the expense of the barons and the bishops, was an unanticipated consequence of the spread of commerce.* Since Smith regarded the sovereignty of a central, civil authority as a prerequisite of liberty, good order, and prosperity, he viewed these historical processes as auspicious.

GOVERNMENT AND THE DIVISION OF POWERS

A central contention of Smith's history of law and government is that individual liberty requires a government *strong* enough to protect citizens from one another, and a system of regular and impartial justice which *limits* the use of government power and protects the rights of the citizen against the sovereign.[39] In a modern commercial society, personal security and the security of property depend on the separation of legislative, judicial, and executive powers.[40]

Unless the judiciary is distinct from the power of the executive, justice is likely to be sacrificed to politics, Smith observed. With the spread of commerce, the law had grown more complex and resort to the law had become more frequent. Consequently those who held political power had been compelled to delegate their judicial responsibilities.[41] Smith regarded the separation of executive and judicial power as a hallmark of modern commercial society. The regular and impartial administration of justice also requires that judges be independent of the legislature, which makes the laws. In contemporary England, Smith observed, something approaching this division of powers had come about. Legislative power lay predominantly with the House of Commons; executive power lay with the king; and, though judges were appointed by the crown, the fact that they were appointed for life provided a considerable degree of judicial independence. These institutional arrangements helped to secure the citizen's rights against the government.[42]

With the spread of commerce and the centralization of the means of coercion, it became possible for government not only to protect person and property—for Smith, the essence of justice—but also to require certain beneficent actions from citizens.[43] In civilized nations, for example, the law obliges parents to support their children, and children to support their parents. It was the power of the central government which created the potential for law to embody the standards of the impartial spectator rather than leaving the weak at the mercy of the strong. Moreover, the law had been interposed to weaken the absolute power of fathers over children, of men over women, and of masters over servants.[44] The role of the lawmaker, Smith declared, was to promote the prosperity of the commonwealth "by establishing good discipline, and by discouraging every sort of vice and impropriety; he may prescribe rules, therefore, which not only prohibit mutual injuries among fellow-citizens, but command mutual good offices to a certain degree."[45] He devoted large portions of his lectures on jurisprudence and The Wealth of Nations to the role of government and law in strengthening the social institutions that foster self-control and benevolence. One of those institutions is the family.

MARRIAGE, LOVE, AND THE FAMILY

In earlier stages of society, the extended blood relations of the clan or tribe are important as the basis of common defense. In civilized societies, where the state provides physical protection, the functional significance of distant, blood relations declines, while the importance of the nuclear family increases.[46] The family, Smith believed, is the primary institution of moral education on which all subsequent moral development depends. For it is in the family that children learn to curb their passions and accommodate their desires to those of other people. Since they are dependent on their parents, they are obliged to learn to limit their passions to a level acceptable to their parents. This is the first of the many experiences of socially induced self-control which together make up the process of education. Smith believed that such early-childhood experiences provide a "chief and most essential part of education, without which being first implanted it would be in vain to attempt the instilling of any others."[47]

Smith viewed the nuclear family made up of parents and children living together under one roof as society's most important moralizing institution. Physical propinquity is essential, because it is less biological relatedness than the frequency and intimacy of relations that give the family its socializing and moralizing influence. Smith criticizes the practice of sending young adolescents away to be educated in colleges, nunneries, or boarding schools:

> Do you wish to educate your children to be dutiful to their parents, to be kind and affectionate to their brothers and sisters? Put them under the necessity of being dutiful children, of being kind and affectionate brothers and sisters: educate them in your own house. . . . Respect for you must always impose a very useful restraint upon their conduct; and respect for them may frequently impose no useless restraint upon your own. Surely no acquirement, which can possibly be derived from what is called a public education, can make any sort of compensation for what is almost certainly and necessarily lost by it.[48]

He also attacked the upper-class practice of sending seventeen and eighteen-year-old boys off on a tour of the Continent, arguing that it weakened character by removing them "from the inspection and control of . . . parents and relations."[49] While Smith's comments on the morally restraining influence of parents on children is familiar enough, his recognition of the restraining influence of children on parents reflects his acute powers of observation and generalization.

Smith devoted a great deal of attention in his lectures on jurisprudence to the changing legal structure of marriage and to the emotional dynamics which each structure was likely to generate. These interests are evident in his discussions of polygamy and of divorce law.

Polygamy was a subject of particular interest to mid-eighteenth-century intellectuals. It was discussed by German professors of natural law, by Montesquieu in his *Persian Letters* of 1721, and by Hume in his 1742 essay "Of Polygamy and Divorces." They knew that, though the Church forbade polygamy, it had been practiced by Europeans in the past and was still practiced in Moslem and other non-European societies. Those who rejected divine revelation as a source of shared law debated whether certain institutional arrangements might be preferred on grounds of natural law and moral superiority.[50] Was monogamy merely a "Eurocentric" predilection, or were there universally valid reasons for preferring it to other institutional arrangements?

Smith drew on these earlier discussions in exploring the psychological dynamics of marital institutions. Polygamy, he maintained, is morally inferior to monogamy because its very structure breeds suspicion and jealousy, which in turn weaken the trust on which civil association and regular government are based.

Polygamy, Smith argued, by creating rivalry among wives for the love of their husband, almost always leads to discord. The number of children produced in a polygamous marriage lowers the intensity of paternal affection for each child. This creates a structural conflict between the husband and his wives, since each wife has a greater psychic investment in her children than the husband has. The imbalance of sexual partners in the family makes it more likely that the wives will be unfaithful, thus fueling jealousy and fear in the husband. Since jealous men fear to expose their wives to the company of other men, social life is kept to a minimum, and the resulting lack of social trust makes it difficult for families to come together and defend common interests. The paucity of civic associations paves the way in turn for arbitrary and despotic government, Smith concluded.[51]

Smith traced the influence of law on the changing psychological structure of the institution of marriage. In early Rome, he noted, the husband wielded supreme power over his wife, children, and slaves. The power of divorce was his alone. Later, as Roman society became richer and wealthy heiresses more common, new legal arrangements evolved which made marriage more contractual, granted women greater control over their fortunes and gave them the power of divorce as well. The effect of these relaxed laws of divorce, Smith maintained, had been morally harmful: the ideal of chastity was devalued as women moved from husband to husband, and female infidelity increased.[52] With the barbarian conquest the power of husbands over wives was reinstituted. Only the male had the right to divorce his spouse, and female adultery was punishable by divorce or even death. Male adultery was regarded less seriously and was without legal consequence. Smith explained this imbalance by the predominance of male power. It was the men who made the laws, and they were inclined "to curb the women as much as possible and give themselves the more indulgence."

The Christian clergy subsequently brought a measure of relief to women. Since priests were not allowed to marry, Smith explained, they were less likely to identify with the husbands and were thus more impartial in judging between husbands and wives. The laws governing marriage were accordingly made more equitable, and infidelity by either partner became grounds for separation.[53] Over time, under the influence of the Church, marriage became almost indissoluble. This increased the "respectability" of the wife and entitled her to a share of her husband's inheritance.[54]

The permanence of marriage, Smith suggested, prompted a fresh cultural evaluation of the passion of love. For when divorce laws were lax and it was easy to move from one partner to another, "the choice of the person was of no very great importance." But when marriage became indissoluble, the choice of one's spouse had a direct effect on one's future happiness. Since that choice was often based on love, that passion became a matter of greater cultural interest and appeared more frequently in works of imaginative literature.[55]

Laws which make divorce easy are likely to have an injurious effect on family life, Smith observed. The constant possibility of being rejected by one's spouse is bound to weaken the partners' trust and confidence in each other and to weaken their sense of involvement in a joint enterprise. The effect of divorce on children is likely to be harmful too, since stepmothers naturally tend to have less affection for stepchildren and are inclined to favor their own children, thus breeding jealousy. Though Smith felt that the laws of his day made divorce too difficult to obtain, he believed that strictness was preferable to laxity. He thought infidelity a legitimate cause for divorce, because it breeds continual distrust within a marriage.[56] He approved of the law which held that only legitimate children could inherit property, since the desire to leave their estate to their children provided a major incentive for men to marry. To permit illegitimate children to inherit property would weaken the institution of marriage, he believed.[57]

In his treatment of marriage and the family, Smith demonstrated how the changing structures of power allow the standard of the impartial spectator to be institutionalized in law. According to the judgment of the impartial spectator bolstered by the historical record, the family was an indispensable institution in the moral education of children, the law should assure men and women equal rights within the family, and the law should preserve the psychological incentives for men and women to express their progenitive drives through wedlock and to remain in marriage. He recommended those conclusions as a guide to the actions of the legislator.

CHAPTER TEN

The Moral Balance Sheet of Commercial Society

AS WE HAVE SEEN, MANY passages in *The Wealth of Nations* convey Smith's views about the moral advantages of commercial society. But it is in *The Theory of Moral Sentiments* that he conducts his most explicit and detailed exploration of those advantages. "Before we can feel much for others, we must in some measure be at ease ourselves. If our own misery pinches us very severely, we have no leisure to attend to that of our neighbour,"[1] Smith noted. For this reason, wealth is a prerequisite for the sympathy and concern for others expressed in politeness, sensibility, and benevolence. Yet Smith saw in the market additional moral benefits beyond providing a level of material prosperity which made the practice of the benevolent virtues possible. Most importantly, the market was an effective institutional mechanism for the encouragement of self-control and the channeling of the passions in socially beneficent directions.

In a commercial society based on exchange, every man "becomes in some measure a merchant."[2] Smith's evaluation of the moral effects of commercial society is reflected in his description of the character traits which merchants are likely to develop. His two books present rather different portraits of the merchant, in keeping with the different purposes and intended audiences of those books. In *The Wealth of Nations*, the merchant usually pursues his economic self-interest at the expense of the public good by circumventing the competition of the market and by attempting to influence the politician to erect protectionist barriers to trade. The challenge for the legislator is to control the merchant for the sake of the public good by eliminating trade restraints which serve particular interests and by channeling the merchant's activities through the competitive market so as to meet the needs of consumers. Yet even in *The Wealth of Nations,* in which Smith's remarks about merchants are generally critical, there are glimpses of a more positive side. Commerce leads the merchant to develop habits of "order, economy, and attention" which "render him much fitter to execute, with profit and success, any project of improvement."[3]

The progress of society from rudeness to civilization, Smith observes, has been retarded by the contempt in which merchants were held, a view he set out to overturn.[4] Regular and frequent market relations tend to guide self-interest toward the keeping of contractual promises, making honesty the best policy:

> Whenever commerce is introduced into any country, probity and punctuality always accompany it. . . . This is not at all to be imputed to national character, as some pretend. . . . It is far more reducible to self-interest, that general principle which regulates the actions of every man, and which leads men to act in a certain manner from views of advantage. . . . Where people seldom deal with one another, we find that they are somewhat disposed to cheat, because they can gain more by a smart trick than they can lose by the injury which it does their character [reputation]. . . . Whenever dealings are frequent, a man does not expect to gain so much by any one contract as by probity and punctuality in the whole, and a prudent dealer, who is sensible of his real interest, would rather choose to lose what he has a right to than give any ground for suspicion. . . . When the greater part of people are merchants they always bring probity and punctuality into fashion, and these are the principal virtues of commercial nations.[5]

In *The Theory of Moral Sentiments,* the merchant appears in a far more favorable light, as a character likely to act with prudence and propriety. Those qualities, though motivated by self-interest, are channeled by the market into benign and even commendable impulses. Since in a commercial society every man becomes in some measure a merchant, the qualities of self-control, planning, and commitment to one's promises spread throughout society.

Just as the search for approval leads men to adapt their behavior to social rules, so the pursuit of self-interest in the market, with its division of labor and the resulting interdependence of the participants, leads men to adapt their behavior to the expectations of others. *In short, one of the functions of the market is to discipline society.* It disciplines those who sell their labor and those who sell more tangible commodities. "The real and effectual discipline which is exercised over a workman, is not that of his corporation [guild]," Smith wrote, "but that of his customers. It is the fear of losing their employment which restrains his frauds and corrects his negligence."[6] To succeed in the market, men must develop the moderate level of self-command which Smith calls "propriety."[7] The market also promotes prudence, discipline in the pursuit of self-interest, and the ability to defer short-term gratification for long-term benefits.[8]

Smith applied his theory of the passions to explain the social dynamics of commercial society. To the human desire for the sympathetic approval of others, Smith added one additional theorem, based upon observation: men were disposed to sympathize more readily with the rich and powerful than with the poor and lowly, he found. Though this disposition was morally questionable, it served as a source of social stability. It prompts men to adopt a "habitual state of deference to those whom they have been accustomed to look upon as their natural superiors." In a deferential society like Smith's own, this propensity reinforced "the distinction of ranks and the order of society."[9]

At the root of the attempt to "better our condition" Smith finds the desire "to be observed, to be attended to, to be taken notice of with sympathy . . . and approbation." The better off men appear to be, the more likely they are to be well regarded by others.[10] Though Smith sometimes refers to this desire as "vanity," he usually describes it in less pejorative terms, as the desire for recognition by others. It was this desire that explained the emulation of one's betters so characteristic of the Britain of his day.[11] The dominant motive for engaging in economic activity — beyond providing for one's bodily needs—is the non-material desire for social status, Smith declared. "Precious" commodities were often valued because their scarcity made them accessible only to the rich, and hence distinguished their owners in the eyes of others or in their own eyes.[12]

As we saw in the passage on the "invisible hand" from *The Theory of Moral Sentiments,* Smith believed that the desire for wealth, status, and power is based on a faulty estimate of their value. And yet it is this desire which motivates human beings to exert themselves and even to strive for excellence. Members of the upper classes, who already command the attention of others, have no need to exert themselves; they need only to act "with the most exact propriety" to retain that attention.[13] Among the lower ranks of society, however, it is the desire for wealth and power that calls forth many of the virtues. It leads men to acquire professional knowledge and to display industry; it prompts them to act on ordinary occasions with "probity and prudence, generosity and frankness." Even in monarchies, Smith noted, government is often staffed by industrious, able men drawn from the lower and middle ranks of society. These upwardly mobile men of "spirit and ambition" search for extraordinary occasions in which to distinguish themselves. They are the movers and shakers. They are more likely to welcome conflict than men of established rank who have nothing to gain and who are less used to cultivating the virtues of "patience, industry, fortitude, and application of thought" typical of upwardly mobile men in search of fortune and fame.[14]

Smith observed that "moralists in all ages" had complained that the "great mob of mankind are the admirers and worshippers . . . of wealth and greatness."[15] At times, Smith himself echoed that complaint. But one of the moral advantages of commercial society, he believed, was that it obliged those "in the middling and inferior stations of life" who were neither rich and powerful nor wise and of superior virtue—that is, most people—to channel their desire for wealth and distinction into decent behavior. The following passage, which Smith added to the edition of *The Theory of Moral Sentiments* he completed shortly before his death, conveys his belief that the moral promise of commercial society lies in the positive directions into which its institutions channel the passions:

> In the middling and inferior stations of life, the road to virtue and that to fortune, to such fortune, at least, as

men in such situations can reasonably expect to acquire, are, happily in most cases, very nearly the same. In all the middling and inferior professions, real and solid professional abilities, joined to prudent, just, firm, and temperate conduct, can very seldom fail of success. . . . Men in the inferior and middling stations of life, besides, can never be great enough to be above the law, which must generally overawe them into some sort of respect for, at least, the more important rules of justice. The success of such people, too, almost always depends upon the favour and good opinion of their neighbours and equals; and without a tolerably regular conduct these can very seldom be obtained. The good old proverb, therefore, That honesty is the best policy, holds, in such situations, almost always perfectly true. In such situations, therefore, we may generally expect a considerable degree of virtue; and, fortunately for the good morals of society, these are the situations of by far the greater part of mankind.[16]

The greatest achievement of the invisible hand of social institutions in commercial society is to convert the potentially base desire for status and approbation into relatively virtuous forms of conduct.

Smith contrasts these virtuous forms of conduct with the conduct promoted by pre-market sources of wealth and power, "the courts of princes" and "the drawing-rooms of the great." There, success depends less upon "the esteem of intelligent and well-informed equals" than upon "the fanciful and foolish favour of ignorant, presumptuous, and proud superiors." While in commercial society promotion is based on "merit and abilities," in aristocratic and court society it is based on flattery and "the abilities to please."[17] A moral advantage of commercial society, therefore, is that it channels self-interest into more virtuous forms of behavior. As compared to societies in which success depends on flattery, fawning, and deceit, in commercial society success depends on honesty, industry, merit, and ability. Consequently it was less likely to promote that corruption of moral sentiments of which moralists had always complained.[18]

For Smith, the most liberating effect of the rise of commercial society was the replacement of relations of direct personal dependency with the cash nexus, the contractual relations which limit the legal power of men to dominate one another.

Smith loathed slavery. Historically, he points out, slaves had been treated most harshly in societies which were opulent but controlled by a free, slave-owning minority. "No human person," he concludes, would wish for a society whose freedom was made possible by the bondage of slaves.[19] He describes contemporary slave traders and slave owners as "the refuse of the jails of Europe, . . . wretches who possess the virtues neither of the countries which they come from, nor of those which they go to, and whose levity, brutality, and baseness, so justly expose them to the contempt of the vanquished."[20] His analysis of slavery, whether or not it was economically sound, casts light on his view of less extreme forms of subservient relations. He maintained that slavery, as practiced in the British colonies in the West Indies and North America, was actually less economically efficient than the use of free labor. The maintainance of the slave was managed by his master, the maintainance of the free laborer by the laborer himself. The rich slave owner was less likely to develop the habits of frugality than the laborer. Free labor, therefore, actually costs less than slave labor. The institution of slavery had persisted into his own day, Smith reasoned, because "The pride of man makes him love to domineer. . . . Wherever the law allows it, and the nature of the work can afford it . . . he will generally prefer the services of slaves to that of freemen."[21] The reason slavery was most common in enterprises where profits were high was that only under conditions of high profit could proprietors afford so uneconomical a source of labor. Smith's arguments subsequently became staples of abolitionist literature in Europe and in the colonies.

In discussions of the vestiges of unfree labor in the coal and salt mines of Scotland, Smith again maintained that the use of legally bound miners was less efficient than the use of free labor. The reason mine-owners persisted in using an economically inefficient work-force was their "love of domination and authority over others, which I am afraid is natural to mankind, a certain desire of having others below one, and the pleasure it gives one to have some persons whom he can order to do his work rather than be obliged to persuade others to bargain with him."[22] The need for institutions that would control the urge to domineer contributed to his moral advocacy of commercial society based on free, wage labor. Legal servitude, he pointed out, though almost entirely extirpated from Great Britain, was still the lot of most people in most of the world. Commerce by itself does not produce liberty or free labor, he stressed, as was evident in eastern Europe. There, in the absence of strong central government, commercial development reinforced the urge to domineer, resulting in commercial agriculture with unfree labor.[23] It was the *combination* of legal security of person and property, free labor, and the market, which produced the virtues which Smith valued in commercial society as it had developed in northwestern Europe.

Commercial society made it possible, for the first time in history, for men to live a morally decent life, in which they were rich enough to engage in some measure of benevolence and in which they could live according to the rules of propriety and prudence, deferring gratification, controlling their appetites, and developing that "steady perseverance in the practice of frugality, industry, and application, though directed to no other purpose than the acquisition of fortune."[24] Commercial society, in Smith's portrait, did not make most men highly virtuous and noble—but then no society could. It did, however, hold out the potential of a society in which most men would be decent, gentle, prudent, and free. Yet that potential was threatened by forces within commercial society itself. Indeed, the pursuit of individual wealth might lead to consequences which threatened the very virtues upon which commercial society depends.

For members of the merchant class, the danger came from the experience of making money too quickly and too easily. Smith criticized the extraordinarily high profits created by monopolies because they seemed to "destroy that parsimony which in other circumstances is natural to the character of the merchant. When profits are high, that sober virtue seems to be superfluous, and expensive luxury to suit better the affluence of his situation." The rapid and painless acquisition of wealth fosters an attitude of "Light come, light go." Its effect is to diminish frugality and industry among merchants, leading them to dissipate their capital rather than investing it in a productive manner which would contribute to the wealth of the nation. Smith pointed to the examples of Spain and Portugal, in which a merchant class which had profited from the windfall profits of colonial trade failed to develop those habits of character which led to reinvestment and national wealth.[25] Unlike the competitive market, in which gradual and uncertain profits promote frugality and parsimony, the experience of quick and easy profits threatens the very process of capital accumulation. Competition makes prudence and self-control necessary; monopoly makes them superfluous.

Smith believed that the possession of excessive wealth weakens the incentive to save and invest with care, and encourages purposeless consumption, or "prodigality." In one of his denunciations of slavery, for example, he contrasted "the disorders which generally prevail in the economy of the rich" to "the strict frugality and parsimonious attention of the poor."[26] He did not see this as a serious danger to commercial society, however, since he believed that prodigality and the imprudent use of wealth by some was "always more than compensated by the frugality and good conduct of others." For the motivation to save came from that powerful "desire of bettering our condition, a desire which, though generally calm and dispassionate, comes with us from the womb, and never leaves us till we go into the grave."[27]

The real danger to commercial society posed by those who grew rich quickly and easily, lay in the human propensity to sympathize with the rich and the powerful rather than with the poor, the lowly, or the wise.[28] Because of this propensity, the behavior of the rich and the famous often serve as a model for those who are poorer and less powerful. "The owners of the great mercantile capitals are necessarily the leaders and conductors of the whole industry of every nation," Smith wrote, "and their example has a much greater influence upon the manners of the whole industrious part of it than that of any other order of men. . . . [I]f his employer is attentive and parsimonious, the workman is very likely to be so too; but if the master is dissolute and disorderly, the servant who shapes his work according to the pattern which his master prescribes to him, will shape his life too according to the example which he sets him."[29] For the lifestyles of the rich to become models for the rest of society would be disastrous. Here was another reason to promote competition in the marketplace. Prudent behavior on the part of the economic elite would be more likely to emerge in response to the hard-earned profits characteristic of the competitive market than in response to the easy profits fostered by legal monopoly.

*   *   *

For the most part, the ordinary man's search for distinction and pre-eminence kept the economy humming, and elicited decent behavior. But two sorts of people, Smith noted, are beyond the quest for social distinction—for entirely opposite reasons. On the one hand, there is the man "so confirmed in wisdom and real philosophy, as to be satisfied that, while the propriety of his conduct renders him the just object of approbation, it is of little consequence though he be neither attended to, nor approved of."[30] Motivated not by the desire for the approval of others but by the desire to be the sort of person *worthy* of approval, such individuals attain a level of morality which it is unrealistic to expect from most of their fellow men and women. These, Smith wrote, are "a select, though, I am afraid, but a small party."

In addition to the average man restrained by public opinion and the wise man restrained by the ideals of his own conscience, Smith distinguishes another type beyond the quest for social distinction—the man whose egoism is restrained neither by public opinion nor by conscience. Such men, unaware of the baseness of their conduct and incapable of feeling disgrace, are regularly guilty of disgraceful actions.[31] Such a person is "so habituated to the idea of his own meanness, and so sunk in slothful and sottish indifference, as entirely to have forgot the desire . . . for superiority." Because he does not even aspire to the approval of society, he is free of the restraints imposed by propriety: free that is to engage in vicious and self-destructive behavior.[32]

Because Smith was so attuned to the role of social surroundings and of human models in the creation of morally decent character, he was particularly alert to the social sources of moral pathology in commercial society. In his recommendations to the legislator, Smith emphasized the need for social institutions that restrain egoism, and the dangers inherent in the emulation of the "loose" lifestyles of the rich and the powerful. If one task of the legislator was to maximize economic benefits by preventing the circumvention of the market, his other task was to maximize the moral benefits of commercial society by fostering institutions to counteract the characteristic moral hazards of that society.

CHAPTER ELEVEN

The Visible Hand of the State

BECAUSE ADAM SMITH ARGUED SO persuasively against direct government involvement in the economy, his awareness of the crucial significance of the state is often overlooked. He argued against government involvement less as a matter of *principle* than as a matter of *strategy*, and he was willing to depart from that strategy when there were compelling reasons for government regulation, as in the case of banking, currency, and even interest rates.[1] Smith tries to persuade the legislator to refrain from setting prices, wages, and tariffs less because such regulations contravene some abstract system of "rights" than because the strategy of restraint works better in promoting economic growth and the distribution of goods that will benefit consumers. Moreover, he felt that many state regulations promoted special interests at the expense of the public interest.

For Smith, the state is the most important institution on which commercial society depends, because the authority and security provided by government are essential for the flourishing of "liberty, reason, and the happiness of mankind. . . ."[2] He believed that, even if the state relinquished its economic role in enforcing tariffs, wage rates, and other trade restrictions, the size and functions of the state would grow with the development of commercial society. The benefits of commercial society required a large state, and the wealth generated by a well-functioning market economy would make the economic burden of the state bearable. This was stated most explicitly in Smith's lectures on jurisprudence:

> We may observe that the government in a civilized country is much more expensive than in a barbarous one; and when we say that one government is more expensive than another, it is the same as if we said that the one country is farther advanced in improvement than another. To say that the government is expensive and the people not oppressed is to say that the people are rich. There are many expenses necessary in a civilized country for which there is no occasion in one that is barbarous. Armies, fleets, fortified palaces, and public buildings, judges, and officers of the revenue must be supported, and if they be neglected, disorder will ensue.[3]

Given this view, it is not surprising that Smith devoted hundreds of pages in The Wealth of Nations to analyzing the functions of government and how to pay for them. Nor is it surprising that he devoted most of the years from the publication of The Wealth of Nations to the end of his life to collecting revenue for the state. The position of Commissioner of Customs for Scotland, to which he was appointed in 1778, was no sinecure. Smith actively sought the appointment, and he was considered ideally suited for it by the expertise on taxation and public finance he had exhibited in The Wealth of Nations. Though the post demanded much of his time, he seems to have enjoyed the work.[4]

As we have seen, customs and excise were important sources of revenue for the fiscal-military state of Smith's day, and Smith approved of their use to pay for the costs of defense and trade.[5] He opposed using customs duties as an instrument of monopoly to favor home industries over imports, but he had no objection to their being used as a source of government revenue and considered numerous suggestions for streamlining their collection.[6] The system of collecting customs duties was ineffective against smugglers, who avoided paying duties on the long list of goods that were subject to taxation. Smith suggested that smuggling could be curtailed and government revenue maintained by reducing the number of items subject to customs duties—thus reducing the incentive to smuggle—and by making the system of collection more difficult to evade. He suggested shifting to the system used to collect excise taxes, under which the goods to be taxed would be stored at specified locations open to customs officials who could ascertain that the duties paid by each importer were in keeping with the volume of his imports. The main barrier to such a reform, Smith wrote, was "Faction, combined with the interest of smuggling merchants."[7] Here was another matter on which the legislator should be guided by the disinterested and public-spirited social scientist.

Smith's views on the functions of the modern state followed from his analysis of the anticipatable *negative* consequences of the central institutions of modern commercial society. The growth of the market and the resulting intensification of the division of labor were the source of much of what was good about civilized society, but they were also the source of a number of intrinsic dangers, which it was the duty of the legislator to obviate.

The need for national defense grows more urgent as economic development proceeds. History shows that as a society grows richer, it becomes a more attractive target to its poorer neighbors. Moreover the division of labor on which opulence depends leaves many men unfit for military service. Fortunately, the division of labor and the growth of affluence that exacerbated the problem of national defense also provided their potential solution—if legislators put the proper mechanisms into place, at increasing expense to the state.

In hunting and shepherding societies, Smith reasoned, every man was both a warrior and a hunter, and the skills needed for civilian pursuits were closely related to the skills needed for waging war. And in agricultural societies the hard physical conditions of civilian life made it relatively easy for men to adapt to the soldierly life. Wars were usually fought after seedtime and before harvest, a time when most young, able-bodied men were willing to serve without additional remuneration. Consequently war did not impose a great expense on government. In medieval Europe, under feudal law, great lords fought, and paid for, the wars of their sovereign, and again the direct cost to the government was relatively low.

In the most advanced stage of history—that of commercial

society—both the likelihood of being attacked and the cost of fighting a war increase dramatically. When most men are smiths, carpenters, or weavers, time spent soldiering is a substantial blow to family income. Even farmers are likely to devote most of their time to earning their livelihood. Thus men are less prepared for war by their ordinary employment, their occupations leave them less time to devote to military exercises, and they cannot afford to go off to war at their own expense. In short, "the great body of the people becomes altogether unwarlike" at the very time when their collective wealth invites invasion by neighboring states.[8]

Thus the social and cultural advance of nations creates the potential for disaster, for the conquest of the civilized and the refined by the rude and the barbarous. For Smith and his contemporaries this was no hypothetical conjecture. It was the historical experience of advanced societies in the West, as Smith reminded his students time and again in his lectures.[9] Athens had fallen to the more primitive Macedonians, who under the leadership of Philip and Alexander had devoted themselves to the development of a standing army and the arts of war.[10] At a time when Rome stood at the height of civilization, the decay of its standing army into "a corrupt, neglected, and undisciplined militia" opened the way to conquest by the barbarous German and Scythian forces.[11]

Although the advance of civilization had been interrupted by successive regressions, Smith believed that the division of labor and national opulence would make it possible to avoid another such reversal. The division of labor, he reasoned, had made the conduct of war more complex and more specialized. Yet it was not in the interest of private citizens to devote themselves fully to the art of war, because it brought no profit in time of peace. Only the state, acting in wisdom, could induce men to devote themselves fully to military matters—a wisdom often lacking in the societies of the past.[12] Here was yet another case in which the legislator, guided by the social scientist drawing on past experience, could foresee and forestall the negative unanticipated consequences of social developments.

In the civic republican tradition, the preferred solution to the problem of defense was the militia, in which citizens were to develop virtue and learn to risk their lives for the common weal. In the Scotland of Smith's day, this solution was again recommended, especially by intellectuals like Adam Ferguson who linked commerce with corruption and were more pessimistic than Smith about the cultural and moral benefits of commercial society.[13] Smith believed that evidence pointed to the military superiority of a modern standing army over a militia. An army of professional soldiers could apply specialization to the military arts and would inculcate the qualities of "regularity, order, and prompt obedience to command" demanded by modern warfare.[14]

An opulent society can afford to devote a portion of its wealth to the cost of maintaining a professional army. The development of modern firearms had made warfare ever more expensive, giving wealthy nations an additional advantage over poor nations in preparing for war. *Thus the invention of gunpowder had unintended positive consequences: it created the opportunity for modern civilized states to avoid the historical pattern of defeat at the hands of less civilized societies.* Smith's remarkable conclusion once again put him at odds with traditional wisdom:

> In ancient times the opulent and civilized found it difficult to defend themselves against the poor and barbarous nations. In modern times the poor and barbarous find it difficult to defend themselves against the opulent and civilized. The invention of fire-arms, an invention which at first sight appears to be so pernicious, is certainly favourable both to the permanency and to the extension of civilization.[15]

Smith's acute historical awareness of the link between national defense and the preservation of civilization led him to characterize the art of war as "certainly the noblest of the arts" and to insist that defense should take precedence over economic considerations in setting trade policy. Though he was highly critical of the Navigation Acts, he approved of the provisions which gave British ships a monopoly over the transportation of British goods, holding that those provisions ensured a supply of the sailors and ships necessary for British defense. He endorsed these laws despite the fact that they obliged British consumers to pay higher prices for imported goods.[16]

In great modern states, Smith realized, a large portion of government revenue would necessarily go to the preparation for war and the protection of commerce. Yet he was critical of the "mercantilist" quest for empire and for the protected trade which was the main impetus behind the expansion of the fiscal-military state.

Smith regarded many of the wars of his day as unnecessary, ill advised, and inimical to the growth of the wealth of the nation. He attributed this in part to the incentives created by a system of government funding which he believed disguised the real costs of war. Rather than raise taxes in time of war—a policy likely to dampen popular support for the war—British governments preferred to pay for war by borrowing money and adding to the national debt.[17] In the long run, Smith argued, the taxes needed to pay the interest on the debt would be greater than war-time taxes would have been. Moreover, politicians were readier to incur new debt than to find new revenues to pay off existing debt: "To relieve the present exigency is always the object which principally interests those immediately concerned in the administration of public affairs. The future liberation of the public revenue, they leave to the care of posterity."[18] Since money paid in taxes was money which would not be invested in the economy, Smith reasoned, the ultimate effect of paying for war by running large deficits was to retard economic growth.[19] Like most eighteenth-century political economists, Smith was deeply concerned about the growth of the national debt. He concluded that on the whole the British system of taxation was better than that of other European states, since it permitted a sizable debt without doing great harm to the national economy. Yet he explored various methods of shrinking the existing debt.[20]

The best way to cope with military expenses, Smith thought, was to pay for wars through wartime taxation. In the short run, to be sure, such a policy would reduce the new capital available for investment. But in the long run, he reasoned, it would promote economic growth by easing the burden of taxation needed to service the government debt. Moreover, forcing taxpayers to bear the real and immediate costs of warfare would create public pressures which would make politicians more wary of going to war and more inclined to conclude wars once they had begun.[21] Keeping a war going was often attractive for noneconomic reasons, Smith believed; for citizens far from the scene of battle who read about the exploits of their armed forces, war had a certain entertainment value. It prompted "a thousand visionary hopes of conquest and national glory." Characteristically trying to channel self-interest toward the public good, Smith urged that wars be funded in a way that would create incentives to avoid unnecessary military adventures.

Next to providing for national defense, Smith believed that the most important function of government was to provide justice and security under the law. Essential to national opulence were legal and political institutions to safeguard peace, protect liberty and property, and allow for market exchange among independent producers. It was to an account of the historical development of such institutions that he devoted his lectures on jurisprudence. And in The Wealth of Nations, he analyzed the history of Spain, Portugal, and China to show how their laws and institutions had retarded economic development and perpetuated poverty despite favorable circumstances.[22]

It was to the security of property that Smith attributed much of Britain's burgeoning wealth. That security made it worthwhile for every individual to make "the natural effort . . . to better his own condition."[23] When men "are secure of enjoying the fruits of their industry, they naturally exert it to better their condition, and to acquire not only the necessaries, but the conveniencies and elegancies of life," he wrote.[24] Without a regular and reliable system of justice it was impossible for merchants and manufacturers to enforce contracts and the payment of debts.[25] As we have seen, Smith regarded confidence in the impartiality of justice as a key factor in economic growth and applauded the separation of the judicial branch from the executive branch of government.[26]

Just as military expenditures rose as society advanced, so too did the costs of administering justice. Property, Smith recognized, can be acquired either by just means, through market exchange, or through unjust means, to the benefit of one party at the expense of the other. As the nation's wealth increases, there is more property to be acquired and stronger motivation to seize it by force or stealth prompted by "avarice and ambition in the rich, in the poor the hatred of labour and the love of present ease and enjoyment."[27] It is the task of government to close off such tempting non-market avenues to wealth at the expense of justice.

Since only the state can protect property and make "private" property possible, those with the greatest amount of property have the greatest amount of interest in maintaining the state,

Smith reminded his readers. Consequently, he argued, taxation should vary with the level of personal wealth.[28] The legislators to whom Smith was appealing were among the wealthiest members of society, a fact which must be kept in mind in reading his rhetorical description of the costs of neglecting the expense of justice:

> Wherever there is great property, there is great inequality. For one very rich man, there must be at least five hundred poor, and the affluence of the few supposes the indigence of the many. The affluence of the rich excites the indignation of the poor, who are often both driven by want, and prompted by envy to invade his possessions. It is only under the shelter of the civil magistrate that the owner of that valuable property, which is acquired by the labour of many years, or perhaps of many successive generations, can sleep a single night in security. He is at all times surrounded by unknown enemies, whom, though he never provoked, he can never appease, and from whose injustice he can be protected only by the powerful arm of the civil magistrate continually held up to chastise it.[29]

Here surely was a passage that might prompt those with the deepest of pockets to reach into them and come up with the needed funds!

Another governmental function which was bound to expand with the advance of commercial society was the provision of what Smith called "institutions for facilitating the commerce of society"—what we call "infrastructure." Roads, canals, bridges, and harbors benefit society as a whole, but are too expensive or unprofitable to be undertaken by individuals. Though Smith believed that providing such facilities was the proper business of government, he sought to match the burden of their expense to those who gain most from them. For example, he suggested charging user tolls proportionate to the wear and tear caused to roads and bridges.[30] In other cases, he suggested legal changes which would allow some infrastructural facilities to be provided by private interests. To meet the need for banking and insurance services which required more capital than could be provided by limited partnerships, Smith recommended the creation of joint-stock companies with limited legal liability to assemble the large amounts of capital required.[31]

By providing for defense, justice, and infrastructure, government would create the preconditions for a market economy and for "that universal opulence which extends itself to the lowest ranks of the people."[32] Yet the very process that brought about an increase in national wealth was fraught with negative consequences which the legislator must anticipate and mitigate.

Smith's emphasis on the positive functions of government in *The Wealth of Nations* has often been downplayed, and the extent to which his proposals demanded new governmental expenditures has rarely been recognized. Nor did Smith regard the functions of government enumerated in Book V of *The Wealth of Nations* as exhaustive. In keeping with the purposes of that book, Smith's discussion there refers primarily to functions related to the expenditure of government revenue. Smith refers elsewhere in his work, as we have seen, to government's role in "promoting the prosperity of the commonwealth, by establishing good discipline, and by discouraging every sort of vice and impropriety; [it] may prescribe rules, therefore, which not only prohibit mutual injuries among fellow-citizens, but command mutual good offices to a certain degree." This was a matter of discretion in which there were risks in erring in either direction. "Of all the duties of a law-giver, however, this, perhaps, is that which it requires the greatest delicacy and reserve to execute with propriety and judgment. To neglect it altogether exposes the commonwealth to many gross disorders and shocking enormities, and to push it too far is destructive of all liberty, security, and justice."[33] On the question of the proper role of government in regulating morality, Smith was as distant from enlightened absolutism as he was from laissez-faire, as we will see when we turn to his policy recommendations.

Foremost among the negative consequences of the process that contributed to the growth of national wealth were the debilitating cultural effects of the division of labor on manual workers. Smith began with the premise that intellectual development is deeply influenced by the nature of work. Writing at a time when there was no general education and when the schedule of workers in manufacturing left little leisure time, Smith observed:

> The man whose whole life is spent in performing a few simple operations, of which the effects too are, perhaps, always the same, or very nearly the same, has no occasion to exert his understanding, or to exercise his invention in finding out expedients for removing difficulties which never occur. He naturally loses, therefore, the habit of such exertion, and generally becomes as stupid and ignorant as it is possible for a human creature to become. The torpor of his mind renders him, not only incapable of relishing or bearing a part in any conversation, but of conceiving any generous, noble, or tender sentiment, and consequently of forming any just judgment concerning many even of the ordinary duties of private life. Of the great and extensive interests of his country he is altogether incapable of judging; and unless very particular pains have been taken to render him otherwise, he is equally incapable of defending his country in war. The uniformity of his stationary life naturally corrupts the courage of his mind, and makes him regard with abhorrence the irregular, uncertain, and adventurous life of a soldier. It corrupts even the activity of his body, and renders him incapable of exerting his strength with vigour and perseverance, in any other employment than that to which he has been bred. His dexterity at his own particular trade seems, in this manner, to be acquired at the expence of his intellectual, social, and martial virtues. But in every improved and civilized society this is the state into which the labouring poor, that is, the great body of the people, must necessarily fall, unless government takes some pains to prevent it.[34]

This is a harrowing view. If Smith had subscribed to it absolutely, his verdict on capitalism would certainly have been that its gains were far outweighed by its losses. Indeed this passage—taken out of context—has frequently been cited by critics of capitalism (including Karl Marx) as testimony to the alienating effects of capitalism. Yet the passage is far from

Smith's last word on the moral effects of commercial society, and in other parts of *The Wealth of Nations* his evaluation of those effects is far more positive. In an earlier discussion of the division of labor, for example, Smith speaks of technological improvements made at the suggestion of factory workers.[35] In arguing against the notion that only low wages would force the poor to work regularly, Smith maintains that "Where wages are high . . . we shall always find the workmen more active, diligent, and expeditious, than where they are low; in England, for example, than in Scotland; in the neighborhood of great towns, than in remote country places."[36] In *The Theory of Moral Sentiments* his estimate of the cultural effects of the market is even more positive.

We must remember that in this gloomy passage Smith is writing what he called rhetorical discourse, which in order to persuade "magnifies all the arguments on the one side, and diminishes or conceals those that might be brought on the side contrary to that which it is designed that we should favour."[37] The key to Smith's purpose lies in the last phrase: *"unless government takes some pains to prevent it."* Smith then presents a list of expensive recommendations for new public expenditures. Having alarmed his readers, he suggests the means of dispelling their anxiety.

As an antidote to the mental degradation caused by the division of labor, Smith recommended universal public schooling, largely at government expense, so that even poor people could acquire the skills of reading, writing, and arithmetic. This suggestion contradicted the advice of enlightened intellectuals like Voltaire, and was at odds with the views of the dominant British classes, who feared that schooling would discourage deference.[38] Smith did not suggest compulsory schooling. Instead, he offered a plan to make schooling more accessible and more useful, and to provide incentives for parents to have their children educated. Such incentives were necessary because the spread of manufacture based upon the division of labor, by making it possible for children to be employed at income generating tasks, led many parents to send even very young children out to work.[39] So the division of labor, in addition to narrowing the horizons of the worker, created economic incentives to neglect education.[40] Hence the need for the public to "facilitate . . . encourage, and . . . even impose upon almost the whole body of the people the necessity of acquiring those most essential parts of education."[41]

In formulating recommendations for public policy, Smith once again examined the historical and comparative record to suggest institutional means to counteract the anticipatable negative consequences of new developments.

Smith recommended the setting up of public schools supported partly at public expense and partly by the payment of very low fees. The English charity schools, which he approved of, were privately supported institutions which provided education to poor children but were not universally available. Smith took as his model the parish schools of Scotland, which had been established early in the eighteenth century in an effort to advance the spread of literacy. These schools were maintained partly at public expense and partly by fees, which were kept low to enable poor parents to provide for the education of their children.[42]

The ancient Greeks and Romans had required their young men to take military and gymnastic training in order to strengthen their martial spirit and prevent the "mental mutilation" of cowardice from spreading through society like a "loathsome and offensive disease." Smith favored a militia for these character-building reasons, even though its utility in warfare was limited under modern conditions. But for Smith the Greek and Roman militias were primarily a model with a different contemporary analogue. Under modern conditions it was necessary for a civilized society with a wide division of labor to create a system of public incentives to prevent the emergence of a *new* form of degradation, "the gross ignorance and stupidity which, in a civilized society, seem so frequently to benumb the understandings of all the inferior ranks of people. A man without the proper use of the intellectual faculties of a man is, if possible, more contemptible than even a coward, and seems to be mutilated and deformed in a still more essential part of the character of human nature." Education, he believed, would perform that function. Not only would education benefit individuals, it would benefit the state as well. The better educated people became, the less likely they would be to respond to "the delusions of enthusiasm and superstition" that lead to religious war. They would also be "more disposed to examine, and more capable of seeing through, the interested complaints of faction and sedition" and thus less likely to engage in rash revolts against the government. Finally,

Smith thought, an educated population would behave in a more decent and orderly manner. These qualities, in turn, would make for greater social cohesion through shared respectability. As the respectable behavior of the lower orders made them feel capable of obtaining the respect of their social superiors, they would become more deferential toward their superiors.[43]

Thus the visible hand of the state would counteract the potentially stultifying effects of the invisible hand of the market. To encourage people to acquire an education, Smith suggested that the government offer small premiums and badges to students who did well in school. He also recommended that the government impose entrance examinations for various occupations which would require the lower classes to demonstrate their literacy and a knowledge of the basics of arithmetic, geometry, and mechanics, and would require the middle and upper classes to display some knowledge of science and philosophy. In the case of those who could afford to pay for their own education, the government should set educational requirements for entry into the professions, and allow those who needed to meet them to find the most suitable teachers. Thus, Smith recommended that government set educational goals but that it rely on the superior knowledge of individuals motivated by self-interest to pursue those goals as efficiently as possible.[44]

In designing the provision of public services Smith tried to devise marketlike mechanisms which subjected providers to the discipline of competition and tied payment to the actual performance of services. "Publick services are never better performed than when their reward comes only in consequence of their being performed, and is proportioned to the diligence employed in performing them," he noted.[45] "In every profession, the exertion of the greater part of those who exercise it, is always in proportion to the necessity they are under of making that exertion."[46] As an incentive for judges to conduct speedy and efficient legal proceedings, Smith advised that they be paid a set fee, and then only after a trial had been concluded. He recommended that the salaries of professors and teachers be paid in part by their students, as an incentive for them to teach well.[47] He suggested giving students with scholarships a choice of the college they wanted to attend, as an incentive for colleges to provide the best education.[48]

Because the costs of defense, justice, infrastructure, and

education all increase as society advances, Smith accepted taxation as inevitable.[49] He would have agreed with Justice Holmes that taxes are the price we pay for civilization. He did not of course conclude that the level of civilization rises with the level of taxation. On the contrary, he tried to devise tax policies which would generate the revenue necessary to cover the government's necessary functions, with as little waste as possible. "Each tax ought . . . to be so contrived," he wrote, "as both to take out and to keep out of the pockets of the people as little as possible, over and above what it brings into the publick treasury of the state."[50]

For Smith, the market was the most striking example of a social institution which channels human passions to public benefits. In the areas in which government activity was necessary to maintain the prerequisites of market activity or to counteract the negative consequences of the market, Smith tried to design institutional means to channel private interests to favorable public outcomes.

CHAPTER TWELVE

Applied Policy Analysis: Adam Smith's Sociology of Religion

SMITH'S ANALYSIS OF RELIGION IN *The Wealth of Nations* is one of the clearest and perhaps least expected applications of his characteristic approach to the role of institutions in channeling the passions and to the unintended consequences of social action.[1] In *The Theory of Moral Sentiments* Smith had sought to answer the question "Why be moral if you no longer believe in heaven or hell?" for men who had ceased to hold those beliefs. But his philosophical answer, he realized, was not accessible to all. For Smith, religion expressed in metaphorical terms the reality that acting justly and beneficently is the source of greatest reward and happiness while acting ignobly brings its own punishment. The fact that religion expresses this insight not in terms of the rewards and punishments of conscience but in terms of rewards and punishments in the afterlife makes it all the more useful for influencing the behavior of those beyond the reach of philosophy. The core truth of religion is that by acting justly and beneficently we fulfill the purposes of our creation. And so, Smith concludes, "religion enforces the natural sense of duty."[2]

In *The Wealth of Nations*, Smith dealt with the social effects of Christian religious institutions despite his skepticism of revealed truth. His most extended exploration of the social functions of religion comes in his discussion of government expenses for the support of "institutions for the instruction of people of all ages."

Religious institutions, he asserts, provide "a species of instruction of which the object is not so much to render the people good citizens in this world as to prepare them for another and a better world to come."[3] While Smith is (probably deliberately) vague as to the *reality* of the afterlife, he discusses the social-psychological *utility* of belief in the afterlife in promoting virtuous behavior in *The Theory of Moral Sentiments*.[4] In *The Wealth of Nations* his concern is with the influence of religion on public order and public morals, both of which were necessary if the lower orders were to enjoy the economic and moral benefits of commercial society.

Smith examines the major established, dissenting, and sectarian Christian denominations of his day and explains their failure or success in terms of the incentives they provide in what might be called the market for souls. As elsewhere, he shows that good intentions may lead to negative results from the perspective of the actor, and that goals may be more readily achieved through institutions designed to create beneficent public outcomes.

Smith presents his own version of the Polybian cycle of growth, decay, and conquest from without, applying it not to states but to churches. The appeal of a prosperous, well-established church, he maintains, declines over time as a result of its very prosperity and security. Either through the generosity of private donors or through government support, the church is provided with benefices which provide clergymen with income and allow them to pursue higher education. But the unanticipated effect of guaranteeing the income and improving the learning of clergymen is to decrease their incentive and ability to bring their religious message to the mass of the population. Since they will receive their income regardless of how effectively they preach and proselytize, Smith observed, they have as little incentive to exert themselves as had the professors Smith had known at Oxford. Refinement and learning are qualities which recommend the clergy to the elite but which diminish their appeal to the masses.

The resulting vacuum at the lower end of the spiritual market, Smith observes, is filled by "a set of popular and bold, though perhaps stupid and ignorant enthusiasts." While the established clergy might be more learned and elegant, "the arts of popularity, all the arts of gaining proselytes, are constantly on the side of its adversaries." It was this process, Smith thought, which explained the successful challenge of the Dissenters to the established Church of England in the seventeenth century. Now that the dissenting churches were themselves becoming well endowed, they were losing their edge to the less learned, more popular Methodists.[5] By contrast, Smith observes, the continuing popularity of the Catholic Church on the Continent could be traced to the fact that the parish clergy depended upon parishioners for part of their income and hence had an economic incentive to meet the religious needs of their flock. In periods when the fortunes of the Church had been in decline, Smith noted, the popularity of the Church had been revived by the mendicant orders, which depended for their sustenance wholly on voluntary contributions: "It is with them as with the hussars and light infantry of some armies—no plunder, no pay."[6]

In describing these entrepreneurs of the holy spirit, Smith's tone was nearly as skeptical as when he was describing worldly merchants. And he found an analogue in the world of religion to the monopolies by which merchants profited at the expense of the common good.

In his analysis of religious institutions, Smith was issuing a rejoinder to David Hume, whom he described in *The Wealth of Nations* as "by far the most illustrious philosopher and historian of the present age."[7] Hume had argued that in regard to most professions government need play no regulatory role, since customers in the market would judge the quality of the services offered. But Hume made a major exception in the case of the clergy, arguing that the very diligence of clergymen would be dangerous, "because, in every religion except the true, it is highly pernicious, and it has even a natural tendency to pervert the true, by infusing into it a strong mixture of superstition, folly, and delusion." Hume, a religious skeptic, did not believe that the doctrine of the established Church was "true," but he was deeply concerned with the effects of religion on public order and public morals. In order to hold the support of their followers, he wrote, preachers of nonestablished sects would profess "the most violent abhorrence of all other sects" and would propagate doctrines geared to "the passions and credulity of the populace." Hume recommended that in the interest of public order and public morals the government should pay the salaries of the established clergy, "to bribe their indolence." Their function was "merely to prevent their flock from straying in quest of new pastures."[8] Struck by the religiously motivated strife in seventeenth-century England, Hume feared the zeal of clergymen as a source of faction and civil war. The state, he believed, should fund the established faith in order to maintain spiritual quality-control and political order.

Smith accepted Hume's goals but suggested a very different mechanism for achieving them. What would happen, he asked, if politicians "dealt equally and impartially with all the different sects" and "allowed every man to chuse his own priest and his own religion as he thought proper?" The result, he predicted, would be "a great multitude of religious sects" in which each teacher would strive to increase the number of his disciples. And the multiplicity of sects, Smith argued, would prevent the outcomes Hume feared:

> The interested and active zeal of religious teachers can be dangerous and troublesome only where there is either but one sect tolerated in the society, or where the whole of a large society is divided into two or three great sects. . . . But that zeal must be altogether innocent where the society is divided into two or three hundred or perhaps as many thousand small sects, of which no one could be considerable enough to disturb the publick tranquillity.

The consequences, Smith suggested, might well be different from the intentions of the sectarians, with results beneficial to the public. "Seeing themselves surrounded on all sides with more adversaries than friends," Smith hypothesized, the preachers of each denomination would become more impartial and moderate than the clergy of an established church, who "see nothing round them but followers, disciples, and humble admirers." The relative weakness of each denomination would prompt it to seek the tolerance of others and would thus create a disposition toward tolerance in society at large. The denominations might even discover that there were "concessions which they would find it both convenient and agreeable to make to one another." Ultimately, they would reduce their doctrine "to that pure and rational religion, free from every mixture of absurdity, imposture, or fanaticism, such as wise men have in all ages of the world wished to see established." Thus zeal and fanaticism might promote toleration, moderation, and rational religion—for Smith the most beneficent of outcomes.[9]

Here is another example of Smith's strategy of pitting

otherwise malicious passions against one another to produce a socially beneficent outcome. Voltaire had used this strategy in arguing for religious pluralism in his *Letters on England* of 1733: "If there were only one religion in England there would be danger of despotism, if there were two they would cut each other's throats, but there are thirty, and they live together in peace and happiness."[10] Smith refined the notion, explained the mechanism, and showed that religion would cost the government less and serve the common good more if Hume's suggested monopoly of faith was replaced by a free market in denominations.

As we have seen, Smith believed that society plays an important role in moralizing behavior. Hence his emphasis in *The Theory of Moral Sentiments* on the influence of what would later be termed reference groups and role models:

> This natural disposition to accommodate and assimilate, as much as we can, our own sentiments, principles, and feelings, to those which we see fixed and rooted in the persons whom we are obliged to live and converse with, is the cause of the contagious effects of both good and bad company. The man who associates chiefly with the wise and the virtuous, though he may not himself become either wise or virtuous, cannot help conceiving a certain respect at least for wisdom and virtue; and the man who associates chiefly with the profligate and the dissolute, though he may not himself become profligate and dissolute, must soon lose, at least, all his original abhorrence of profligacy and dissolution of manners.[11]

It was these considerations which were foremost in his analysis of the social function of religious sects in *The Wealth of Nations*.

Smith was writing in an era when the expansion of urban manufacture was drawing people from the countryside into the cities. The speed with which these new communities came into being far outstripped the capacity of the established Church of England to adapt. Formerly, most parishes had depended on paternalistic landowners for financial support. But there were no such landowners to be found in the new urban centers, where the parish structure was inadequate. The gap was eventually filled by the Methodists, who concentrated their energies on the lower classes and were most successful in the new industrial centers.[12] The Methodist preachers performed what Smith deemed a vital social function, and Smith presented his own analysis of their success.

Sectarian preachers, Smith claimed, succeeded among the lower classes because their dependence on the contributions of their flock gave them a material incentive to proselytize and because the message they delivered was well suited to the social needs and intellectual attainments of their audience. That message the established clergy were no longer capable of delivering.

There were, broadly speaking, two systems of morality in society, Smith observed, one "loose," the other "austere."

> In the liberal or loose system luxury, wanton and even disorderly mirth, the pursuit of pleasure to some degree of intemperance, the breach of chastity, at least in one of the two sexes, etc. provided they are not accompanied with gross indecency, and do not lead to falsehood or injustice, are generally treated with a good deal of indulgence, and are easily either excused or pardoned altogether. In the austere system, on the contrary, those excesses are regarded with the utmost abhorrence and detestation.

These moral systems were correlated to one's economic position in society. The rich in general and particularly "people of fashion" tended to favor the loose system. The more successful among the common people, by contrast, tended toward the austere system, because they knew that liberal morals would be disastrous for them:

> The vices of levity are always ruinous to the common people, and a single week's thoughtlessness and dissipation is often sufficient to undo a poor workman for ever, and to drive him through despair upon committing the most enormous crimes. The wiser and better sort of the common people, therefore, have always the utmost abhorrence and detestation of such excesses, which their experience tells them are so immediately fatal to people of their condition.

In discussing the opportunities in commercial society open to "the common people" or "the poor," Smith distinguished between those whose morals disposed them to reap the rewards of commercial society and those whose morals did not. In his comparison of the lot of the common people in an opulent, commercial society to the lot of the king of a tribe of poor savages, it was the "industrious and frugal peasant" who benefited from society's wealth.

Smith believed that the moral environment of the poor was a key factor in determining whether or not they would benefit from universal opulence.[13] In *The Theory of Moral Sentiments*, he showed how conscience and self-mastery develop from internalizing the moral approval of others. In this sense being in the public eye is a spur to moral conduct. A man of "rank and fortune" who seeks to avoid disgrace is reinforced in his moral behavior by his awareness that others "attend to every part of his conduct." Urbanization, however, threatened the poor by removing the social reinforcement of decent and prudent behavior. Smith compared the situation of a man of low social standing in the countryside with his situation in the city:

> While he remains in a country village his conduct may be attended to, and he may be obliged to attend to it himself. In this situation, and in this situation only, he may have what is called a character to lose. But as soon as he comes into a great city, he is sunk in obscurity and darkness. His conduct is observed and attended to by nobody, and he is therefore very likely to neglect it himself, and to abandon himself to every sort of low profligacy and vice.

The new evangelical sects offered one solution to this problem. Because of their small size and their focus on moral behavior, they rescued their members from anonymity and made their conduct the concern of a "respectable society" with its own sanctions against those who failed to live up to its moral code. Moreover, in order to win over members of the lower classes for whom the austere system of morality had a natural appeal, the clergy of the new sects favored this system over the liberal system characteristic of the upper classes. Motivated by self-interest, the evangelical preachers were led to reinforce the austere system of morality which the common people required in commercial society.[14]

Although Smith applauded the moralizing role of the evangelical sects, he feared that their effect might be *too* austere, or what he called "unsocial," and that they might promote that suspicion of enlightened culture which he called "the poison of enthusiasm and superstition." He suggested two remedies. The first was for the state to promote "the study of science and philosophy" by requiring those of "middling or more than middling rank and fortune" who sought to enter the professions to pass a test on these subjects. "Science is the great antidote to the poison of enthusiasm and superstition," he wrote, "and where all the superior ranks of people were secured from it, the inferior ranks could not be much exposed to it." Second, to alleviate "that melancholy and gloomy humour which is almost always the nurse of popular superstition and enthusiasm," Smith recommended the amusement and diversion provided by painting, poetry, music, dancing, and drama.

In the case of both remedies, Smith showed his typical preference for having the government set goals and limits and then leaving it to the market to meet them. Thus the state was to set the standards of philosophical and scientific knowledge required for admission into the professions but would leave it to those seeking entry into the professions to find their own teachers. Government could use market mechanisms in the cultural realm as well in order to structure institutions to encourage morally beneficent outcomes. It could promote public diversions simply "by giving entire liberty to all those who for their own interest would attempt, without scandal or indecency, to amuse and divert the people. . . ." The phrase "without scandal or indecency" reminds us that Smith assumed that government would set limits on the market for entertainment. Without such limits human passions would lead in directions at odds with Smith's civilizing project.

In religious policy the most effective strategy would be for government to restrict itself to keeping the peace in the competition among religious faiths "to hinder them from persecuting, abusing, or oppressing one another."[15] After presenting this ideal solution of a free market in religion, Smith considered how his goals might best be promoted under existing conditions, in which most states had an established religion. As is so often the case in *The Wealth of Nations,* he drew on historical and comparative evidence in order to determine which methods of funding religion would be most effective in promoting the morality of the citizenry.

The clergy of the established churches of England and the Lutheran German states, Smith points out, were appointed by the patronage of the court, the nobility and the gentry, and were therefore attuned to the views of their distinguished patrons. They were learned and genteel, and contemptuous of the "fanaticism" of the sects. These qualities, which appealed to their upper-class patrons, left the established clergy less fit to appeal to the common people. "They are listened to, esteemed and respected by their superiors; but before their inferiors they are frequently incapable of defending, effectually and to the conviction of such hearers, their own sober and moderate doctrines against the most ignorant enthusiast who chooses to attack them."[16] Smith was describing a religious culture of the learned which had reacted against the extremism and irrationalism of seventeenth-century sectarianism by moving in the direction of "natural religion."[17] In the Church of England this tendency was known as "latitudinarianism," and in the Scottish Kirk as "Moderatism." John Witherspoon, a Scottish divine who emigrated to America and became president of Princeton University, wrote this amusingly critical description of the preaching of the typical Moderate clergyman:[18]

1. His subjects must be confined to social duties.
2. He must recommend them only from rational considerations, namely the beauty and comely proportions of virtue, and its advantages in the present life, without any regard to a future state of more extended self-interest.
3. His authorities must be drawn from heathen writers, none, or as few as possible from scripture.
4. He must be very unacceptable to the common people.

Many of Smith's friends were members of the Moderate clergy, and his own rationalistic, natural religion was an extreme version of their faith.[19] But he recognized that the problem posed by the fourth of Witherspoon's points was real enough.

Of all the major European churches, Smith judged that the Calvinist Presbyterians were perhaps the most successful in combining learning and theological moderation with the ability to attract a wide popular following. He attributed this in part to the structure of incentives in the Scottish Kirk. While the patronage of the powerful played a role in the election of clergy, the confirmation of ministers required popular consent. And, since benefices in Scotland were pretty much the same for everyone, aspiring clergymen had little incentive to fawn on powerful patrons or to appeal to popular extremism in search of election. In addition, the meager but adequate salary of the clergy meant that they too had to adhere to the austere system of morals, adding to their appeal to the common people. The Scottish Kirk thus optimized the qualities Smith deemed appropriate to the clergy: learning and theological moderation, advocacy of austere morality, and the ability to appeal to the populace.[20]

Smith's analysis of religion provides a capstone of his overall project, which Walter Bagehot characterized with tongue half in cheek as "showing how, from being a savage, man rose to become a Scotchman."[21]

CHAPTER THIRTEEN

"A Small Party":
Moral and Political Leadership in
Commercial Society

COMMERCIAL SOCIETY, IN WHICH EVERY man becomes to some degree a merchant, encourages the spread of characteristics associated with the prudent pursuit of self-interest—the "inferior virtues" of moderation, self-control, frugality, and decent behavior toward others. But that does not mean that the rarer and more demanding virtues, such as valor, strong benevolence, and fortitude, are obsolete. While Smith taught that the road to national wealth lay in commerce rather than in conquest, he believed that the nation still needed the ability to defend itself and therefore required the fortitude and bravery of the military hero. While well-designed institutions minimize the need for ongoing government intervention in social and economic life, commercial society still requires the informed prudence and wisdom of statesmen and legislators devoted to the public weal.[1] In *The Theory of Moral Sentiments*, Smith reminded his readers of the superiority of these virtues and the greater approbation and self-approbation that ought to attend them. And *The Wealth of Nations* was written not for men who sought to increase their own wealth but for those who might be motivated to advance the public good by increasing the wealth of the nation and strengthening its character-building institutions.[2]

Much of the institutional analysis contained in *The Wealth of*

Nations, The Theory of Moral Sentiments, and the lectures on jurisprudence is devoted to describing and prescribing how institutions should be structured to develop the inferior virtues. Yet time and again Smith insists that the survival and prosperity of society depend on the cultivation of the superior virtues among at least some of its members. Though he devotes little explicit attention to the institutional means by which this can be achieved, that lapse is more apparent than real. Implicit in Smith's works is the assumption that superior virtue, insofar as it is susceptible to cultivation, can be developed through exposing those who have developed the inferior virtues through institutional means to the stimulus of moral philosophy. To those who are morally and intellectually capable of learning its lessons, moral philosophy teaches that superior virtue may earn them the more intense approbation of their fellow men and assure them the self-approbation that comes with knowing that one has acted not only acceptably but excellently.

The great strength of commercial society, as Smith perceives it, is its ability to control the passions by promoting the inferior virtues associated with striving for rank and fortune and with the prudent pursuit of self-interest. The virtues of "those who are contented to walk in the humble paths of private and peaceable life" are "temperance, decency, modesty, and moderation . . . industry and frugality."[3] The characteristic type of commercial society is the prudent man, who

> is not always very forward to listen to the voice even of noble and great ambition. . . . [He] would be much better pleased that the public business were well managed by some other person, than that he himself should have the trouble, and incur the responsibility, of managing it. In the bottom of his heart he would prefer the undisturbed enjoyment of secure tranquillity, not only to all the vain splendour of successful ambition, but to the real and solid glory of performing the greatest and most magnanimous actions.[4]

The prudent man's pursuit of his own health, fortune, rank, and reputation produces a character worthy of our "cold esteem," but these virtues are neither very ennobling nor very endearing.[5] Smith's prudent man closely resembles the "bourgeois" who was to be the target of so much cultural criticism in the years ahead.[6] Yet Smith did not characterize the prudent man as lacking in virtue; to do so would be to disdain the qualities of prudence, deferred gratification, and self-control that make men gentle in their relations with one another and that prompt them to create the universal opulence which makes possible a decent life for the many. It was this disdain, characteristic of the civic republican tradition, that Smith sought to dispel.

Commercial society is based on the assumption that the benevolence of most people is limited, and that it declines in strength as distance increases from family to friends to neighborhood to country. Although commercial society provides for the "inferior prudence" required for the pursuit of self-interest, it also demands that at least some of its members acquire that "superior prudence" which combines prudence "with many greater and more splendid virtues, with valour, with extensive and strong benevolence, and with a sacred regard to the rules of justice, and all these supported by a proper degree of self-command."[7] Smith values the actions of the man of inferior prudence "contented to walk in the humble paths of private and peaceable life," but he values more highly "the more splendid actions of the hero, the statesman, or the legislator."[8]

Smith stressed the significance of institutions which habituate individuals to develop decent behavior. In Smith's civilizing project, state institutions of coercive social control were rendered less necessary by the self-restraints which were the products of non-political institutions such as the family, the market, and the chapel. Yet he believed that those institutions of moral education needed to be augmented by an intellectual elite which offered a rational explanation and rhetorical encouragement of the inferior virtues of prudent self-control, as well as the superior virtues of benevolence, self-sacrifice, and public-spiritedness. "The wise and the virtuous," Smith believed, were inevitably a "small party."[9] Yet the members of that small party played a number of crucial roles in promoting the moral and economic wealth of the nation.

The term "intellectual"—with its modern connotation of an independent man of letters who tries to mold public opinion and the opinion of legislators—did not come into wide use until the closing years of the nineteenth century. But the type long preceded the term. Smith wrote relatively little about intellectuals and their proper political role. But his conception of that role, including his own, is implicit in the rhetoric of his books and in the observations scattered through them. To reconstruct that conception, we must assemble the fragments into a coherent whole.

THE INTELLECTUAL AS MORALIST

One such fragment appears in *The Theory of Moral Sentiments*, in Smith's description of "the wise and virtuous man." In judging our own behavior, Smith writes, we may orient ourselves to either of two standards of proper behavior. The lower standard is the one that is attained by most of those around us. The higher standard is that of moral perfection, insofar as each of us is capable of understanding that ideal. The ability to comprehend the nature of moral perfection varies with our capacity to reflect on our observations of the character and conduct of those around us, and hence to perfect our sense of what is morally just and proper. The wise and virtuous man aspires to this higher standard and directs his attention to understanding its implications.[10] Because he is aware of his own imperfection, he does not treat those who are more imperfect with scorn or contempt. Instead, he attempts "by his advice and by his example" to "promote their further advancement."[11]

Smith believed that this impulse is deeply ingrained in human nature. "The desire of being believed, the desire of persuading, of leading and directing other people, seems to be one of the strongest of all our natural desires. . . ." This desire to influence the judgments of others marks a stage in the rise to perfection. "As from admiring other people we come to wish to be admired ourselves; so from being led and directed by other people we learn to wish to become ourselves leaders and directors," Smith writes. And just as the desire to be regarded as admirable by others motivates us to act admirably, the desire to be believed by others motivates us to act in a manner worthy of belief.[12] The "great ambition" to guide the conduct of others, therefore, is both morally legitimate and a goad to moral self-improvement.

Smith's purpose in *The Theory of Moral Sentiments* is to encourage the desire to become the proper object of self-approval among those who are potentially virtuous.[13] Just as the style and rhetoric of *The Wealth of Nations* are designed to motivate legislators to advance the public interest, so the style and rhetoric of *The Theory of Moral Sentiments* are designed to make its readers more virtuous. The market was to structure the incentives for material gain so that man's search for the attention of others would lead him toward decent forms of behavior. Social settings such as the family, neighborhood and chapel provided a structure of incentives in which the passion for approbation would lead toward some degree of benevolent behavior. But what structure of incentives could develop the passion of self-approbation, the desire to act in a way we know we ought to approve of even if those around us do not?

Smith gives an implicit answer to this question in *The Theory of Moral Sentiments*, where he criticizes the "casuistry" of moralizing works that try to determine the precise degree of vice and virtue but fail "to animate us to what is generous and noble . . . to soften us to what is gentle and humane."[14] The proper role of "books of morality" is to excite emotions in the heart, to present moral cases in a way that will make us *want* to act as we *ought* to.[15] Smith's strategy is to reveal the implicit logic of social judgment in what he calls "common life" by describing the social disapproval and self-disapproval provoked by bad deeds, and the approbation and self-approbation aroused by good ones. The lesson of *The Theory of Moral Sentiments* is that self-command pays: it gratifies either the desire for approbation, or—more valuably—the desire for self-approbation. The intention is to strengthen the reader's sense that self-satisfaction results from acting virtuously.

One role of the intellectual, then, is that of the moral philosopher who guides the conscience of his readers or listeners.[16] He must direct them toward the proper pursuit of prudence, toward obedience to the rules of justice, and toward benevolence.[17] This role demands the use of reason in order to discover general rules of prudence, justice, and benevolence based upon induction from experience.[18] But the task of the moral philosopher is not merely to distinguish between virtuous and vicious actions: he must do so in such a way as to encourage the members of his audience to improve their own behavior.

Despite Smith's awareness of the limits of rational persuasion as a motive for moral action, he believed that the conceptions of morality offered by philosophers influence the judgments and actions of those who are moved by conscience to try to act virtuously. One responsibility of the moral philosopher is to criticize philosophies that fail to make relevant moral distinctions, because bad philosophy can undermine virtuous behavior. This conviction explains Smith's vigorous criticism of Mandeville. Because Mandeville emphasized the psychological motives behind moral action, his work has "an air of truth and probability which is very apt to impose upon the unskillful." Mandeville's system, Smith complains, is "wholly pernicious" in that it seems to eliminate entirely the distinction between virtue and vice.[19] "The question concerning the nature of virtue necessarily has some influence upon our notions of right and wrong in many particular cases," Smith noted. By reducing all virtuous actions to egoistic vices, Mandeville undermined the desire to act virtuously.[20]

The deleterious effect of Mandeville's philosophy, Smith believed, could be traced to his inability to make relevant distinctions. His fallacy was "to represent every passion as wholly vicious, which is so in any degree and in any direction." For example, he labeled as vices "the love of pleasure and the love of sex." Yet, Smith insisted, it is perfectly moral to indulge those passions so long as they are controlled by temperance and marital fidelity.[21] Similarly, by classifying the desire for approbation as "vanity," Mandeville failed to distinguish the morally laudable desire for *earned* approbation from the desire for *unearned* approbation, which is the proper definition of vanity.[22] Though Smith shared Mandeville's emphasis on the passionate sources of behavior, Smith regarded his own moral philosophy as a corrective to Mandeville's intellectual errors and to their morally pernicious effects.

One role of the intellectual, as Smith conceived it, is as moral analyst and guide to individual behavior. The other role is as policy analyst, who makes use of social scientific knowledge to guide the actions of legislators toward the public interest.

The Intellectual and the Politician

Like much else in commercial society, the role of the intellectual as policy analyst is a result of the division of labor. For the variety of occupations in a commercial society present an almost infinite variety of objects to the contemplation of those few, who, being attached to no particular occupation themselves, have leisure and inclination to examine the occupations of other people. The contemplation of so great a variety of objects necessarily exercises their minds in endless comparisons and combinations, and renders their understandings, in an extraordinary degree, both acute and comprehensive. Unless those few, however, happen to be placed in some very particular situations, their great abilities, though honourable to themselves, may contribute very little to the good government or happiness of their society."[23]

Smith suggested no mechanism by which those few could be placed in the "particular situations" in which their abilities could be made to serve the happiness of their society—perhaps because he and other Scottish intellectuals were already in situations of influence thanks to the patronage of the rulers of Scotland and England. To proclaim that fact would be at best superfluous, at worst impolitic. But occupying a position of potential influence merely created the *possibility* of bringing one's intellectual abilities to bear on government. To realize that possibility demanded a style of writing which appealed to potential readers in positions of power—the Townshends and the Buccleuchs, the Shelburnes and the Pitts.

It is Smith's concern for the effect of his writing on his intended audience that accounts for the radically different portraits of the merchant in *The Theory of Moral Sentiments* and *The Wealth of Nations*. In *The Theory of Moral Sentiments* the portrait is positive, whereas in *The Wealth of Nations* the merchant is capable of threatening public welfare by exercising undue political influence. This was a warning to politicians, most of whom were men of landed wealth, to resist the attempts of merchants to get laws passed that would serve their own interests. *The Wealth of Nations* tries to influence the politician by appealing to his concern for the public good and by the aesthetic attraction exerted by the systematic exposition of the "system of natural liberty."

Ultimately it is only the legislator who can prevent special interests from dominating the decisions of government. To do so requires politicians motivated to put the welfare of the country above their personal and particular interests. Under modern conditions politicians have need for men whose intellectual aptitudes and whose position in the division of labor allow them to think systematically about "the science of the legislator." But even with such advisers, the politician needs to be guided by prudence, an awareness of the gap between what is desirable and what is possible.

Smith wrote relatively little about what he regarded as the best structure of government. To portray him either as a supporter or an opponent of modern representative democracy is simply anachronistic: in a country where most people were benighted to the point of illiteracy, the possibility of their participation in government was hardly conceivable. In his lectures of 1762, Smith's few comments on "democracy"—a term he used in the traditional sense of direct popular participation in government— noted that it had not been much of a success the few times that it had been tried and in each case had been abandoned.[24] In his genealogy of commercial society, as we have seen, Smith depicted the consolidation of royal power over the feudal landlords as a gain for civilization. He clearly approved of the division of power as it had developed in England from the Glorious Revolution through the age of Walpole. Legislative power lay in the elected House of Commons, but the monarch could influence the Commons through the preferments at his disposal.[25] In the vocabulary of his day, Smith was a Whig, a supporter of a strong central government dominated by a modernizing and commercialized aristocracy. But he was a sceptical, scientific Whig, uncommitted to any faction.[26]

Smith maintained that the institutions of commercial society guided men's passions into some degree of benevolence, but benevolence was limited, and its intensity diminished with social distance. The other side of the coin of limited benevolence is group self-interest, a reality with which the prudent statesman must reckon. Each state, Smith wrote, is made up of numerous "orders and societies, each of which has its own particular powers, privileges, and immunities." Though all these orders and communities depend upon the state for their prosperity and protection, individuals are naturally concerned to protect the interests of their particular order or community over those of others. "This partiality, though it may sometimes be unjust, may not, upon that account, be useless," Smith remarked. For the effort "to preserve whatever is the established balance among the different orders and societies into which the state is divided . . . contributes in reality to the stability and permanency of the whole system."[27]

The importance of stability pervades Smith's remarks on government. Only a stable government can guarantee the security of person and property which is so essential to the flourishing of commercial society. Under modern conditions, he believed, that stability rests on the opinion the governed have of the governors. The importance of public opinion in a legitimate regime was one of the arguments Smith advanced for the promotion of mass education. It was also central to his view of political prudence: because government in commercial society rested ultimately upon public opinion, he was wary of government attempts to institute radical change, no matter how well intentioned or well advised. He cautioned enlightened monarchs against attempts to hasten reform by usurping the power and privileges of the nobility, of cities and provinces, or of the other established orders of society.[28]

Smith believed that statesmen needed to be guided by ideals as they set policy, and he tried to make his social science attractive to them. But he warned of the dangers of trying to implement those policy ideals all at once. To do so was to commit the error of "the man of system," who "is often so enamoured with the supposed beauty of his own ideal plan of government, that he cannot suffer the smallest deviation from any part of it." Such attempts are bound to fail, Smith warned, because of the resistance arising from existing socio-economic interests and deeply rooted beliefs. The man of system, in other words, is insufficiently attuned to the peculiarities of his countrymen to make proper use of mechanisms for the institutional direction of the passions:

> He seems to imagine that he can arrange the different members of a great society with as much ease as the hand arranges the different pieces upon a chess-board. He does not consider that the pieces upon the chess-board have no other principle of motion besides that which the hand impresses upon them; but that, in the great chess-board of human society, every single piece has a principle of motion of its own, altogether differ-

ent from that which the legislature might choose to impress upon it. If those two principles coincide and act in the same direction, the game of human society will go on easily and harmoniously, and is very likely to be happy and successful. If they are opposite or different, the game will go on miserably. . . .[29]

Systematic social thought necessarily simplifies the motives of human behavior. Men are not like chess-pieces, because of the complexity of human motivations. Hence, unlike the rules of a game, the rules of society are never fully spelled out, and political actions often have unanticipated consequences. *It is the role of social science to anticipate these consequences more fully, but the limits of prediction commend caution in reform.*

And so, even as Smith tried to encourage the politician to act like a good citizen who wishes to "promote, by every means in his power, the welfare of the whole society of his fellow-citizens," he cautioned the benevolent "man of public spirit" to

respect the established powers and privileges even of individuals, and still more those of the great orders and societies, into which the state is divided. . . . He will content himself with moderating, what he often cannot annihilate without great violence. When he cannot conquer the rooted prejudices of the people by reason and persuasion, he will not attempt to subdue them by force. . . . He will accommodate, as well as he can, his public arrangements to the confirmed habits and preju-dices of the people. . . . When he cannot establish the right, he will not disdain to ameliorate the wrong; but like Solon, when he cannot establish the best system of laws, he will endeavour to establish the best that the people can bear.[30]

Smith's policy recommendations reflect his awareness of the need to accommodate existing interests in order to preserve governmental legitimacy and stability. Though he argued strong-ly that most tariffs served private interests, he recommended that the protectionist tariffs then in effect in industries involving large investments of capital and employing many workers be lifted gradually and with adequate warning, thus providing "equitable regard" to the interests of investors and preventing sudden mass unemployment.[31] In both *The Theory of Moral Sentiments* and *The*

Wealth of Nations he cautioned against the excessive use of government force to implement even well-motivated policy reforms; and in *The Wealth of Nations,* he expressed approval of the manner in which the English Parliament was being "managed" through the accommodation of existing interests, in contrast to the forceful attempts of the French monarch to overcome the resistance of the *parlements.*[32]

For Smith, then, one role of the intellectual was to influence men of power, to encourage their public spirit, and to provide them with concepts and information through which they could anticipate the probable consequences of government action. Yet, Smith insisted, even well-motivated and well-informed politicians had to be guided by prudence, the knowledge of the possible, and by sensitivity to the situation of the moment. The "science of a legislator," in which the social scientist specialized, deals with "general principles which are always the same"; but the implementation of policy depends on "the skill of that insidious and crafty animal, vulgarly called a statesman or politician, whose councils are directed by the momentary fluctuations of affairs."[33] In other words, the skills, knowledge, motivations, and considerations of the politician are different from— and no less important than—those of the intellectual.

PART III

FROM SMITH'S TIME TO OURS

CHAPTER FOURTEEN

Critics, Friendly and Unfriendly

WITHIN A FEW YEARS AFTER Smith's death, sweeping political events and shifting economic trends led to major challenges to his ideas by critics friendly and unfriendly. To pursue the friendly critiques of *The Wealth of Nations* would be to write a history of subsequent economic thought. So important an innovator in the field of political economy as Alfred Marshall is reported to have said of his own work, "It's all in Adam Smith."[1] To trace Smith's influence on later economic thought cannot be our purpose here. To pursue the challenges to his moral evaluation of commercial society is beyond the bounds of this chapter.[2] Nevertheless it is worth reviewing, in broad strokes, the directions such criticisms were to take.

One of the most significant criticisms came from a sympathizer, and was penned shortly after the ink had dried on *The Wealth of Nations*. In a critique of Smith's strictures on interest rates in that book, Jeremy Bentham put forth a broader reassessment of the sources of growth in a capitalist economy.[3]

Contrary to his customary position, Smith had recommended that interest rates be capped by government at a rate slightly higher than the lowest going market rate. High interest rates, Smith claimed, would direct most of the money available for loans into the hands of "prodigals and projectors," since they alone would be willing to pay high rates of interest. The "sober people" who expected a lower rate of profit would be frozen out of the loan market. "A great part of the capital of the country would thus be kept out of the hands which were most likely to make a profitable and advantageous use of it," Smith reasoned, "and thrown into those which were most likely to waste and destroy it."[4]

This recommendation reflected Smith's general evaluation of commercial society in terms of its propensity to promote the neo-stoic virtue of prudence. For Smith, "employers of stock" were merchants and manufacturers engaged in "plans and projects." He put "projectors" into a different category.[5] For Smith, "projectors" were those who were willing to take the risks associated with high-interest loans. They did not conform to his model of the prudent man, the human engine of the capitalist economy as he conceived it. The prudent man was more likely to minimize his risks by investing in existing and proven methods of production and distribution. The prudent man, as Smith described him in The Theory of Moral Sentiments, "is naturally contented with his situation, which, by continual, though small accumulations, is growing better and better every day. . . . He does not go in quest of new enterprises and adventures, which might endanger, but could not well increase, the secure tranquillity which he actually enjoys."[6] Smith's aversion to risk-taking and to risk-takers was reflected in his skepticism with regard to joint-stock companies with limited liability, which, he argued, encouraged investors to invest in risky enterprises and thus discouraged prudence.[7] He favored such companies only when they engaged in routine operations and hence were free from the lure of "extraordinary gain."[8]

Bentham's Defence of Usury, written in 1787 and published the next year, included an open letter to Smith attacking Smith's advocacy of a legal limitation on interest rates and criticizing his pairing of the "projector" with the "prodigal."[9] To scorn the "projector," Bentham declared, was to disdain "all such persons as, in the pursuit of wealth, strike out into any new channel, and more especially into any channel of invention," whether by creating new products, improving existing products, reducing production costs, or moving into new markets. Bentham argued that by lumping the "projector" with the "prodigal" as types to be shut out of the money market, Smith had stigmatized "every application of the human powers, in which ingenuity stands in need of wealth for its assistant." It was such innovators who were most in need of capital available only at high rates of interest. They would have to pay more for the money they borrowed because the very novelty of their projects made them less attractive to "prudent" lenders, who preferred the tried and proved to the novel and unknown. Bentham turned Voltaire's argument about the historical relativity of "luxury" against Smith, reminding him that all the innovations "by which our species have been successively advanced from that state in which acorns were their food, and raw hides their clothing, to the state in which it stands at present" had at one time been untried "projects." The lack of available capital to such "projectors" had discouraged innovation in the past, Bentham maintained. Removing limits on interest rates and increasing the availability of lending capital would accelerate the pace of innovation, and with it the material progress of society, he concluded.

Bentham's emphasis on the crucial role of entrepreneurial innovation was not widely shared by nineteenth-century British economists, though it was echoed by the influential French economist Jean-Baptiste Say.[10] At the turn of the twentieth century, a new wave of attention to the role of creative elites in human affairs would lead Joseph Schumpeter to a renewed emphasis on the role of the entrepreneur in capitalist society. Schumpeter's view of the historical development of capitalism was rather different from Smith's. Smith had seen that process as a gradual but steady accumulation of wealth occasioned by the growth of capital and by incremental improvements in production methods. Schumpeter, by contrast, described capitalism as a process of "creative destruction" which advanced in discontinuous leaps and bounds as imaginative entrepreneurs pioneered new technology and new methods of organization.[11]

Why did Smith downplay the role of entrepreneurial innovation in the history of capitalism? This was almost certainly a case in which his moral philosophy blinded him to an important factor. As we have seen, his concern for the moral and economic well-being of the laboring class led him to criticize merchants for circumventing the market in their pursuit of profit at public expense. The grounds for Smith's more positive evaluation of merchants lay in their practice of prudence. In that respect they were very different from the risk-taking, innovative entrepreneurs credited by Bentham and Schumpeter.

Smith's neo-stoic lens also colored his analysis of what motivates the actors on the economic stage of commercial society and may have led him to overlook an important link in the chain connecting benevolence and market activity. In *The Theory of Moral Sentiments,* Smith portrayed the family as the central locus of benevolence in commercial society, and in his lectures on jurisprudence he identified the desire to leave property to one's descendants as the motivation behind much of family law. Yet in *The Theory of Moral Sentiments* and in *The Wealth of Nations,* he attributed economic striving mostly to the desire to win the attention and admiration of others. He says almost nothing about the desire to promote family well-being as a motivating force in economic activity. Here was an area in which sympathetic subsequent theorists would not so much criticize as complement Smith's vision of commercial society.[12]

Smith was convinced that the future of wage-earners in commercial society would be bright so long as government policy permitted capital to grow rapidly enough to outpace the rate of population increase and thus ensure employment and rising real wages. As we have seen, Smith wrote at a time when the living standard of the laboring classes was on the rise. By the time of his death in 1790, however, the situation had begun to change. Shortly thereafter, in 1794–95 and 1800–01, food prices shot up. Shortages led to food riots and the threat of widespread disorder. In 1798, Thomas Malthus, in his *Essay on the Principle of Population,* expressed doubts about the likelihood that material comfort could be provided for the bulk of the population, thus leading to the characterization of economics as "the dismal science." And Edmund Burke—a friend of Smith's and an advocate of a freer economy—offered an even more somber forecast of the inevitability of periodic privation among the poor in his *Thoughts and Details on Scarcity* (written in 1795 and published posthumously in 1797).

In the meantime, the French Revolution had shocked Burke into reflecting on the fragility of the institutions of Whig England, of which both he and Smith generally approved (though Smith had been more reserved and skeptical in his approval). Burke now concluded that Smith had overlooked some of the most important historical factors which had made "civilization" and stability possible in England. The contribution of commerce to the rise of civilization had been made possible by developments and institutions which Smith had slighted: the improvement in manners associated with "chivalry" and embodied in the inherited aristocracy, and the role of the Established Church in holding together the ranks of society.[13] Burke was expressing a theme that would recur many times in modern conservative thought—namely, that the stability of commercial society depends on traditions and institutions which predate the market itself.

Smith's argument that mutual benefits flow from international trade unrestricted by protectionist tariffs or export subsidies was refined and extended by David Ricardo in his theory of comparative advantage, presented in his *Principles of Political Economy and Taxation* (1817). Others, meanwhile, were formulating what was to be a persistent critique of Smith's view of international economic relations. Critics maintained that all things being equal, Smith was right about the benefits of international free trade, but since all things were not equal, some departures from Smith's model were required. Alexander Hamilton, for example, in his "Report on Manufactures" (1791), argued that agriculture was an unstable basis for the American economy, because the European nations from which Americans purchased manufactured goods did not provide a reliable, long-term market for American agricultural exports. To encourage the growth of manufacturing in the United States, Hamilton recommended a system of government subsidies (bounties) and protective tariffs that would strengthen domestic production for home consumption and for export.[14] Among those impressed by Hamilton's vision was the German political refugee Friedrich List, who argued that advanced nations would always be able to produce manufactured goods more cheaply than their less developed trading partners. Thus, he argued in *Outlines of American Political Economy* (1827), the only way a nation could develop a manufacturing base was to protect "infant industries" by imposing tariffs on imported manufactured goods. List returned to Europe in 1832, where his writings provided an impetus for the *Zollverein*, the customs union out of which a unified Germany was eventually to emerge.[15] The argument on behalf of balanced national economic development has remained the great counter to the theory of international free trade ever since.

A more fundamental critique of Smith's claims appeared in the writings of the early-nineteenth-century socialists, culminating in the works of Karl Marx. Marx claimed that cyclical contractions in the supply of capital would lead to an oversupply of workers, a rise in unemployment, and a depression of wages to the subsistence level (though he indicated that this minimal level would move upward with changing social conceptions of subsistence). Marx's critique of what Smith had called "commercial society" predated his economic concerns and were fundamentally moral and philosophical. For Marx the division of labor and the specialization on which commercial society is based were morally intolerable, as was self-interest itself.[16] He declared that the "liberty" provided by commercial society was no liberty at all. Workers had exchanged the personal dependence of serfdom for impersonal dependence on the market, which for Marx was a distinction without a difference. Just as Smith had invidiously dubbed the commercial policy of his time "the mercantile system," a reference to those whose interests he believed it to favor, Marx dubbed the market economy of his day "the capitalist system," to signal his contention that the system served the owners of capital at the expense of the workers.

Marx's economic predictions turned out to be flawed, partly as a result of his reliance on the labor theory of value. That theory was in accord with his philosophical assumptions about man's place in the world, but it was being abandoned by most economists because of its lack of explanatory power.[17] But Marx's moral critique of an economy based on self-interest, and of the constraints on self-realization imposed by the division of labor—a critique which reflected the influence of civic republicanism and romanticism—retained its appeal even after the subsequent history of capitalism and its Marxist alternatives had negated his economic analysis.

In the two centuries from Smith's time to ours, there have been repeated oscillations between optimistic views and pessimistic views of the material benefits arising from a market economy. The death knell of capitalism has served as an ostinato to the rising theme of capitalist vitality. To some degree, these oscillations reflect the alternating pattern of expansion and contraction in standards of living related to international conflict, demographic transitions, the pace of technological innovation, and a host of other factors. In the long run (and frequently in the short run as well), Smith's optimism regarding the material benefits of commercial society has been vindicated. But each

short-run contraction has spawned warnings of inevitable decline and proclamations of the limits of growth. Such pessimism
has often appeared even when the lot of the poor was improving,
due in part to a lack of historical perspective, in part to the gap
between objective evidence and the perceptions of the compas-
sionate.[18]

The acceptance or rejection of Smith's defense of free trade
has had a profound effect on international relations from his time
to ours. For most of the eighteenth century, foreign conquest and
monopoly of foreign trade were regarded as the major sources of
national wealth, and international relations were seen a zero-
sum competition for scarce resources. Smith put forward a
convincing case that free international trade would work to the
benefit of all, and thus placed international relations on a more
pacific basis. This view continued to influence British policy for
much of the following century, and the policy of the ascendant
liberals on the European continent as well.

The final decades of the nineteenth century saw a turning
away from the Smithian view of international relations. Under
the influence of social Darwinist doctrines, relations between
nations once again came to be viewed as a struggle for resources
to be secured through military hegemony. Motivated by social
Darwinist views and by the trade restrictions that were their
international corollary, nations from Russia to the United States
embraced a new imperialism. Germany, having achieved national unity only recently and thus having missed out on the earlier
stages of European colonial expansion which gave Britain,
France, and Holland their colonial holdings, now demanded its
own "place in the sun." The tensions fed by this view of
international relations led inexorably to the First World War.
After that massive blood-letting, the western nations turned once
again toward free trade. But economic depression soon led to
renewed protectionism: in 1930 the Congress of the United
States, responding to pressure from the National Association of
Manufacturers and the American Federation of Labor, imposed
the Smoot-Hartley tariffs, making it difficult for foreign nations
to sell their goods in the American market. The British responded
with their own system of "Imperial Preference." The Japanese,
who needed to export in order to survive, concluded that they
required their own zone of protected trade, and with their 1937
invasion of Manchuria set out to create their "Asian Co-

Prosperity Sphere." The Germans too established a protected economic zone, a *"Grossraum,"* stretching across Europe and into Russia.

After the Second World War, American policy makers, recognizing the link between pre-war protectionism and the descent into war, set about creating a regime of international trade with minimal tariffs. It was this regime which fostered the recovery of western Europe and Japan, and the rise of many nations from poverty to participation in that "universal opulence" which it had been Smith's goal to extend.

Adam Smith distinguished "the mean principle of national prejudice" from "the noble one of the love of our own country." It was below the dignity of a great nation, he wrote, to view with envy

> the internal happiness and prosperity of the other, the cultivation of its lands, the advancement of its manufactures, the increase of its commerce, . . . its proficiency in all the liberal arts and sciences. . . . These are all real improvements of the world we live in. Mankind are benefited, human nature is ennobled by them. In such improvements each nation ought, not only to endeavour itself to excel, but from the love of mankind, to promote, instead of obstructing the excellence of its neighbours. These are all proper objects of national emulation, not of national envy or prejudice.[19]

Smith believed that men of wisdom should put cosmopolitan, long-term interests above immediate pressures and international envy. Whether economic relations among nations will again revert to the assumption that "when one gains, the other must lose" remains an open question. Advocates of that view bear the burden of explaining why it will not again lead to military conflict as it has repeatedly in the past.

CHAPTER FIFTEEN

Some Unanticipated Consequences of Smith's Rhetoric

DURING THE DECADE AFTER SMITH'S death in 1790, members of Parliament often cited *The Wealth of Nations* as an authoritative source, and by 1800 there was already a "superstitious worship of Smith's name."[1] On the hundreth anniversary of the book's publication, Walther Bagehot wrote that Smith was one of those rare intellectuals with the ability to "describe practical matters in such a way as to fasten them on the imagination, and not only get what they say read, but get it remembered and make it part of the substance of the reader's mind ever afterwards." Smith "carried political economy far beyond the bounds of those who care for abstract science, or who understand exactly what it means. He has popularized it in the only sense in which it can be popularized without being spoiled; that is, he has put certain broad conclusions into the minds of hard-headed men, which are all which they need know and all which they for the most part will ever care for, and he has put those conclusions there ineradicably."[2]

What were the broad conclusions which, in Bagehot's words, were most ineradicably placed into the minds of hard-headed men by *The Wealth of Nations*? They were conclusions about "the system of natural liberty" that Smith put forth most unequivocally and simply, as in the following passage, with which Smith ended his powerful critique of mercantilism:

All systems either of preference or of restraint, therefore, being thus completely taken away, the obvious
and simple system of natural liberty establishes itself of
its own accord. Every man, as long as he does not
violate the laws of justice, is left perfectly free to pursue
his own interest his own way, and to bring both his
industry and capital into competition with those of any
other man, or order of men. The sovereign is completely discharged from a duty, in the attempting to perform
which he must always be exposed to innumerable
delusions, and for the proper performance of which no
human wisdom or knowledge could ever be sufficient;
the duty of superintending the industry of private
people, and of directing it towards the employments
most suitable to the interest of society.[3]

Smith used the term "natural liberty" in order to impress
upon his readers the beauty of a coherent system deduced from a
few premises. Indeed, he was so successful in making the general
case against government restraints on trade that his readers all
too often ignored the complexity of his conception of commercial
society and his frequent qualifications of "natural liberty." That it
was essential for government in a commercial society to provide
for the common defense, for a legal system to protect person and
property, and for the infrastructure necessary for commerce; that
government must encourage and even coerce its citizens to
acquire an education; that government should foster non-governmental institutions that develop character in its citizenry; that
government must ensure the decency of popular entertainments
—all were overlooked. Subsequent commentators were to re-
mark time and again on the gap between Smith's policy recommendations and what is usually taken as his "laissez-faire"
message.

The "restraint" against which Smith was inveighing in the
passage quoted above meant export and import duties, not the
restraint of the individual and his passions. Leaving every man
"perfectly free to pursue his own interest his own way" referred
to economic interest—Smith was not suggesting that moral
instruction is unnecessary, or that the pursuit of self-interest will
by itself lead to a morally commendable spontaneous order. In
speaking of the inability of the sovereign to direct the minutiae of

economic life, he was not dismissing the role of social science in government policy or suggesting that society could do without the wisdom and virtue of the politician.

So impressed were eighteenth-century intellectuals with the new-found ability of man to uncover the invariable laws of nature that they often used the terms "nature" and "natural" ambiguously. Those terms denoted both what was *factual* and what was *normative:* the structure of reality, and the way things ought to be.[4] The search for natural law and natural theology was often colored by an explicit providentialism, the belief that the deep structure of the world was fundamentally beneficient.[5] For Smith, the "natural" is the normative—what *ought* to be made to happen for the benefit of all. Only in the commercial stage of society can the natural propensity to truck, trade, or barter be fully exercised and have its most beneficial effects. But the wise and the virtuous, those who devise and those who implement the science of the legislator and moral philosophy, have crucial roles to play in moving commercial society toward the "natural" benefits it makes possible.

In his account of ancient stoicism in *The Theory of Moral Sentiments*, Smith criticized the providentialist belief that a beneficent creator had so designed creation as to free us from concern over the results of our actions.[6] But his rhetoric of "natural liberty" was so compelling that it led many readers to take just such a view. Ironically, that rhetoric would later be taken as a warrant for the notion that "doing what comes naturally" would result in providential outcomes. The need for institutions to direct the passions, the role of social science in designing institutions, the obligation of government to combat the dangers inherent in commercial society—all would be overlooked. Thus Smith's rhetoric of "natural liberty" had the paradoxical effect of making his message appear both more conservative and more libertarian than he intended it to be.

Smith's view of the proper role of social science was close to what the twentieth-century philosopher Karl Popper has called "piecemeal social engineering." "The task of the piecemeal social engineer," Popper writes, "is to design social institutions, and to reconstruct and run those already in existence. . . . [He] recognizes that *only a minority of social institutions are consciously designed while the vast majority have just 'grown', as the undesigned results of human actions.* But however strongly he may be impressed by this important fact . . . he will look upon them from a 'functional' or 'instrumental' point of view." Popper distinguishes "piecemeal social engineering" from "universal non-interventionism." Those who hold the latter view are so aware of the undesigned origins of institutions and the unanticipated negative consequences of deliberate action that they counsel a passive acceptance of existing institutions. He also distinguishes it from holistic planning, which is insufficiently cognizant of the limits of knowledge and the unanticipated consequences of social action.[7] Because Smith was so effective in demonstrating the unintended positive social consequences of the market and other institutions, he is often claimed as a patron saint by those inclined toward universal non-interventionism.

Smith would have trouble recognizing himself in that role. Moreover, as a neo-stoic advocate of the institutional direction of the passions, he would rub his eyes in amazement at the self-described "liberals," "classical liberals," and "libertarians" who invoke his "natural liberty" to justify the legalization of everything from pornography to guns to hard drugs.

Perhaps the gravest unanticipated consequence of Smith's rhetoric of "natural liberty" is the transformation of that phrase to mean the reverse of what Smith meant by it. As we have seen, Smith's evaluation of commercial society and his policy prescriptions were grounded in his civilizing project. He valued the market, the family, and other social institutions for their role in creating that imperfect but attainable level of virtue which he called "decency." He also believed that commercial society required some men to achieve higher levels of virtue which it was the role of the moral philosopher to cultivate. A prerequisite for the exercise of any level of virtue was what Smith called "self-command," "self-control," or "self-government."

In making his plea for "natural liberty," Smith assumed that political liberty is possible because natural man is social man. Man is endowed by nature with imagination and the desire for sympathy. *Imagination* allows him to put himself in the position of others and to judge his own conduct accordingly. *Sympathy* allows him to share the emotions of others and to control his own behavior in accordance with shared social standards. For Smith, these moral faculties are more than just one set of passions among others. "They were set up within us to be the supreme arbiters of all our actions, to superintend all our senses, passions, and appetites, and to judge how far each of them was either to be indulged or restrained."[8] When we obey moral rules, we experience the rewards of self-approbation or self-satisfaction; when we violate them, we experience "the torments of inward shame" and self-condemnation.[9] The standards by which we judge ourselves have their origin outside ourselves, whether they are the lower standards adhered to by most people around us or the higher standards that accord with the standards of the ideal spectator.

In either case, to be virtuous is to make our conduct conform to an external model which we have internalized. In describing the man of wisdom, Smith says that "he almost identifies himself with, he almost becomes himself that impartial spectator, and scarce even feels but as that great arbiter of his conduct directs him to feel."[10] Having studied the nature of propriety by observing and reflecting upon his own actions and the actions of others, the wise man "endeavours as well as he can, to assimilate his own character to this archetype of perfection" and "to fashion his own character and conduct" according to this model.[11]

Smith therefore assumed that to be a person of moral worth is to make one's conduct conform to a standard oriented beyond the immediate, natural passions of the self. His great achievement was to explain how the combination of original passions and social institutions make such self-control possible. For Smith, to be the sort of individual worth being is to model oneself on standards that are shared or worth sharing. A decent society is one in which those around us have enough control over their passions to respect our needs, a control which they have learned from social institutions. The more virtuous their character, the more we can count on them to live up to shared expectations. "Vice," Smith wrote, "is always capricious: virtue only is regular and orderly."[12] The highest happiness—the pleasure of self-approval—comes from the self-esteem that follows from knowing we have acted virtuously; to be true to oneself, then, is to act in a manner which fulfills a public role.[13]

The complex linkage between limited government, the market economy, social control, and self-control which together made up Smith's civilizing project endured into the nineteenth century, sometimes under the rubric of liberalism, sometimes, as in the United States, under the old label of Whiggism.[14] Yet over the course of that century, liberalism was transformed by the threefold challenge of Radicalism, Utilitarianism, and Romanticism. "Radicalism," in nineteenth-century Europe, advocated the extension of voting rights to all adult males. This democratic tendency, which was in its infancy in Smith's day, did not meet with Smith's approval; but with the spread of education he might well have come to approve of it in the century which followed. It is certainly possible to approve of the extension of voting rights on Smithian grounds—though with the expectation that the pursuit of particular economic interests at the expense of the general interest would be not so much eliminated as extended to include not only landowners, merchants and manufacturers, but workers, farmers and government employees as well.

Utilitarianism and romanticism represented far greater threats to Smith's civilizing project, not least because they were so easily mistaken for it. Jeremy Bentham, the founder of Utilitarianism, sought, like Smith, to formulate a science of the legislator and sometimes regarded himself as Smith's pupil. But what a pupil learns may be quite different from what his teacher tries to teach. Bentham sought a single normative standard by which to judge legislation and which could be combined with a clear, simple science of human motivation. Legislation was to be formulated according to the "greatest happiness principle"— "the greatest happiness of the greatest number." And that happiness—or "well-being," as he called it in *Deontology* (1814) can be measured as "the *difference* in *value* between the sum of the pleasures of all sorts and the sum of the pains of all sorts" which a man experiences over a period of time.[15] The precision Bentham sought was attainable only on the assumption that happiness is basically homogeneous. "Quantity of pleasure being equal, push-pin is as good as poetry," he declared in one of his most telling aphorisms. While Smith's deistic humanism had judged commercial society according to the standards of the civilizing project, Bentham's utilitarianism eliminated the possibility of standards beyond sensual pleasure for judging character. Indeed, it tended to discredit qualitative distinctions, to make them appear as intellectually suspect and morally sinister, and promoted a model of moral thinking which tries to do without them altogether.[16]

What escaped Bentham, wrote a nineteenth-century critic,

was the fact that man is a being capable "of desiring for its own sake the conformity of his own character to his standard of excellence, without hope of good or fear of evil from other source than his own inward consciousness." Bentham, in other words, had no way of accounting for the role of conscience. Nor did he have philosophical grounds from which to argue that some pleasures are more worth having than others:

> If he thought at all of the deeper feelings of human nature, it was but as idiosyncrasies of taste, with which neither the moralist nor the legislator had any concern, further than to prohibit such as were mischievous among the actions to which they might chance to lead. To say either that man should, or that he should not, take pleasure in one thing, displeasure in another, appeared to him as much an act of despotism in the moralist, as in the political ruler.[17]

The man who penned these words shortly after Bentham's death in 1838 was John Stuart Mill. Mill had been educated as a Utilitarian by his father, and would later attempt to recast Utilitarianism in a more philosophically defensible form by abandoning Bentham's premise of the equal value of all pleasures. Yet far from renewing Smith's civilizing project, Mill further distanced liberalism from it. In his best-known essay, *On Liberty* (1859), he declared that "The sole end for which mankind are warranted, individually or collectively, in interfering with the liberty of action of any of their number, is self-protection." In the relationship between society and the individual, he ruled out all "compulsion and control, whether the means used be physical force in the form of legal penalties, or the moral coercion of public opinion."

On Liberty marks a key point at which liberalism was transformed by the incorporation of Romanticism—at the expense of Smith's civilizing project. Though the liberal terms were left intact, they were given new meanings which were in many ways alien to Smith's civilizing project and the Whiggish liberalism that followed from it.[18] In *On Liberty*, liberalism became the defense of "individuality," which Mill hailed as "one of the principal ingredients of human happiness, and quite the chief ingredient of individual and human progess. . . . In proportion to the development of his individuality, each person becomes more valuable to others." Among the elements Mill attributed to individuality were "spontaneity, originality, choice, diversity, desire, impulse, peculiarity, and even eccentricity."[19] Mill thereby defined the new liberalism as the rejection of shared standards in the name of a doctrine which held that the individual is most worthy when he is least like others.

This new criterion of evaluating individual worth reflected the influence of Romanticism. It had begun with new standards of aesthetic judgment, standards which were soon applied to the moral evaluation of the artistic genius. Eventually, the new standards were generalized and democratized.

According to the aesthetic canons of Smith's time, the artist was to orient his creation to the nature, needs, and springs of pleasure in his audience. This required judgment, the study of past models, and artful restraints. There were important parallels between these artistic canons and Smith's conception of moral excellence, which called for the virtuous man to orient himself to the needs of others through incorporating the standards of the "impartial spectator." A superior understanding of these standards demanded observation and the study of models ancient and contemporary; their realization demanded moral restraint.

The new, "expressive" theories of art developed by the Romantics, by contrast, gave pride of place to the poet's natural genius, creative imagination, and spontaneous emotional intensity.[20] According to the Romantic ideal, shared rules are fetters on the Promethean self. For the Romantic, the model individual does not strive to embody shared standards of virtue, he is a genius who need not be bound by the rules of society, indeed who is most himself when he revolts against shared standards.

To be true to oneself no longer meant bringing one's conduct into line with shared, public standards, or with the standards of the impartial spectator. It meant acting "authentically," and authenticity was measured by divergence from shared models. In *On Liberty* Mill integrated this new understanding into liberalism. "If a person possesses any tolerable amount of common sense and experience, his own mode of laying out his existence is the best, not because it is the best in itself, but because it is his own mode."[21] Whereas Smith had advocated limiting government power in order to free non-governmental institutions to channel the passions in socially beneficial directions, Mill advocated limiting government power in order to ensure a free sphere of private life where romantic impulses and expressions of personality could emerge.[22] For Mill, the individual was to be liberated not only from the power of *government* but from the influence of *public opinion*.

The outlook which elevated the expression of the individual's deepest and most particular passions has been called "expressive individualism." Being different became the sign of authenticity. Shared standards and institutional obligations were seen as a burden on the self. The origins of expressive individualism lay in Romanticism, but its highest development came with Nietzsche and Emerson. For Nietzsche, the creative few are philosopher-artists who create themselves and their own morality. In America, the ideal of the individual as the creative artist of his own life was democratized by Emerson. In the Emersonian tradition life is an ongoing experiment in which custom and convention are barriers to the development of the imperial self, which is most authentic when it is different, unique, fluid, and unconstrained by socially shared morality.[23] For expressive individualism, liberty is the freedom to "do your own thing." Its superior virtues are authenticity and difference; its inferior virtues are bohemianism and eccentricity.

Because of this altered meaning of "liberty," an unanticipated consequence of Smith's rhetoric was his identification with conceptions of the good life he would have found abhorrent if not incomprehensible.

CHAPTER SIXTEEN

The Timeless and the Timely

IF SMITH'S NEO-STOIC EVALUATION OF the moral effects of capitalism strikes us as counterintuitive, it may be because we lack the necessary historical and comparative perspective. In the popular mind—and not only in the popular mind—capitalism is more often than not associated with unleashed greed and the pursuit of pleasure. Max Weber was voicing a most Smithian sentiment when he criticized that view:

> The impulse to acquisition, the pursuit of gain, of money, of the greatest possible amount of money, has in itself nothing to do with capitalism. This pursuit exists and has existed among waiters, physicians, coachmen, artists, prostitutes, dishonest officials, soldiers, brigands, crusaders, gamblers, and beggars—among "all sorts and conditions of men," in all times and in every land on earth where the objective possibility of it has existed or exists. This naive conception of capitalism ought to be given up once and for all in the nursery school of cultural history. Unbridled avarice is not in the least the equivalent of capitalism, still less of its "spirit." Capitalism may actually amount to the *restraint*, or at least the rational tempering, of this irrational impulse.[1]

Even today not everyone has graduated from the nursery of cultural history. One need not embrace Smith's (or Weber's) view of capitalism to appreciate Smith's account of the restraining, disciplining effect of the market economy, or its power to guide self-interest toward concern for the needs of others. As countries around the world attempt the great leap forward into capitalism, they become aware of the social discipline and work-orientation it demands. The link of self-interest to mutual concern expressed by the sales clerk's "Can I help you?" and "Have a nice day" is often scorned—except by those who have lived in societies where sales clerks, for lack of institutional incentives, habitually ignore potential customers. Seen from the heights of moral rigorism, such commercially motivated solicitude is evidence of a lack of true charity and altruism. Seen historically and comparatively, the market's ability to create a self-interested regard for others may be preferable to the more brutal means by which self-interest has been pursued, or the explicit indifference which most often characterizes the relations of morally imperfect individuals toward one another.

Since Smith's day, his morally informed social science has fragmented into discrete disciplines and subdisciplines. The gains in the precision of analysis have been great, but the losses in overall understanding have been substantial. The bulk of *The Wealth of Nations* has been absorbed into the discipline of economics, which benefited hugely from Smith's efforts to systematize economic knowledge. Smith's exploration of the influence of social institutions on personality has become the subject matter of sociology and social psychology. In their efforts to become value-neutral, however, all three disciplines have eschewed the vocabulary of character and virtue, which implies that some modes of behavior are more laudable than others, a question regarded as beyond the purview of social science. The question of what constitutes excellence in character has become a sub-field of the sub-field of ethics within the field of philosophy. Contemporary political philosophy, for the most part, resorts to highly formalized criteria of justice in trying to describe the good society, with little reference to the complex web of subpolitical mechanisms so prominent in Smith's work. Smith's assumption that even modern commercial society—perhaps especially such a society—requires "superior prudence" in its governing elites smacks of antidemocratic heresy, at least to those more swayed by democratic dogma than by reflection on successful democratic practice.

Smith was critical of "the propensity to account for all appearances from as few principles as possible," a tendency "which is natural to all men, but which philosophers in particular are apt to cultivate with a peculiar fondness, as the great means of displaying their ingenuity."[2] This propensity has led to the simplification and distortion of Smith's vision by various academic disciplines and political ideologies that have attempted to routinize and democratize ingenuity. Economists tend to assume that economic behavior can be accounted for by treating all individuals as rational profit-maximizers, an assumption they often ascribe to Smith. But they overlook his many departures from this model in *The Wealth of Nations* and *The Theory of Moral Sentiments* or else dismiss them as irrelevant to economic analysis. The recent contribution of economists to trans-disciplinary social scientific thought has taken the form of methodological imperialism, in which the language and assumptions used to analyze economic behavior are applied to institutions such as the family and politics. To conceive of children as consumer durables, the quantity and quality of which vary with the psychic gains they provide, is, Smith would have noted, ingenious.[3] But instead of contributing to the explanation of human behavior, it seems merely to extend to new areas the tautological premises of many economists, who "assume that individuals attempt to maximize utility, and define utility as that which the individual attempts to maximize."[4] It is similarly ingenious to describe voters as utility maximizers, and to describe politicians as aggregators of economic interests. But so narrow a view of human motivation does nothing to explain why citizens often vote against their economic self-interest or on the basis of non-economic values, or why ideology and the process of legislative deliberation often determine the votes of legislators.[5]

Smith's great analytic motif, the unanticipated consequences of human action, has been parcelled out among diverse academic disciplines and political ideologies. For many economists there is one great unintended but quite anticipatable consequence of human action, and it is the socially beneficial consequence of market competition. It is among sociologists that the theme of the unanticipated consequences of human action

has been most explicitly treated, along with its corollary of the
latent (unintended or unstated) functions of social institutions
that exist alongside their manifest (intended or stated) purposes.[6]
When the consequences of government social policy fall short of
its anticipated consequences, it is often because legislators have
failed to appreciate the latent functions of existing social institutions.[7]

Many conservatives have adopted Smith's belief in the
unintended, socially positive outcomes of the market as their
guiding maxim, along with the belief that the unintended
consequences of government action tend to be negative.[8] Con-
versely, many liberals tend to overlook the negative consequences of government action, often substituting good intentions
for sound policy. As a result, those who are most attuned to the
unintended positive consequences of the market and the unintended negative consequences of government action are least
inclined to participate in government, either as civil servants or
as elected legislators. Those, on the other hand, who are most
willing to serve as civil servants or legislators tend to be more
conscious of the negative consequences of the market and the
positive consequences of government action.[9] Both camps depart
from Smith's program of cultivating men of public spirit who
would be moved to participate in government, aided by social
scientific knowledge, aware that the most effective means of
promoting the common weal is often by market mechanisms yet
cognizant that the market requires an extensive framework of
public services in which to function.

To highlight the timeliness of Adam Smith's work is to run the
risk of anachronism, of wrenching his views out of their historical
context; to ignore its timeliness is to reduce the study of his
thought to antiquarianism. Those who regard Smith as a patron
saint often fail to *think like Adam Smith* because they are quite
satisfied to *like what Adam Smith thought* (or more often, what they
suppose him to have thought). Trying to find what is timely in
Smith by thinking as Smith thought is a less certain but
potentially more rewarding enterprise.

Smith did not try to develop a science of economics free of
moral judgments or ethical considerations. As we have seen, his
policy recommendations were shot through with moral purposes. But his science of political economy was not a moralistic

science: he tried to bring about improvement not through preaching but through designing institutions which would strengthen the incentive to act in a socially beneficial manner. His attention to the gap between intentions and consequences provides a powerful antidote to the tendency to substitute moral indignation for social analysis. The authors of the *Federalist Papers*, perhaps the most successful practitioners of psychological institutionalism, followed the lead of Hume and Smith in seeking to design institutions which would pit the passions against one another and channel self-interest to serve the public good.[10]

Smith's importance for social science lies not only in the fact that he was a psychological institutionalist, but in the fact that he was so *adept* a psychological institutionalist. Many others have tried their hand at using institutions to direct human passions, often with results that were either futile or nightmarish. Among the monuments to futility was the "philanstery" of the nineteenth-century visionary socialist, Charles Fourier, an elaborately designed community intended to liberate and utilize the passions while keeping them in equilibrium.[11] In the category of nightmare there was Jeremy Bentham's "Panopticon," which sought to replace the faulty social controls of society with the more powerful and omnipresent controls of encompassing incarceratory institutions.[12]

If Smith was successful as a psychological institutionalist, it was because he concentrated on understanding the workings of existing institutions rather than attempting to design entirely new institutions on the basis of purported social scientific knowledge. For the most part he limited his suggestions for reform to institutions which had demonstrated their essential soundness. Even his more novel suggestions drew upon historical models which had proved their worth through experience. This cognitive modesty helps explain the effectiveness of his suggestions and why, for all the significance he attached to the rise of commercial society, he looked so often to the ancient Greeks and Romans for guidance.

As we have seen, Smith predicted that the costs of government would increase as it undertook functions that were essential to the public welfare—including defense, justice, education, transportation, and other projects that were in the collective interest but were unprofitable for individuals or corporations to undertake. The number and scale of such projects have indeed increased with the development of capitalism and, under the heading "public goods," have become a subject of economic theory and of public policy. Smith also suggested the manner in which public goods should be provided. In providing education, for example, the government should not involve itself in running the schools, paying the teachers, and directing students to particular schools and particular teachers. That approach would deny the consumers of public services the ability to choose and would destroy the incentive of the providers of such services to provide them efficiently. Smith advised government to set standards, to provide the better part of the costs of education to those least able to afford it, and whenever possible to allow citizens to choose how they would acquire the education necessary to pass standardized tests.

Smith's preference is for public goods to be provided through the market, even when government provides its citizens with the means to purchase such goods in the marketplace. A contemporary example of this strategy would be the market provision of universal education through the use of school vouchers, provided by government for use at private schools. Were this strategy politically unacceptable on one or another ground (including grounds of entrenched interests), a second-best Smithian solution would be the provision of choice within a public school system.[13] For when the market is judged to be an inadequate mechanism, the Smithian predisposition is to design structures of incentives which create some of the disciplining effects of consumer choice upon the providers of public services.

Perhaps the most important updating of Smith's thought is Arthur Cecil Pigou's theory of "social costs," first suggested in his *Economics of Welfare* of 1920 and refined by later analysts. Pigou pointed out that the real costs of a commodity include not only the "private costs" reflected in the market price, but also the costs of negative "externalities." These are by-products of industrial activity which—in the absence of regulation—are not reflected in the market price but are borne by people who have no role in the production or consumption of the commodity. One might say that Smith's failure to recognize this problem indicates that his work is irrelevant to contemporary industrial societies. Or one might say that since Smith did not view it as a problem, there is no reason for us to view it as a problem. (This would be a sign of Smithian fundamentalism.) It would be most in keeping with the spirit of Smith's work to recognize the reality of such disharmonies of private and social costs, and then to attempt to use law to restructure the private costs, so that the real costs are borne by those who make and consume the commodities which create the negative by-products. (This is what economists call "internalizing the externalities.") One contemporary application of this method is the imposition of a tax on polluters equal to the cost imposed by the polluter on others.

Government regulation of private economic activity may be imposed in a more or less Smithian manner. One approach is for the government to set standards and to specify how they are to be met. This is the approach usually favored by activists who lobby the government to impose regulations and by the lawyers who write the legislation. In a more Smithian approach, the government sets the standards and leaves it to the diverse actors in the market to devise the most economically efficient means of meeting them.[14] This approach creates a structure of incentives to guide private interests toward a socially desirable outcome. Take the example of environmental pollution. The moralistic response to pollution is that it is reprehensible and that the government should forbid it regardless of the costs. Smith would probably agree that pollution is reprehensible but would try to control it in a way that would allow the market to minimize the costs of doing so. In one recent application of this Smithian approach, the government has set permitted levels of air pollution, along with a system of "pollution permits" which can be bought and sold, allowing different firms to optimize their costs by spending more on permits, on pollution-control devices, or by shutting down the sources of pollution.

Smith objected to excessive government intervention in economic and social life because laws are often enacted to serve private interests at the expense of the public interest, and because legislators do not have the information they need to coordinate economic activities. On these matters he was persuasive, but not dogmatic. Neither problem could be eliminated, he realized, but they could both be ameliorated. Only very recently have economists devoted their attention to guaging the actual effectiveness of governmental measures, rather than applauding or condemning such measures on ideological grounds.[15]

*   *   *

Smith did not believe that even well-functioning market institutions by themselves would produce a society of decent men and women. That task required additional institutions which socialized the individual, taught him to control his passions, and fostered benevolence. The beginning—though not the end—of a Smithian approach to contemporary social policy would evince a certain prejudice in favor of those socializing institutions which Smith thought had demonstrated their indispensability. But it would also demand a continual reevaluation of the effectiveness of such institutions in light of changing historical circumstances and the possibility of adapting institutions to provide incentives for morally desirable and socially necessary behavior. Last but not least, a Smithian approach would consider how government public policy might ameliorate the negative effects of market processes on such institutions.

Smith regarded the family as the most effective socializing institution, since it is there that children take their first steps toward self-command. First under the influence of parental authority and then out of the habitual sympathy which arises from frequent interactions with siblings, children learn to curb their passions and accommodate their desires to those of others. The effect of divorce and remarriage on children is likely to be harmful, he suggested. Because of the importance of family stability, Smith recommended legal arrangements that would enhance the security of the marital partners and thus promote their confidence and trust that they were both part of a joint enterprise. He thought that laws which made divorce easy for either partner to obtain endangered that trust and confidence. A major psychological incentive for men to marry was the desire to have children who could inherit their property. Removing the legal disabilities upon illegitimate children, he argued, therefore weakened the institution of monogamous marriage.

These considerations have been largely ignored in attempts to reform family law in recent decades. The costs to women, to children, and to society of substituting "expressive individualism" for Smith's psychological institutionalism are becoming apparent.[16] It is difficult to imagine how children will acquire self-control and concern for others when they are deprived of effective parental influence. A Smithian approach would be to ask how the law, government welfare policies, tax policies, and market institutions could be redesigned to create a structure of incentives that would heighten family stability.

Smith was concerned that the processes at work within commercial society might undermine the very qualities of character which are its greatest achievement and on which its success depends. In arguing against monopoly profits, he noted that wealth acquired too quickly and too easily made "sober virtue" seem superfluous. Elsewhere, as we have seen, he remarked on the tendency of the lower ranks of society to emulate the "loose" lifestyle of the rich and powerful, a lifestyle that was morally abhorrent, and socially disastrous for the lower classes. In his time and place, Smith regarded these trends more as a potential danger than as an acute threat to the character type he sought to promote. We can readily imagine how Smith would view an entertainment industry in which "the lifestyles of the rich and famous"—the mores of a subculture marked by the rapid acquisition of wealth and the practice of "loose" morals—have become a staple of mass culture that competes with family, schools, and religion for moral influence.

Unlike Plato and Rousseau, Smith did not disparage public amusements nor did he require that they promote virtue. He did, however, suggest that the law should prohibit "scandal or indecency" in the otherwise free market for public entertainment. And he spoke of the role of government in "promoting the prosperity of the commonwealth, by establishing good discipline, and by discouraging every sort of vice and impropriety; [it] may prescribe rules, therefore, which not only prohibit mutual injuries among fellow-citizens, but command mutual good offices to a certain degree." The role of legislators in this area, Smith warned, demands "the greatest delicacy and reserve to execute with propriety and judgement. To neglect it altogether," he wrote, "exposes the commonwealth to many gross disorders and shocking enormities, and to push it too far is destructive of all liberty, security, and justice."[17] Rather than maintaining a delicate reserve in discouraging "vice and impropriety" the recent tendency of government has been to ignore this function entirely. Indeed it has become a mark of enlightenment to stigmatize as cultural Neanderthals those who believe that the state has a proper role in limiting indecency. It is worth recalling that Smith—a leading light of the Scottish Enlightenment and a proponent of the free market and of "natural liberty"—assumed that government would set limits on expression in the cultural market.

Smith's views have often been distorted by being associated with the tendency of nineteenth-century liberalism and twentieth-century libertarianism to regard the pursuit of self-interest as intrinsically good and government as intrinsically evil. This tendency was quite foreign to Smith and to the Scottish Enlightenment. Smith's moral and political philosophy might serve as a corrective to contemporary neo-liberal theory which conceives of liberty as nothing more than the capricious indulgence of one's passions and holds that any effort by the government to restrain such behavior will inevitably lead to tyranny.[18] Smith's many comments on the evil and folly of politicians and legislators were no more a condemnation of government than his many criticisms of merchants were a condemnation of commerce. The right to indulge one's passions was not what he meant by "natural liberty." He assumed that some degree of governmental prohibition of immoral action is necessary, but he tried to minimize the need for such restraint by encouraging the cultivation of social control and individual conscience. If government policy abandons the support of the institutions which foster decency, citizens will be obliged to choose between an all-powerful state to ensure a modicum of security and a Hobbesian war of all against all.

Smith contended that the greatest happiness comes from acting in a manner we know to be virtuous, while the greatest misery comes from knowing we have violated moral law. For Smith, this was a result of the constitution of the human mind. Like the propensity to truck, trade, and barter to improve our fortune, the satisfaction of acting according to moral law, and the inner pain that comes from violating it, can be inferred from human experience. It is on the veracity of this assumption that much of modern social thought deviates from Smith's moral philosophy.

Smith believed that one of the important roles of the intellectual is to draw moral distinctions between modes of behavior. Much of contemporary social science—especially economics—champions the opposite view.[19] While Smith devoted much of *The Theory of Moral Sentiments* to demonstrating how and why we become benevolent, contemporary economists who turn to public policy sometimes seem to agree with Mandeville that benevolence and altruism are illusory.[20] According to one acute observer of the discipline, "Economists of the past thought it was part of their task to remind their readers that there are high and low pleasures, that many of the high ones require reason and the sometimes-painful acquisition of knowledge, that we aspire to tastes better than our current ones, and that such aspirations are sometimes hindered by profit-seeking businesses that cater to vices and over-emphasize the importance of what money can buy. Today's economists are more likely to feel a professional obligation to combat such sentiments than to support them."[21] Here again, Smith offers a corrective to the unanticipated negative consequences of the discipline he helped spawn. Within other academic disciplines descended from moral philosophy, it has become fashionable to treat all moral codes merely as functions of systems of power. The need for the institutional direction of the passions is implicitly discounted, social control is treated as intrinsically suspect, and the preference for some standards of behavior over others is assumed to be arbitrary.[22] In questioning the premises of such fashionable assumptions, a re-examination of Smith's works would indeed be timely.

Perhaps the greatest institutional transformation that has taken place since Smith's day is the diffusion of political influence by the spread of voting rights. Political representation is much broader than in Smith's day. And democracy, despite its poor historical record, reviewed by Smith in his lectures, has become the norm, albeit it a form much attenuated from the ideals of classical republicanism—and perhaps more successful for that very reason. To a degree rarely articulated in democratic theory, representative democracy may well owe its success to its ability to exercise some control over the governors while safeguarding against an excessively expressive citizenry[23]—a fact appreciated by the framers of the American Constitution. For reasons which remain to be fully analyzed, capitalism seems to be a necessary (though by no means sufficient) prerequisite for representative democracy. Smith wrote *The Wealth of Nations,* as we have seen, to encourage legislators to resist the pressures of economic groups attempting to use political power to advance their own interests. The combination of representative democracy and commercial society does not so much eliminate this problem as transform it, as more interests come to exert political influence.

One role for the intellectual, Smith suggested, was to serve as a member of what Hegel was to call "the universal class"—the professional bureaucracy devoted to the common good. To be sure, Smith's conception of this role was more modest than Hegel's. For Hegel, the function of the universal class was to moralize society. For Smith, that goal could be achieved, only partially and indirectly, by creating a legal framework in which non-governmental institutions could channel the passions toward socially desirable outcomes. Smith himself took a government post during the last decade of his life, and similar roles have been filled by his intellectual successors.

Smith was remarkably prescient in identifying the promise of capitalism, and his work contributed in no small measure to the fulfillment of that promise. The difficulties and dangers to which Smith pointed remain with us. That he did not solve them may reflect the fact that they are incapable of resolution. But some insoluble problems are more benign than others, and it was Smith's judgment that the problems posed by commercial society are preferable to the alternatives. As we have seen, Smith believed that commercial society is better suited to advance what the stoics had called the inferior virtues—in other words, that it is more likely to be morally decent. But he realized that a decent society would not come about through the market alone, nor were even the best-designed institutions adequate to the task. That task demanded that moralists like himself offer an intellectually coherent and emotionally compelling account of the standards of virtue and vice, of decency and indecency, of the sources of shared respectability. The fulfillment of the promise of a decent society depended as well on the willingness of some to pursue the public good, and on the knowledge, wisdom, and prudence of those so motivated. In this sense, too, an awareness of Smith's work in the context of his time may help us to appreciate both its timelessness and its timeliness.

Notes

KEY TO SOURCES
AND CITATIONS

Full author, title, and bibliographical information are provided for each work the first time it is cited in each chapter. All subsequent references provide the author's surname and a short title. Unless otherwise indicated, Cambridge refers to Cambridge, England.

All references to Smith's works and to his correspondence are to the *Glasgow Edition of the Works and Correspondence of Adam Smith*, published in hardcover by Oxford University Press. All volumes except the volume of *Correspondence* are published in softcover by Liberty Classics, Indianapolis.

Correspondence = *The Correspondence of Adam Smith*, ed. E. C. Mossner and I. S. Ross (1977, with additional material 1987).

ED = "'Early Draft' of Part of *The Wealth of Nations*," published as an appendix to *LJ*.

EPS = *Essays on Philosophical Subjects*, ed. W. P. D. Wightman and J. C. Bryce (1980).

LJ = *Lectures on Jurisprudence*, ed. R. L. Meek, D. D. Raphael, and P. G. Stein (1978).

LRBL = *Lectures on Rhetoric and Belles Lettres*, ed. J. C. Bryce (1983).

TMS= The Theory of Moral Sentiments, ed. A. L. Macfie and D. D. Raphael (1976, with minor corrections 1979).

WN= An Inquiry into the Nature and Causes of the Wealth of Nations, ed. R. H. Campbell and A. S. Skinner, two volumes continuously paginated (1976, with minor corrections 1979).

Citations from *The Theory of Moral Sentiments* and from *The Wealth of Nations* include references to the standard book, chapter, part, and paragraph divisions used in the Glasgow edition, as well as to page numbers in that edition.

INTRODUCTION
BACK TO ADAM?

1. See, for example, Mary Ann Glendon, *Rights Talk: The Impoverishment of Political Discourse* (New York, 1991).

2. See, for example, the recent work of political theory by William A. Galston, *Liberal Purposes: Goods, Virtues, and Diversity in the Liberal State* (Cambridge, 1991), which provides an excellent critique of the view that the liberal state can be "neutral" in regard to the types of character fostered; and James Q. Wilson, *On Character* (Washington, 1991), by a leading public policy analyst, whose work has increasingly emphasized the centrality of character-building institutions. In a similar vein, see Christopher Lasch, "The Fragility of Liberalism," *Salmagundi*, 92 (Fall, 1991), pp. 5–18.

3. For arguments on all sides of the issue, see James Tully (ed.), *Meaning and Context: Quentin Skinner and his Critics* (Princeton, 1988).

4. The question of the relationship of Smith's rhetoric to the *substance* of his moral thought is explored in Charles L. Griswold, Jr., "Rhetoric and Ethics: Adam Smith on Theorizing about the Moral Sentiments," *Philosophy and Rhetoric*, Vol. 24, #3 (1991), pp. 213–37.

5. The most relevant works by these authors are Jacob Viner, "Adam Smith and Laissez Faire" (1928), reprinted in Jacob Viner, *Essays on the Intellectual History of Economics*, ed. Douglas A. Irwin (Princeton, 1991); Nathan Rosenberg, "Some Institutional Aspects of the Wealth of Nations," *Journal of Political Economy*, Vol. 18, #6 (Dec. 1960), pp. 557–70, and "Adam Smith and the Stock of Moral Capital," *History of Political Economy*, Vol. 22, #1 (1990), pp. 1–17; Donald Winch, *Adam Smith's Politics: An Essay in Historiographic Revision* (Cambridge, 1978), and "Science and the Legislator: Adam Smith and After," *The Economic Journal*, Vol. 93 (Sept. 1983), pp. 501–20, and "Adam Smith's 'enduring particular result'; A political and cosmopolitan perspective," in Istvan Hont and Michael Ignatieff, (eds.), *Wealth and Virtue: The Shaping of Political Economy in the Scottish Enlightenment* (Cambridge, 1983), pp. 253–69, and "Adam Smith and the Liberal Tradition," in Knud Haakonssen (ed.), *Traditions of Liberalism* (St. Leonards, Australia, 1988),

pp. 83–101; Istvan Hont and Michael Ignatieff, "Needs and justice in the 'Wealth of Nations'," in Istvan Hont and Michael Ignatieff (eds.), *Wealth and Virtue: The Shaping of Political Economy in the Scottish Enlightenment* (Cambridge, 1983); Knud Haakonssen, *The Science of a Legislator: The Natural Jurisprudence of David Hume and Adam Smith* (Cambridge, 1981); Laurence Dickey, "Historicizing the 'Adam Smith Problem': Conceptual, Historiographical, and Textual Issues," *Journal of Modern History*, Vol. 58, #3 (Sept. 1986), pp. 579–609; Gertrude Himmelfarb, *Victorian Minds* (New York, 1968), *The Idea of Poverty: England in the Early Industrial Age* (New York, 1984), and *Poverty and Compassion: The Moral Imagination of the Late Victorians* (New York, 1991); Albert O. Hirschman, *The Passions and the Interests: Political Arguments for Capitalism Before Its Triumph* (Princeton, 1977), and *Rival Views of Market Society and Other Recent Essays* (New York, 1986); J. G. A. Pocock, *The Machiavellian Moment: Florentine Political Thought and the Atlantic Republican Tradition* (Princeton, 1975), and *Virtue, Commerce, and History* (Cambridge, 1985).

Other recent works which take issue with the image of Smith as an advocate of "laissez-faire" and call attention to the substantial role of government in his work include David McNally, *Political Economy and the Rise of Capitalism* (Berkeley, 1988), Chapters 4 and 5; Jerry Evensky, "The evolution of Adam Smith's views on political economy," *History of Political Economy*, Vol. 21, #1 (1989), pp. 123–45; and, in a more exaggerated fashion, Spencer J. Pack, *Capitalism as a Moral System: Adam Smith's Critique of the Free Market Economy* (Aldershot, 1991).

6. Joseph Schumpeter, *History of Economic Analysis*, ed. Elizabeth Boody Schumpeter (New York, 1954), pp. 184–85.

7. These are portions of Smith's *Lectures on Jurisprudence*, a compilation of two sets of student notes from the years 1762–64, and the "Early Draft" of *The Wealth of Nations*, thought to date from about 1763.

8. On the significance of the changes between the 1759 and 1790 versions of *The Theory of Moral Sentiments*, see Dickey, "Historicizing the 'Adam Smith Problem'"; and John Dwyer, *Virtuous Discourse: Sensibility and Community in Late Eighteenth-Century Scotland* (Edinburgh, 1987), pp. 168–85. Evensky, "The evolution of Adam Smith's views on political economy," offers a plausible reconstruction of the trajectory of Smith's development.

CHAPTER 1
COSMOPOLITAN PROVINCIAL:
SMITH'S LIFE AND SOCIAL MILIEU

1. Madame Riccoboni to Robert Liston, in *Mme Riccoboni's Letters to David Hume, David Garrick, and Sir Robert Liston, 1764–1783*, ed. James C. Nicolls, *Studies on Voltaire and the Eighteenth Century*, Vol. 149 (1976), p. 71, quoted in Deidre Dawson, "Is Sympathy so Surprising? Adam

Smith and French Fictions of Sympathy," *Eighteenth Century Life*, Vol. 15, #1 and #2 (1991), pp. 147–62.

2. Madame Riccoboni to David Garrick, quoted in John Rae, *Life of Adam Smith* (1895, reprinted New York, 1965, with an Introduction "Guide to John Rae's *Life of Adam Smith*" by Jacob Viner), pp. 211–12.

3. Voltaire, *Oeuvres complètes*, ed. Beaumarchais, 70 vols. (Kehl, 1784–89), 21:1.71, quoted in Dawson, "Is Sympathy so Surprising?," p. 147.

4. Hugh Blair to Adam Smith, April 3, 1776, in *Correspondence*, p. 188.

5. Information on Smith's life is drawn from Dugald Stewart, "An Account of the Life and Writings of Adam Smith, L.L.D." (1793), reprinted in *EPS*; Rae, *Life of Adam Smith*; R. H. Campbell and A. S. Skinner, *Adam Smith* (New York, 1982); and D. D. Raphael, *Adam Smith* (New York, 1985).

6. On the links between education, patronage, and government service in the Scotland of Smith's day, see Robert Wuthnow, *Communities of Discourse: Ideology and Social Structure in the Reformation, the Enlightenment, and European Socialism* (Cambridge, MA, 1989), pp. 254–64, which summarizes a great deal of recent research on the topic.

7. Paul Langford, *A Polite and Commercial People: England 1727–1783* (Oxford, 1989), pp. 325–26.

8. Campbell and Skinner, *Adam Smith*, pp. 13–14.

9. *WN*, V.i.f.34, p. 772; *WN*, V.i.f.46, p. 781.

10. The essay was published posthumously in 1795 and may be found in W. P. D. Wightman (ed.), *Essays on Philosophical Subjects*, in the Glasgow Edition.

11. On Smith's contacts with the merchant community of Glasgow, see Rae, *Life of Adam Smith*, pp. 87–89; Campbell and Skinner, *Adam Smith*, pp. 60–64.

12. On the social setting of the Scottish Enlightenment, see John Clive, "The Social Background of the Scottish Renaissance," in his *Not By Fact Alone: Essays on the Writing and Reading of History* (New York, 1989), pp. 149–65; David Daiches, "The Scottish Enlightenment," in David Daiches, Peter Jones, and Jean Jones (eds.), *A Hotbed of Genius: The Scottish Enlightenment 1730–1790* (Edinburgh, 1986), pp. 1–42; Richard Sher, *Church and University in the Scottish Enlightenment* (Princeton, 1985); and Wuthnow, *Communities of Discourse*. On the Select Society in particular, see Roger L. Emerson, "The Social composition of enlightened Scotland: the select society of Edinburgh, 1754–1764," *Studies on Voltaire and the Eighteenth Century*, Vol. CXIV (1973), pp. 291–329.

13. From *Gentleman's Magazine* (Aug. 1790, p. 792), quoted in Smith, *Lectures on Rhetoric and Belles Lettres*, ed. J. C. Bryce (Oxford, 1983), p. 7.

14. On the conscious attempt of Hume and other members of the

Scottish Enlightenment to assimilate into English culture, see Campbell and Skinner, *Adam Smith*, p. 35; Emerson, "Social Composition"; Viner, "Introduction" to Rae, *Life of Adam Smith*, p. 15. On the role of Scots in English life in this period, see Langford, *A Polite and Commercial People*, pp. 325ff.

15. See Duncan Forbes, "Sceptical Whiggism, Commerce, and History," in Andrew S. Skinner and Thomas Wilson (eds.), *Essays on Adam Smith* (Oxford, 1975); Winch, *Adam Smith's Politics*, Chs. 2–4; J. G. A. Pocock, "Hume and the American Revolution," in his *Virtue, Commerce, and History* (Cambridge, 1985).

16. On the Anglican self-understanding of the regime, see J. C. D. Clark, *English Society 1688–1832* (Cambridge, 1985).

17. Duncan Forbes, "Scientific Whiggism: Adam Smith and John Millar," *Cambridge Journal*, Vol.7 (1953–54).

18. For useful overviews, see Rosalind Mitchison, "Scotland 1750–1850," in *The Cambridge Social History of Britain 1750–1950, Vol.1, Regions and Communities*, F. M. L. Thompson (ed.) (Cambridge, 1990), pp. 155–71; and Eric Richards, "Scotland and the Uses of the Atlantic Empire," in Bernard Bailyn and Philip D. Morgan (eds.), *Strangers within the Realm: Cultural Margins of the First British Empire* (Chapel Hill, 1991), esp. pp. 67–91.

19. *The Letters of David Hume*, ed. J. Y. T. Greig (Oxford, 1932, two volumes), Vol. 1, p. 255.

20. On Smith's direct role in supervising the college years of the sons of English peers, see *Correspondence*, pp. 26–32, 36–38, 41–42, 58–67, 69–73, 95–96. This role was to be repeated by Smith's students and successors at Scottish universities, who educated three Victorian prime ministers. See Anand C. Chitnis, *The Scottish Enlightenment and Early Victorian English Society* (London, 1986), pp. 44ff.

21. See Leo Strauss, "On Classical Political Philosophy," in Thomas Pangle (ed.), *The Rebirth of Classical Political Rationalism: An Introduction to the Thought of Leo Strauss* (Chicago, 1989), pp. 49–62, p. 54.

22. See Quentin Skinner, *The Foundations of Modern Political Thought, Volume One: The Renaissance* (Cambridge, 1978), pp. 213ff.

23. Dugald Stewart, "An Account of the Life and Writings of Adam Smith, L.L.D.," in *EPS*, p. 311.

24. *WN*, IV. intro. 1, p. 428.

25. Lewis Namier and John Brooke, *Charles Townshend* (London, 1964), p. 34.

26. Smith to Shelburne, Feb. 12, 1767, in *Correspondence*, p. 124.

27. See, for example, Sir Grey Cooper to Smith, Nov. 7, 1777, in *Correspondence*, pp. 227–28.

28. The story is related by John Rae, *Life of Adam Smith*, p. 405, who expresses some doubt as to its authenticity. The influence of Smith on Pitt's trade policy in the 1780s is undoubted. See Bernard Semmel, *The*

Rise of Free Trade Imperialism: Classical Political Economy and the Empire of Free Trade and Imperialism, 1750–1850 (Cambridge, 1970), pp. 30–44. Pitt paid a tribute to Smith's *Wealth of Nations* in a Parliamentary speech of 1791; see *Mr. Pitt's Parliamentary Speeches*, ed. W. Hathaway (London, 1808), Vol. 1, p. 358, quoted in Salim Rashid, "Adam Smith's Rise to Fame: A Reexamination of the Evidence," *The Eighteenth Century*, Vol. 23, #1 (1982), pp. 64–85.

29. Smith to Henry Dundas, Nov. 1, 1779, in *Correspondence*, pp. 241–42.

30. Rae, *Life*, p. 437.

31. On *The Wealth of Nations* as a pedagogic and professorial achievement, see Schumpeter, *History of Economic Analysis*, pp. 181ff. On Smith's relationship to his predecessors in the field of economic thought, see the Guide to Further Reading.

CHAPTER 2

GENTLEMEN, CONSUMERS,
AND THE FISCAL–MILITARY STATE

1. Bernard Bailyn, *Voyagers to the West: A Passage in the Peopling of America on the Eve of the Revolution* (New York, 1986), pp. 166–203.

2. *WN*, V.ii.k, p. 870.

3. N. C. R. Crafts, "The eighteenth century: a survey," in Roderick Floud and Donald McCloskey (eds.), *The Economic History of Britain since 1700. Vol.1: 1700–1860* (Cambridge, 1981), p. 5.

4. See E. A. Wrigley, *Continuity, chance, and change: the character of the industrial revolution in England* (Cambridge, 1988), p. 35.

5. See Wrigley, *Continuity*, p. 31.

6. See J. C. D. Clark, *English Society 1688–1832* (Cambridge, 1985), p. 71; also E. L. Jones, "Agriculture 1700–80," in Floud and McCloskey (eds.), *Economic History of Britain*, pp. 76–86.

7. David Landes, *The Unbound Prometheus: Technological Change and Industrial Development in Western Europe from 1750 to the Present* (Cambridge, 1969), pp. 66ff; and T. M. Devine, "The Scottish Merchant Community, 1680–1740," in R. H. Campbell and Andrew S. Skinner (eds.), *The Origins and Nature of the Scottish Enlightenment* (Edinburgh, 1982), pp. 36–37.

8. P. J. Cain and A. G. Hopkins, "Gentlemanly Capitalism and British Expansion Overseas, I, The Old Colonial System, 1688–1850," *Economic History Review*, 2nd Series, Vol. 39, (1986), pp. 501–25, quoted by Bernard Bailyn and Philip D. Morgan (eds.), *Strangers within the Realm: Cultural Margins of the First British Empire* (Chapel Hill, 1991), p. 13.

9. Joyce Appleby, *Capitalism and a New Social Order: The Republican Vision of the 1790s* (New York, 1984), p. 33.

10. Jones, "Agriculture 1700–80," p. 74.

11. T. C. Smout, "Where had the Scottish economy got to by 1776?" in Istvan Hont and Michael Ignatieff (eds.), *Wealth and Virtue: The Shaping of Political Economy in the Scottish Enlightenment* (Cambridge, 1983), pp. 47–49.

12. Paul Langford, *A Polite and Commercial People: England 1727–1783* (Oxford, 1989), pp. 177–82; on the decline of publicly fixed wage rates, see also *WN*, I.x.c.60, p. 157.

13. Patrick K. O'Brien, "The political economy of British taxation, 1660–1815," *Economic History Review* 2nd Series, Vol. 41, (1988), pp. 1–32, p. 9.

14. Langford, *Polite*, pp. 174–76. R. P. Thomas and D. N. McCloskey, "Overseas trade and empire 1700–1860," in Floud and McCloskey (eds.), *Economic History of Britain*, p. 93.

15. Ralph Davis, "The Rise of Protection in England, 1689–1786," *Economic History Review* 2nd Series, Vol. 19, (1966), pp. 306–17, pp. 313–14.

16. Niels Steensgaard, "The growth and composition of the long-distance trade of England and the Dutch Republic before 1750," in James Tracy (ed.), *The Rise of Merchant Empires: Long-Distance Trade in the Early Modern World, 1350–1750* (Cambridge, 1990), pp. 102–52, pp. 145, 151, 168; R. P. Thomas and D. N. McCloskey, "Overseas trade and empire 1700–1860," in Floud and McCloskey (eds.), *Economic History of Britain*, pp. 90–191.

17. *WN*, V.iii. 92, pp. 946–47.

18. Thomas and McCloskey, "Overseas trade and empire 1700–1860," pp. 94–102.

19. D. E. C. Eversley, "The Home Market and Economic Growth in England, 1750–1780," in E. L. Jones and G. E. Mingay (eds.), *Land, Labour and Population in the Industrial Revolution* (London, 1967), p. 255. See more generally the excellent survey by Daniel Baugh, "Poverty, Protestantism, and Political Economy: English Attitudes toward the Poor, 1660–1800," in Stephen B. Baxter (ed.), *England's Rise to Greatness, 1660–1763* (Berkeley, 1983), pp. 63–108, pp. 81–90.

20. Langford, *Polite*, p. 150, and Neil McKendrick, "Introduction," in McKendrick, John Brewer, and J. H. Plumb, *The Birth of a Consumer Society: The Commercialization of Eighteenth-Century England* (Bloomington, 1982), pp. 9ff.

21. Neil McKendrick, "Commercialization and the Economy," *ibid.*, p. 23.

22. Neil McKendrick, "Home Demand and Economic Growth: A New View of the Role of Women and Children in the Industrial Revolution," in Neil McKendrick (ed.), *Historical Perspectives. Studies in English Thought and Society* (London, 1974), pp. 152–210.

23. McKendrick, in *Birth of a Consumer Society*, pp. 28–29.

24. Neil McKendrick, "Introduction," in McKendrick, *Birth of a Consumer Society*, pp. 1–2; Langford, *Polite*, pp. 67ff.

25. See Nathan Rosenberg, "Adam Smith on Profits—Paradox Lost and Regained," in Andrew S. Skinner and Thomas Wilson (eds.), *Essays on Adam Smith* (Oxford, 1975), pp. 377–89, pp. 388–89.

26. W. A. Cole, "Factors in Demand 1700–80," in Floud and McCloskey (eds.), *Economic History of Britain*, p. 58; Landes, *Unbound Prometheus*, pp. 58–59.

27. For examples, see Istvan Hont and Michael Ignatieff, "Needs and justice in the 'Wealth of Nations,'" in Istvan Hont and Michael Ignatieff (eds.), *Wealth and Virtue: The Shaping of Political Economy in the Scottish Enlightenment* (Cambridge, 1983), p. 5; and Langford, *Polite*, p. 150.

28. Baugh, "Poverty," pp. 85–86. See also the discussion in Rosenberg, "Adam Smith on Profits—Paradox Lost and Regained," pp. 378–79.

29. *WN*, I.viii. 35–42, pp. 95–99.

30. Langford, *Polite*, p. 690.

31. Langford, *Polite*, pp. 704–10.

32. Langford, *Polite*, pp. 692–93.

33. John Brewer, *The Sinews of Power: War, Money, and the English State, 1688–1783* (New York, 1989), p. 40.

34. Carolyn Webber and Aaron Wildavsky, *A History of Taxation and Expenditure in the Western World* (New York, 1986), Chapter 5; Fernand Braudel, *The Wheels of Commerce* (New York, 1982), pp. 521ff.; Charles P. Kindelberger, *A Financial History of Western Europe* (London, 1984), pp. 151–53.

35. P. G. M. Dickson, *The Financial Revolution in England. A Study in the Development of Public Credit 1688–1756* (London, 1967), p. 514.

36. Dickson, *Financial Revolution*, pp. 17ff. See J. G. A. Pocock, *The Machiavellian Moment, Florentine Political Thought and the Atlantic Republican Tradition* (Princeton, 1975), pp. 446–61, 467–75.

37. Langford, *Polite*, 692–97; Brewer, *Sinews of Power, passim*.

38. Langford, *Polite*, pp. 709–10; Davis, "Rise of Protection," pp. 307–14; O'Brien, "Political Economy," p. 24; Brewer, *Sinews of War*, pp. xxi, 169, 248–49. For a striking example of the merchants's use of politics, see the case of Samuel Touchet, a merchant adventurer who became financial adviser to Townshend at the Exchequer, from which position he tried to obtain a monopoly of the African slave trade. Namier and Brooke, *Charles Townshend*, p. 130. On the most politically significant merchant company of the era, see Lucy S. Sutherland, *The East India Company in Eighteenth-Century Politics* (Oxford, 1952).

39. Langford, *Polite*, pp. 442–47.

1. I have used the term "traditions" instead of such near-synonyms as "paradigms," "languages," or "discourses."

2. Père Thomassin, *Traité du Négoce et de l'Usure* (1697), pp. 96ff., quoted in Bernard Groethuysen, *The Bourgeois: Catholicism vs. Capitalism in Eighteenth-Century France* (New York, 1968), pp. 191–92.

3. Charles Davenant, "Essay upon the Probable Methods of Making a People Gainers in the Balance of Trade" (1699), in *Works*, II, p. 275; quoted in J. G. A. Pocock *The Machiavellian Moment* (Princeton, 1975), p. 443.

4. Aristotle, *Politics*, Lord Edition, Book 1, Ch. 9; Book 7, Ch. 9. See also Thomas L. Lewis, "Acquisition and anxiety: Aristotle's case against the market," *Canadian Journal of Economics*, Vol. 11, #1 (1978), pp. 69–90.

5. See S. C. Humphreys, *Anthropology and the Greeks* (London, 1976), pp. 139–50.

6. See Richard Mulgan, "Liberty in Ancient Greece," in Zbigniew Pelczynski and John Gray (eds.), *Conceptions of Liberty in Political Philosophy* (London, 1984), pp. 7–26, esp. pp. 8–10; Abram N. Shulsky, "The 'Infrastructure' of Aristotle's *Politics*: Aristotle on Economics and Politics," in Carnes Lord and David K. O'Conner (eds.), *Essays on the Foundations of Aristotelian Political Science* (Berkeley, 1991), pp. 74–111, esp. 83–87, 106–07; Joseph Schumpeter, *History of Economic Analysis*, (New York, 1954), p. 60.

7. See John W. Baldwin, *The Medieval Theories of the Just Price: Romanists, Canonists, and Theologians in the Twelfth and Thirteenth Centuries* (Philadelphia, 1959), pp. 12–16.

8. Quoted in Raymond de Roover, "The Scholastic Attitude Toward Trade and Entrepreneurship," *Explorations in Entrepreneurial History*, 2nd Series, Vol. 1, #1 (Fall, 1963), pp. 76–87.

9. John Gilchrist, *The Church and Economic Activity in the Middle Ages* (New York, 1969), pp. 52–53; Baldwin, *Medieval Theories*, p. 35. Lester K. Little, *Religious Poverty and the Profit Economy in Medieval Europe* (Ithaca, 1978), p. 53.

10. Quoted in Jacob Viner, *Religious Thought and Economic Society* (Durham, 1978), pp. 35–36.

11. Viner, *Religious Thought*, 37–38. On Libanius of Antioch and his influence, see also Jacob Viner, *The Role of Providence in the Social Order* (Princeton, 1972), pp. 36–37.

12. Baldwin, *Medieval Theories*, p. 8.

13. See Schumpeter, *History of Economic Analysis*, pp. 91–94; De Roover, "Scholastic Attitude," pp. 76–79; John F. McGovern, "The Rise of New Economic Attitudes—Economic Humanism, Economic

Nationalism—During the Later Middle Ages and the Renaissance, A.D. 1200–1500," *Traditio,* Vol. XXVI (1970), pp. 217–54, p. 230; Little, *Religious Poverty,* pp. 176ff; Julius Kirshner, "Raymond de Roover on Scholastic Economic Thought," in Kirshner (ed.), *Business, Banking, and Economic Thought in Late Medieval and Early Modern Europe* (Chicago, 1974), p. 19. Kirshner's introductory essay provides a useful review of the scholarship on scholastic economic thought and a balanced critique of de Roover's work.

14. De Roover, "Scholastic Attitude," *passim;* McGovern, "New Attitudes," p. 230; R. H. Tawney, *Religion and the Rise of Capitalism* (London, 1926), pp. 30ff.; Little, *Religious Poverty,* p. 181, exaggerates the extent of their embrace of commerce.

15. See Alasdair MacIntyre, *Whose Justice? Which Rationality?* (Notre Dame, 1988), p. 157.

16. MacIntyre, *Whose Justice?,* pp. 162, 199; see Aquinas, *Summa theologica,* IIa–IIae, 61–66.

17. De Roover, "Scholastic Attitude," p. 80.

18. On avarice as the root of the cardinal sins in Aquinas' *Summa theologica* see Morton Bloomfield, *The Seven Deadly Sins* (n.p., 1952), pp. 87–88.

19. Cited in De Roover, "Scholastic Attitude," p. 80. See also Viner, *Religious Thought,* pp. 35–38; and Schumpeter, *History,* pp. 60, 92, 99.

20. For examples, see Simon Schama, *The Embarrassment of Riches: An Interpretation of Dutch Culture in the Golden Age* (New York, 1987), pp. 329ff.; J. H. Hexter, "The Historical Method of Christopher Hill," in his *On Historians* (Cambridge, MA, 1979), pp. 234–36.

21. Stephen Holmes, *Benjamin Constant and the Making of Modern Liberalism* (New Haven, 1984), pp. 1, 179.

22. MacIntyre, *Whose Justice?,* p. 163.

23. This quintessence of the civic tradition is drawn from Jeff A. Weintraub, "Virtue, Community and the Sociology of Liberty: The Notion of Republican Virtue and Its Impact on Modern Western Social Thought" (Ph.D. diss., Berkeley, 1979), Chapter 1; and the succinct summaries in J. G. A. Pocock, "Cambridge paradigms and Scotch philosophers," pp. 235–52, 235–36, and in John Robertson, "The Scottish Enlightenment at the limits of the civic tradition," pp. 137–78, 138–40, both in Istvan Hont and Michael Ignatieff (eds.), *Wealth and Virtue: The Shaping of Political Economy in the Scottish Enlightenment* (Cambridge, 1983); and Forrest McDonald, *Novus Ordo Seclorum: The Intellectual Origins of the Constitution* (Lawrence, Kansas, 1985), pp. 70–71.

24. On the image of Sparta, see Elizabeth Rawson, *The Spartan Tradition in European Thought* (Oxford, 1969), esp. pp. 5–8.

25. Baldwin, *Medieval Theories,* p. 17.

26. J. H. Hexter, "Republic, Virtue, Liberty, and the Political Universe of J. G. A. Pocock," in his *On Historians* (Cambridge, MA, 1979), pp. 255–303, 294–303; Pocock, "Cambridge Paradigms," pp. 240–50.

27. On the normative role of theology versus the practical role of civil law in medieval Europe, see Baldwin, *Medieval Theories*, pp. 59–63.

28. See J. G. A. Pocock, "Virtues, rights, and manners: a model for historians of political thought," in his *Virtue, Commerce, and History* (Cambridge, 1985), pp. 43–45.

29. For a concise overview of the problems posed to political theorists by the struggles of the sixteenth and seventeenth centuries, see F. J. C. Hearnshaw, "Introductory: The Social and Political Problems of the Sixteenth and Seventeenth Centuries," in Hearnshaw (ed.), *The Social and Political Ideas of Some Great Thinkers of the Sixteenth and Seventeenth Centuries* (New York, 1967), pp. 9–41; and Theodore R. Rabb, *The Struggle for Stability in Early Modern Europe* (New York, 1973).

30. Richard Tuck, "The 'modern' theory of natural law," in Anthony Pagden (ed.), *The Languages of Political Theory in Early-Modern Europe* (Cambridge, 1987), pp. 99–119; p. 114–19.

31. Grotius, *The Rights of War and Peace*, p. 64, quoted in Tuck, "The 'modern' theory," p. 117.

32. See the discussion of Grotius and his influence in Richard F. Teichgraeber III, *"Free Trade" and Moral Philosophy: Rethinking the Sources of Adam Smith's Wealth of Nations* (Durham, 1986).

33. On the role of civil jurisprudence in Scottish intellectual life, see John Clive, "The Social Background of the Scottish Renaissance," in his *Not By Fact Alone: Essays on the Writing and Reading of History* (New York, 1989), pp. 149–65.

34. Duncan Forbes, "Hume and the Scottish Enlightenment" in S. C. Brown (ed.) *Philosophers of the Enlightenment* (Atlantic Highlands, NJ, 1979), pp. 94–109, p. 98, and Duncan Forbes, *Hume's Philosophical Politics* (Cambridge, 1978), Chapter 1; and Hans Medick, *Naturzustand und Naturgeschichte der bürgerlichen Gesellschaft: Die Ursprünge der bürgerlichen Sozialtheorie als Geschichtsphilosophie bei Samuel Pufendorf, John Locke and Adam Smith* (Göttingen, 1981, reprint of 1973 original edition), pp. 137ff. For earlier adumbrations of this attempt, see Istvan Hont, "The language of sociability and commerce: Samuel Pufendorf and the theoretical foundations of the 'Four-Stages Theory'," in Pagden (ed.), *The Languages of Political Theory* (Cambridge, 1987), pp. 253–76.

35. On the influence of neo-stoicism in early modern Europe, see Wilhelm Dilthey, *Gesammelte Schriften: II Band: Weltanschauung und Analyse des Menschen seit Renaissance und Reformation* (Stuttgart, 1957), and Gerhard Oestreich, *Neo-Stoicism and the early modern state* (Cambridge, 1982).

36. Oestreich, *Neo-Stoicism*, pp. 265ff.

37. Dilthey, *Weltanschauung*, pp. 280–81.

38. On the appeal of Newton as exemplar for the Scottish Enlightenment, see D. D. Raphael, "Adam Smith: Philosophy, Science, and Social Science," in S. C. Brown (ed.), *Philosophers of the Enlightenment* (Atlantic Highlands, NJ, 1979), pp. 77–119, p. 88; Stefan Collini, Donald Winch, and John Burrow, *That Noble Science of Politics* (Cambridge, 1983), pp. 14ff.; and Peter Gay, *The Enlightenment: An Interpretation: Vol.II, The Science of Freedom* (New York, 1969), Chapter 4, "The Science of Man."

39. *TMS*, VI.ii.3.6, p. 237.

40. On the development of this tradition, see Norbert Elias, *The Civilizing Process: Vol. 1, The History of Manners* (New York, 1978); and on one of its variations in France, see Roger Chartier, "From Texts to Manners," in *The Cultural Uses of Print in Early Modern France* (Princeton, 1987).

41. William J. Bouwsma, "The Two Faces of Humanism: Stoicism and Augustinianism in Renaissance Thought," in his *A Useable Past: Essays in European Cultural History* (Berkeley, 1990), pp. 31–42.

42. On the development of neo-Augustinian moralism, see above all Alfred O. Lovejoy, *Reflections on Human Nature* (Baltimore, 1961), pp. 25ff. Also useful are Paul Benichou, *Man and Ethics: Studies in French Classicism* (Garden City, New York, 1971); Louis Schneider, *Paradox and Society: The Work of Bernard Mandeville* (New Brunswick, NJ, 1987), pp. 67–76; Thomas Horne, *The Social Thought of Bernard Mandeville: Virtue and Commerce in Early Eighteenth-Century England* (New York, 1978), Chapter 2; Laurence Dickey, "Pride, Hypocrisy and Civility in Mandeville's Social and Historical Theory," *Critical Review*, Vol. 4, #3 (1990), pp. 387–431; and Jacob Viner, *The Role of Providence in the Social Order: An Essay in Intellectual History* (Princeton, 1972), pp. 56–57.

43. Jean Domat, *Lois civiles dans leur ordre naturel*, trans. W. Strahan (1722), p. XX, quoted in Terence Hutchison, *Before Adam Smith: The Emergence of Political Economy, 1662–1776* (New York, 1988), pp. 102–03.

44. Dale Van Kley, "Pierre Nicole, Jansenism, and the Morality of Enlightened Self-Interest," in Alan Charles Kors and Paul J. Korshin (eds.), *Anticipations of the Enlightenment in England, France, and Germany* (Philadelphia, 1987), pp. 69–85. On Jansenism and Nicole, see also Anthony Levi, *French Moralists* (Oxford, 1964), Chapter 8.

45. On the search for the irrational and egoistic motives of rational and virtuous action in the seventeenth and early eighteenth centuries, see also the introduction by F. B. Kaye to Bernard Mandeville, *The Fable of the Bees or Private Vices, Publick Benefits*, two volumes (Oxford, 1924; reprinted Indianapolis, 1988), pp. lxvii–cxiii; as well as Jean Ehrard, *L'Idée de nature en France a l'aube des Lumières* (Paris, 1970), pp. 223–41,

and Lester G. Crocker, *An Age of Crisis: Man and World in Eighteenth Century French Thought* (Baltimore, 1959), pp. 218–324.

46. This paragraph draws upon Lovejoy, *Reflections*, pp. 131–70.

47. Quoted in Lovejoy, *Reflections*, pp. 162–63.

48. Mandeville, *Fable* I, p. 208.

49. For an acute analysis of Mandeville's institutional strategy, see Nathan Rosenberg, "Mandeville and Laissez-Faire," *Journal of the History of Ideas*, Vol. 24 (1963), pp. 183–96.

50. For a useful survey of English writings on this theme, see Milton L. Myers, *The Soul of Modern Economic Man: Ideas of Self-Interest Thomas Hobbes to Adam Smith* (Chicago, 1983). Smith's acquaintance with the French literature exploring the passionate basis of moral behavior was in part direct, in part mediated through Mandeville, and in part mediated through the work of David Hume, who drew on Bayle, Nicole, Malebranche, and other late-seventeenth-century French sources. Regarding French influences on Hume, see Peter Jones, *Hume's Sentiments: Their Ciceronian and French Context* (Edinburgh, 1982), pp. 1–43. On the development of strategies for channeling the passions, see also David Levy, "Adam Smith's 'Natural Law' and Contractual Society," *Journal of the History of Ideas*, Vol. 39 (1978), pp. 665–74.

51. Mandeville, *Fable* I, p. 145.

52. Quoted in Lovejoy, *Reflections*, p. 42.

53. Josiah Tucker, *The Elements of Commerce and Theory of Taxes* (1755), quoted in Hutchison, *Before Adam Smith*, p. 230.

54. Lovejoy, *Reflections*, pp. 40–41, 64. For more on the genesis and development of such strategies, see Albert O. Hirschman, *The Passions and the Interests: Political Arguments for Capitalism before Its Triumph* (Princeton, 1977), Part I.

55. Charles Davenant, *An Essay on the East India Trade* [1696], in *Works*, Vol. 1, p. 90, quoted in Istvan Hont, "Free trade and the economic limits to national politics: neo-Machiavellian political economy reconsidered," in John Dunn (ed.), *The Economic Limits to Modern Politics* (Cambridge, 1990), pp. 41–120, p. 68.

56. John de Witt [Pieter de la Court], *The True Interest and Political Maxims of the Republic of Holland*, published in English translation in London, 1746, and reprinted, New York, 1972, p. 60. I thank J. G. A. Pocock for calling my attention to this book.

57. David Hume, "Of Civil Liberty," in Eugene Miller (ed.), *David Hume: Essays Moral, Political and Literary* (Indianapolis, 1985), pp. 88–89.

58. Smith *LRBL*, p. 62.

59. Smith, *LRBL*, p. 146.

60. *TMS*, IV.i.11, pp. 185–87.

61. For acute observations on the recurrent suspicion of new wealth, see Albert O. Hirschman, *Shifting Involvements: Private Interest*

and Public Action (Princeton, 1982), Chapter 3. Among the most useful examinations of the notion of "luxury" in eighteenth-century thought are Ellen Ross, "The Debate on Luxury in Eighteenth-Century France: A Study of the Language of Opposition to Change" (unpub. Ph.D. diss., University of Chicago, 1975); Simeon M. Wade, Jr., "The Idea of Luxury in Eighteenth-Century England" (unpub. Ph.D. diss., Harvard University, 1968); John Sekora, *Luxury: The Concept in Western Thought, Eden to Smollett* (Baltimore, 1977); and André Morize, *L'Apologie du Luxe au XVIIIe Siècle et "Le Mondain" de Voltaire. Étude critique sur "Le Mondain" et ses Sources* (1909; reprint, Geneva, 1970). Line references to "Le Mondain" and "Défense de Mondain" are to this edition.

62. Sekora, *Luxury*, pp. 39–44.

63. M. M. Goldsmith, "Liberty, luxury, and the pursuit of happiness," in Anthony Pagden (ed.), *The Languages of Political Theory in Early-Modern Europe* (Cambridge, 1987), pp. 225–52, p. 236; M. M. Goldsmith, *Private Vices, Public Benefits. Bernard Mandeville's Social and Political Thought* (Cambridge, 1985), p. 26.

64. Lucien Febvre, *"Civilisation:* evolution of a word and a group of ideas," in Peter Burke (ed.), *A New Kind of History. From the Writings of Febvre* (New York, 1973), pp. 219–57.

65. David Hume, *An Enquiry Concerning the Principles of Morals* (1751), ed. J. B. Schneewind (Indianapolis, 1983), pp. 73–74. Voltaire, *Philosophical Dictionary*, article "Virtue."

66. "Mondain," 1.14.

67. Voltaire, "Observations sur Mm. Jean Lass" (1738), in Moland, ed., *Ouvres complètes*, Vol. XX, p. 363, quoted in Ross, *Debate*, p. 64.

68. *Philosophical Dictionary* (Gay translation), article "Luxury."

69. "Defense," 1.55–72. For contemporary eighteenth-century variations of this argument, see Werner Sombart, *Luxury and Capitalism* (Ann Arbor, 1967; German original, 1913), pp. 113–15.

70. "Mondain," 1.19–24.

71. *LJ* (A), p. 83.

72. This paragraph and the next draw heavily on the discussion in Hont and Ignatieff, "Needs and justice in the 'Wealth of Nations,'" pp. 26–44. See also Richard Tuck, *Natural Rights Theories: Their Origin and Development* (Cambridge, 1979), pp. 72–75 on Grotius, and pp. 158–62 on Pufendorf, who developed the position that "general agreements for social utility confer rights," which is close to that of Smith.

73. David Hume, *An Enquiry Concerning the Principles of Morals*, Chapter 3, Part II.

74. This formulation is from Thomas Horne, *Property Rights and Poverty: Political Argument in Britain, 1605–1834* (Chapel Hill, 1990), p. 119.

75. *WN*, I.viii. 35–36, p. 96.

CHAPTER 4
THE MARKET: FROM SELF-LOVE
TO UNIVERSAL OPULENCE

1. *WN*, IV. Intro. p. 428.

2. Dugald Stewart, "Account of the Life and Writings of Adam Smith, LL.D.," in *EPS*, p. 309.

3. Stewart, "Account," p. 310. On this theme, see also Duncan Forbes, "Sceptical Whiggism, Commerce, and Liberty," in Andrew Skinner and Thomas Wilson (eds.), *Essays on Adam Smith* (Oxford, 1975), pp. 179–201. On the upward evaluation of "ordinary life" in early modern thought, see Charles Taylor, *Sources of the Self* (Cambridge, MA, 1989), pp. 211–18; on the transformation of Christian charity into practical benevolence, pp. 84–85, 258, 281.

4. *WN*, I.xi.b.41, p. 177.

5. John Locke, *Essay Concerning Civil Government*, §42.

6. *ED*, pp. 562–63.

7. *WN*, I.i.11, p. 22–24.

8. "It is the great multiplication of the productions of all the different arts, in consequence of the division of labour, which occasions, in a well-governed society, that universal opulence which extends itself to the lowest ranks of the people." *WN*, I.i.19, p. 22.

9. *WN*, I.i.4, p. 16; IV.ix,35, p. 676.

10. *WN*, I.i.5, p. 17; on the importance of the development of machinery in bringing about greater productivity, see also *WN*, II. 3–4, p. 277.

11. *WN*, I.i.9, pp. 21–22.

12. See *ED*, p. 570.

13. On Watt's steam engine, see David S. Landes, *The Unbound Prometheus: Technological Change and Industrial Development in Western Europe from 1750 to the Present* (Cambridge, 1969), pp. 99–104. On Watt and his relationship to Joseph Black, see R. G. W. Anderson, "Joseph Black," in David Daiches, *et al.*, *A Hotbed of Genius: The Scottish Enlightenment 1730–1790* (Edinburgh, 1986).

14. *WN*, I.iii.1, p. 31.

15. *WN*, I.ii.1–2, pp. 25–26.

16. *WN*, I.iv.1, p. 37.

17. *WN*, I.ii.4–5, pp. 28–30.

18. *WN*, I.ii.2, pp. 26–27.

19. *TMS*, VI.ii.intro.2, p. 218; VII.ii.3.18, p. 305; see the discussion of *TMS*, below.

20. *WN*, I.ii.2, p. 26.

21. *WN*, intro. 4, p. 10.

22. See for example his references to contemporary China in *WN*, I.viii.24, p. 90; and to ancient Greece in *TMS*, V.i.2.15., pp. 209–10.

23. *WN*, I.ii.1, p. 25.

24. This phrase comes not from Smith but from Robert K. Merton, "The Unanticipated Consequences of Purposive Social Action," *American Sociological Review*, Vol. 1, 1936.

25. *TMS*, IV.2.6, p. 189.

26. *WN*, II.iii.28, p. 341.

27. *WN*, I.vii.1–6, pp. 72–73.

28. *WN*, I.vii.; I.x.a.1, p. 116.

29. *WN*, I.vii.15, p. 75.

30. *WN*, I.viii.36, p. 96.

31. *WN*, I.viii.35, pp. 95–96; I.ix.9, p. 108.

32. *WN*, I.xi.o.1, p. 260.

33. *WN*, xi.o.9, p. 266.

34. *WN*, I.viii.27, p. 91.

35. *WN*, I.viii.16–21, pp. 86–87; I.viii.57, p. 104; II.intro.3–4, p. 277; II.iii.32, p. 343.

36. *WN*, I.viii.43, p. 99; *WN*, II.iii.6, p. 345. Smith discussed the negative implications of the standard of living of laborers in a "stationary state" in which capital was not increasing, and the dire implications of a "declining state." Some commentators, including most recently the distinguished historian E. A. Wrigley, *Continuity, chance, and change: the character of the industrial revolution in England* (Cambridge, 1988), claim that Smith maintained that on-going improvement in real wages was impossible because of declining marginal returns in agricultural production. (Wrigley, *Continuity*, pp. 3–4, 47–49, 103). But Wrigley appears to be reading the most pessimistic scenarios of Ricardo and Malthus back into Smith. While Smith does conjure up the "stationary state," it is as a specter to be avoided by wise policy, not as an inevitable destination for commercial society. On the mechanisms by which Smith believed that more advanced commercial nations could continue to raise real wages despite the competition of poorer nations with lower wage rates, see Istvan Hont, "The 'rich country–poor country' debate in Scottish classical political economy," in Istvan Hont and Michael Ignatieff (eds.), *Wealth and Virtue: The Shaping of Political Economy in the Scottish Enlightenment* (Cambridge, 1983), pp. 271–315, pp. 288–306.

37. *WN*, I.xi.o.1–8, pp. 264–65.

CHAPTER 5
THE LEGISLATOR AND THE MERCHANT

1. This has been recognized by Nathan Rosenberg, "Some Institutional Aspects of the Wealth of Nations," *Journal of Political Economy*, Vol. 18, #6 (1960), pp. 557–70; George Stigler, "Smith's Travels on the Ship of State," in Andrew S. Skinner and Thomas Wilson (eds.), *Essays on Adam Smith* (Oxford, 1975), pp. 237–46; and Lionel Robbins, *The Theory of Economic Policy in English Classical Political Economy* (London, 1953), p. 56.

6. *WN*, IV.ii.9, p. 456.

7. *WN*, IV.ii.10, p. 456.

8. *WN*, I.x.b.26–34, pp. 124–28.

9. *TMS*, IV.i.8–9, pp. 181–83; for similar comments on the psychic costs of wealth, see *TMS*, I.iii.2.1, p. 51.

10. This argument had been made in Mandeville's *Fable of the Bees*, and in Voltaire's *Défense de Mondain* of 1736.

11. *TMS*, IV.I.10, pp. 183–85, italics added.

12. *TMS*, VI.ii.I.20, pp. 225–26.

13. *WN*, IV.vii.b.61, p. 589.

14. *WN*, V.i.f.5–9, pp. 760–61.

15. *WN*, V.i.g.1, pp. 788–89; also V.i.g.29, pp. 805–06.

16. *WN*, IV.iv, pp. 499–543.

17. *WN*, IV.ix.48–49, pp. 686–87.

18. *WN*, V.ii.k, 33–34, p. 884.

19. *WN*, IV.ix.38, p. 678.

20. This sentence is adapted from Albert O. Hirschman, *The Rhetoric of Reaction* (Cambridge, MA, 1991), p. 36, who puts this insight to a different use.

CHAPTER 7

COMMERCIAL HUMANISM:
SMITH'S CIVILIZING PROJECT

1. On the earlier lineage of this genre, see Norbert Elias, *The Civilizing Process: Volume 1, The History of Manners* (New York, 1978), pp. 51–218; *The Civilizing Process: Volume 2, Power and Civility* (New York, 1982), pp. 229ff; and Roger Chartier, "From Texts to Manners. A Concept and Its Books; *Civilité* between Aristocratic Distinction and Popular Appropriation," in his *The Cultural Uses of Print in Early Modern France* (Princeton, 1987).

2. See the evaluation by Dugald Stewart, "Account," pp. 291–92, and Charles L. Griswold, Jr., "Rhetoric and Ethics: Adam Smith on Theorizing about the Moral Sentiments," *Philosophy and Rhetoric*, Vol.24, #3 (1991), pp. 213–37.

3. See F. M. L. Thompson, *The Rise of Respectable Society: A Social History of Victorian Britain, 1830–1900* (Cambridge, MA, 1988), esp. pp. 276–77, 352–61; and Gertrude Himmelfarb, *Poverty and Compassion: The Moral Imagination of the Late Victorians* (New York, 1991).

4. On the role of the virtues in the humanists, see Quentin Skinner, *The Foundations of Modern Political Thought: Vol.1, The Renaissance* (Cambridge, 1978), pp. 228ff.

5. The term is drawn from J. G. A. Pocock, "Virtues, rights, and manners: a model for historians of political thought," in his *Virtue, Commerce, and History* (Cambridge, 1985), p. 50.

6. *TMS*, V.2.13, p. 209.

7. On the notion in early-modern thought that commerce makes men more "gentle," see Albert Hirschman, *The Passions and the Interests: Political Arguments for Capitalism before Its Triumph* (Princeton, 1977), *passim*, esp. pp. 56–66; and *Rival Views of Market Society and Other Recent Essays* (New York, 1986), pp. 106–09. Though my discussion is greatly indebted to Hirschman, I believe he has underestimated the importance of the related theme of self-control in Smith's works in his discussion of Smith in *Passions*, pp. 100–13.

8. Smith's debt to stoicism is discussed by the editors of the Glasgow Edition of *TMS*, on pp. 5–10 of their introduction, but without any reference to neo-stoicism.

9. See, for example, La Bruyère, *Caractères*, "De l'homme," no. 3, quoted in Franklin L. Baumer, *Modern European Thought* (New York 1977), p. 86.

10. *TMS*, VII.ii.intro.1, p. 266.

11. *TMS*, VII.ii.2.14, p. 299.

12. *TMS*, VII.ii.I.11–14, pp. 270–72; I.i.3.1–10, pp. 16–19.

13. *TMS*, VI.3–5, pp. 212–13.

14. *TMS*, VII.ii.4.5, p. 307.

15. *TMS*, VI.iii.11, p. 241.

16. *TMS*, III.6.4, p. 172.

17. *TMS*, III.6.7, p. 173.

18. *TMS*, VII.ii.3.18, p. 305.

19. *TMS*, VII.ii.intro.2, p. 218.

20. *TMS*, II.i.5.9–10, p. 77.

21. *TMS*, VII.ii.I.42, p. 291; Lovejoy, *Reflections*, pp. 156–57, Norbert Waszek, "Two Concepts of Morality: A Distinction of Adam Smith's Ethics and Its Stoic Origin," *Journal of the History of Ideas*, Vol. XLV, #4 (1984), pp. 591–606.

22. Cicero, *On Duties*, edited and translated by M. T. Griffen and E. M. Atkins (Cambridge, 1991), Book I, 46, p. 20.

23. Cicero, *Of Duties*, Book I, iii, 8, and III, ii, 13–16, pp. 105–06.

24. *TMS*, VII.ii.I, p. 291.

25. *TMS*, VII.ii.3.15–16, p. 304.

26. Edmund Burke, "Letter to a Member of the National Assembly," (1791), in *The Writings and Speeches of Edmund Burke. Volume VIII; The French Revolution 1790–1794* edited by L. G. Mitchell (Oxford, 1989), p. 332.

CHAPTER 8
"THE IMPARTIAL SPECTATOR"

1. *TMS*, II.ii.2.1, pp. 82–83.

2. *TMS*, II.ii.3.4, p. 86.

3. *TMS*, I.i.i.1, p. 9.

4. *TMS*, I.i.2.1, pp. 13–14.

5. *TMS*, I.i.2.–I.i.4, pp. 13–22.

6. *TMS*, I.i.5.1, p. 23.

7. *TMS*, I.i.5, pp. 23–26.

8. *TMS*, II.ii.2.1, pp. 82–83.

9. *TMS*, VI.concl.1–2, pp. 262–63.

10. *TMS*, I.i.5.5, p. 25.

11. *TMS*, III.3.20, p. 145.

12. This point has been recognized by John Dwyer, *Virtuous Discourse: Sensibility and Community in Late Eighteenth-Century Scotland* (Edinburgh, 1987), pp. 53–54.

13. *TMS*, II.ii.3.5, p. 87.

14. *TMS*, II.iii.2, pp. 105–06.

15. *TMS*, III.1.2–3, pp. 109–11.

16. *TMS*, III.4.7, p. 159.

17. *TMS*, III.2.3, p. 114.

18. *TMS*, III.1.2, pp. 109–10.

19. *TMS*, II.5.1, p. 162.

20. *TMS*, II.5.1–2, pp. 162–63.

21. *TMS*, III.ii.1–4, p. 113–15.

22. *TMS*, III.2.6–9, p. 116–17.

23. *TMS*, III.2.32, p. 130.

24. *TMS*, III.3.4, p. 137.

25. *TMS*, III.2.1–8, pp. 113–17.

26. *TMS*, II.ii.2.1–4, pp. 82–84.

27. *TMS*, III.5.6, p. 166.

28. On the significance of Deism, see Charles Taylor, *Sources of the Self* (Cambridge, MA, 1989), Chapter 16, and especially the acute observations on pp. 266–67.

29. *TMS*, VI.ii.I.18, pp. 224–25.

30. This theme is explored most extensively in the *Gorgias*.

31. *TMS*, VI.iii.35, p. 247.

32. *TMS*, VII.ii.4.10, p. 311, emphasis added.

33. The term "social control" was coined by the American sociologist Edward A. Ross in his book *Social Control: A Survey of the Foundations of Social Order* (New York, 1901). The book makes extensive use of the themes and categories of *The Theory of Moral Sentiments* but funnels them through the categories of nineteenth-century naturalism and combines them with a rationalistic constructivism, feminism, eugenicism, and prospective elitism that give the book a very different tone from its eighteenth-century model. In place of the link between the internalization of norms and the development of autonomy, Ross posits a "passion for liberty" in necessary tension with a coercively conceived "social control." On social control in turn-of-the-century American social science, see Dorothy Ross, *The Origins of American Social Science* (Cambridge, 1991), Chapter 7.

For an excellent synoptic interpretation of Smith's thought which stresses the element of social control, see Warren J. Samuels, "The Political Economy of Adam Smith," *Ethics*, Vol. 87, #3 (1977), pp. 189–207.

34. *TMS*, III.2.31–32, pp. 128–30.

35. *TMS*, VI.ii.intro.2, p. 218; VII.ii.2.4, p. 229; III.3.7–9, pp. 138–40.

36. *TMS*, VI.ii.1.1, p. 219.

37. *TMS*, VI.ii.1–9, pp. 219–21.

38. *TMS*, VI.ii.1.16–17, p. 224.

39. *TMS*, VI.ii.2.2, p. 227.

40. *TMS*, VI.concl.1, p. 262.

41. *TMS*, II.ii.2.1, pp. 82–83.

42. *TMS*, II.ii.3.1–4, pp. 85–86.

43. *TMS*, I.i.5.5, p. 25.

44. *TMS*, II.ii.1.8, p. 81.

Chapter 9
The Historical and Institutional
Foundations of Commercial Society

1. *LB* (B), introd., p. 397; see also Knud Haakonssen, *The Science of a Legislator: The Natural Jurisprudence of David Hume and Adam Smith* (Cambridge, 1981), p. 148. This was Smith's understanding of Hobbes, not necessarily Hobbes' actual position.

2. Dugald Stewart, "Dissertation Exhibiting the Progress of Metaphysical, Ethical and Political Philosophy since the Revival of Letters in Europe" (originally published 1816–21) in Vol. 1 of his *Collected Works*, ed. W. Hamilton, 10 vols. (Edinburgh, 1854–58); quoted in Hans Medick, *Naturzustand und Naturgeschichte der bürgerlichen Gesellschaft: Die Ursprünge der bürgerlichen Sozialtheorie als Geschichtsphilosophie bei Samuel Pufendorf, John Locke and Adam Smith* (Göttingen, 1981; reprint of 1973 original edition), p. 146.

3. This argument is persuasively presented by Medick, *Naturzustand*, pp. 137–49. On Kames's linkage of history and jurisprudence, see William C. Lehmann, *Henry Home, Lord Kames, and the Scottish Enlightenment* (The Hague, 1971), Chapters 12–13.

4. "Jurisprudence is that science which inquires into the general principles which ought to be the foundation of the laws of all nations." *LJ* (B), p. 397; *LJ* (A), p. 5; and *TMS*, VII.iv.37, p. 341, where natural jurisprudence is called "a theory of the general principles which ought to run through and be the foundation of the laws of all nations."

5. *LJ* (B), p. 402. See the discussion in Haakonssen, *Science*, pp. 54–62, to whose work I am much indebted for my understanding of the lectures on jurisprudence and their links to *The Theory of Moral Sentiments*.

6. See Haakonssen, *Science*, p. 189.

7. See Haakonssen, *Science*, p. 151.

8. *LJ* (A), p. 17; Haakonssen, *Science*, pp. 106–07.

9. *LJ* (A), pp. 91–94.

10. *TMS*, VII.iv.36–37, pp. 340–41.

11. *LJ* (B), pp. 476ff.

12. *LJ* (A), p. 95; *LJ* (B), pp. 399–401, 459, 476; see also the analysis in Haakonssen, *Science*, pp. 100–01.

13. *LJ* (A), pp. 143, 172–76; see also Haakonssen *Science*, pp. 155–57.

14. *LJ* (A), p. 202.

15. *LJ* (A), p. 208.

16. *LJ* (B), p. 401.

17. *LJ* (A), pp. 213–17; *LJ* (B), pp. 404–08; Haakonssen, *Science*, pp. 157–59.

18. *LRBL*, p. 150.

19. *LRBL*, pp. 151–52.

20. *WN*, V.i.a.6–11, pp. 692–96; and *LJ* (A), pp. 232–33.

21. *LJ* (A), pp. 229ff.

22. *WN*, III.1–3, pp. 397–400.

23. *WN*, III.4, p. 400.

24. *WN*, III.6, pp. 400–01.

25. *WN*, III.ii.7–8, pp. 385–87.

26. *WN*, III.ii.18, p. 393; also III.iv.7, p. 415.

27. *WN*, III.iv.9, pp. 417–18.

28. *WN*, III.iii.6–12, pp. 401–05.

29. *WN*, III.iv.5, p. 413.

30. *WN*, III.iv.10, pp. 418–19.

31. *WN*, IV.iv.15, p. 421.

32. *LJ*(A), iv.165–66, p. 264.

33. *WN*, III.iv.4, p. 412.

34. *WN*, IV.iv.17, p. 422.

35. *WN*, III.i.9, p. 380.

36. *WN*, IV.iv.19–24, pp. 422–27.

37. *WN*, V.i.g.24, pp. 802–03.

38. *WN*, V.i.g.25–28, pp. 803–05.

39. This point is well explicated in Haakonssen, *Science*, pp. 131–33.

40. *LJ* (A), pp. 200ff.

41. *WN*, V.i.b.24–25, pp. 722–23, and additional references on p. 722, note 34.

42. On this development, see *LJ* (A), pp. 269–75; *LJ* (B), pp. 420–22.

43. *TMS*, II.ii.i.8, p. 81.

44. *LJ* (A), p. 175, and *passim*.

45. *TMS*, II.ii.i.8, p. 81.
46. *TMS*, VI.ii.1.12–14, pp. 222–23.
47. *LJ* (A), pp. 142–43; *LJ* (B), p. 438.
48. *TMS*, VI.ii.1.10, p. 222.
49. *WN*, V.i.f.36, pp. 773–74.
50. See Ursula Vogel, "Political Philosophers and the Trouble with Polygamy: Patriarchal Reasoning in Modern Natural Law," *History of Political Thought*, Vol. 12, #2 (1991), pp. 229–51.
51. *LJ* (A), pp. 150–54.
52. *LJ* (A), pp. 143–45.
53. *LJ* (A), p. 147.
54. *LJ* (A), p. 47.
55. *LJ* (A), p. 150.
56. *LJ* (A), pp. 159–60; *LJ* (B), p. 445.
57. *LJ* (A), pp. 171–72; *LJ* (B), p. 448.

CHAPTER 10
THE MORAL BALANCE SHEET
OF COMMERCIAL SOCIETY

1. *TMS*, V.2.9, p. 205.
2. *WN*, I.iv.1, p. 37.
3. *WN*, II.iv.3, p. 412.
4. *LJ* (B), p. 527.
5. *LJ* (B), pp. 538–39.
6. *WN*, I.x.c.31, p. 146.
7. On the distinction between virtue and propriety, see *TMS* I.i.5, pp. 6–7.
8. *TMS*, VI.I, pp. 212–17.
9. *TMS*, I.iii.2.3, pp. 52–53.
10. *TMS*, I.iii.2.1, p. 50.
11. See the works by Langford and McKendrick cited in Chapter 2. On the primacy of emulation as the motivation for economic activity in Smith's analysis of commercial society, see Nathan Rosenberg, "Adam Smith, Consumer Tastes, and Economic Growth," *The Journal of Political Economy*, Vol. 76 (1968), pp. 361–74; and the discussion in J. Ralph Lindgren, *The Social Philosophy of Adam Smith* (The Hague, 1973), pp. 101ff.
12. *WN*, I.xi.c.7, pp. 180–82; *WN*, I.xi.c.31–32, pp. 189–91.
13. *TMS*, I.iii.2.4, p. 53.
14. *TMS*, I.iii.2.5, pp. 55–56; VI.i.7, p. 213.
15. *TMS*, I.iii.3.1, p. 62.
16. *TMS*, I.iii.3.5, p. 63.
17. *TMS*, I.iii.3.6, p. 63.
18. On this point see Allan Silver, "Friendship in Commercial

Society: Eighteenth-Century Social Theory and Modern Sociology,"
American Journal of Sociology, Vol. 95, #6 (1990), pp. 1474–1504, esp. p.
1493.

19. *LJ* (B), pp. 452–53.

20. *TMS*, V.2.9, pp. 206–07.

21. *WN*, III.ii.10, p. 388. See also *WN*, I.vii.41, pp. 98–99.

22. *LJ* (A), p. 192.

23. *LJ* (B), pp. 451–52.

24. *TMS*, IV.2.6–8, pp. 189–90; similarly, III.5.8, pp. 166–67;
VI.i.1–14, pp. 212–16.

25. *WN*, IV.vii.c, p. 61, pp. 612–13. For confirmations of Smith's
analysis by subsequent historians, see John Elliot, "The Decline of
Spain," *Past and Present*, #20 (1961), pp. 52–75; and Bartolomé
Bennassar, *L'homme espagnol: attitudes et mentalites du XVIe au XVIIIe
siècle* (Paris, 1975), pp. 84–116.

26. *WN*, I.viii.41, p. 98.

27. *WN*, II.iii.28, p. 341.

28. *TMS*, I.iii.3.2–7, pp. 62–64.

29. *WN*, IV.vii.c.61, p. 612.

30. *TMS*, I.iii.2.8, p. 57.

31. *TMS*, III.2.11, p. 120.

32. *TMS*, I.iii.2.8, p. 57.

Chapter 11
The Visible Hand of the State

1. For Smith's strictures on banking and currency and their
historical context, see S. G. Checkland, "Adam Smith and the Bankers,"
in Andrew S. Skinner and Thomas Wilson (eds.), *Essays on Adam Smith*
(Oxford, 1975), pp. 504–23.

2. *WN*, V.i.g.24, pp. 802–03.

3. *LJ* (A), p. 239.

4. See Gary M. Anderson, William F. Shughart II, and Robert D.
Tollison, "Adam Smith in the Customhouse," *Journal of Political Economy*, Vol. 93, #4 (1985), pp. 740–59.

5. *WN*, V.i.e.1–4, pp. 731–33.

6. *WN*, V.ii.k.27, p. 882; similarly, V.ii.k.38, p. 885.

7. *WN*, V.ii.k.36–40, pp. 884–86.

8. *WN*, V.i.a.1–15, pp. 689–98.

9. *LJ* (A), pp. 228ff.

10. *WN*, V.i.a.29, pp. 701–02.

11. *WN*, V.i.a.36, p. 704.

12. *WN*, V.i.a.14, p. 697.

13. See the discussion in Richard Sher, *Church and University in the*

Scottish Enlightenment (Princeton, 1985), pp. 218ff, and, more generally, John Robertson, *The Scottish Enlightenment and the Militia Question* (Edinburgh, 1985).

14. *WN*, V.i.a.36–40, pp. 704–06.

15. *WN*, V.i.a.44, p. 708.

16. *WN*, V.i.a.14, p. 697; *WN*, IV.ii.23–30, pp. 463–64. For a more extensive discussion of these matters, see Knud Haakonssen, *The Science of a Legislator: The Natural Jurisprudence of David Hume and Adam Smith* (Cambridge, 1981), pp. 93–95, and 160ff.

17. *WN*, V.iii.37, pp. 919–20.

18. *WN*, V.iii.26, p. 915.

19. *WN*, V.iii.51–56, pp. 926–28.

20. *WN*, V.iii.58–59, pp. 928–29.

21. *WN*, V.iii.50, pp. 925–26.

22. *WN*, IV.v.b.43–45, pp. 540–41; I.ix.15, pp. 111–12.

23. *WN*, IV.v.b.44, p. 540.

24. *WN*, III.iii.12, p. 405.

25. *WN*, V.iii.7, p. 910.

26. *WN*, V.i.b.25, p. 722; see also *LJ* (B), pp. 59–91; *WN*, III.iv.15, p. 421.

27. *WN*, V.i.b.2, p. 709.

28. *WN*, V.ii.b.3, p. 825.

29. *WN*, V.i.b.2, p. 709.

30. *WN*, V.i.d.4, pp. 724–25; V.i.i.4, p. 815.

31. *WN*, V.i.e.33–40, pp. 756–58.

32. *WN*, I.i.19, p. 22.

33. *TMS*, II.ii.1.8, p. 81.

34. *WN*, V.i.f.50, p. 782.

35. *WN*, I.i.8, pp. 20–21; see also *LJ* (A), p. 351.

36. *WN*, I.viii.44, p. 99.

37. *LRBL*, p. 62.

38. See Jacob Viner, "Man's Economic Status," in his *Essays on the Intellectual History of Economics*, ed. Douglas Irwin (Princeton, 1991), pp. 286–87, on the attitude of the British upper classes toward popular schooling; for the quote from Voltaire, see p. 283. In keeping with his attempt to convince the upper classes of the desirability of universal education, Smith in 1785 publicly endorsed the initiative of the Sunday School Society to encourage Sunday education for the lower orders. See Thomas Laqueur, *Religion and Respectability: Sunday Schools and Working Class Culture, 1780–1850* (New Haven, 1976), p. 35; and John Rae, *Life of Adam Smith* (1895; reprinted, New York, 1965), p. 407.

39. On economic incentives for child labor, see Neil McKendrick, "Home Demand and Economic Growth: A New View of the Role of Women and Children in the Industrial Revolution," in Neil McKendrick

(ed.), *Historical Perspectives. Studies in English Thought and Society* (London, 1974).

    40. *LJ* (B), pp. 539–40.
    41. *WN*, V.i.f.54, p. 785.
    42. *WN*, V.i.f.55–57, pp. 785–86.
    43. *WN*, V.i.f.61, p. 788.
    44. *WN*, V.i.f.55–57, pp. 785–86; V.i.g.14, p. 796.
    45. *WN*, V.i.b.20, p. 719.
    46. *WN*, V.i.f.ii.4, p. 759.
    47. *WN*, V.i.f.ii, pp. 758ff, and V.i.f.55, p. 785.
    48. *WN*, V.i.f.ii.412, p. 762.
    49. *WN*, V.ii.a.14–15, p. 821.
    50. *WN*, V.ii.b.6, p. 826.

CHAPTER 12
APPLIED POLICY ANALYSIS:
ADAM SMITH'S SOCIOLOGY OF RELIGION

1. The most acute analyst of the institutional theme in Smith's work is Nathan Rosenberg. See especially his "Some Institutional Aspects of the Wealth of Nations," *Journal of Political Economy*, Vol. 18, #6 (1960), pp. 557–70; and "Adam Smith and the Stock of Moral Capital," *History of Political Economy*, Vol. 22, #1 (1990), pp. 1–17. Yet Smith's institutional analysis of religion has received remarkably little attention from Rosenberg or from most other commentators. One of the few general interpretations of Smith to pay attention to the issue is by Joseph Cropsey, *Polity and Economy: An Interpretation of the Principles of Adam Smith* (1957; reprinted Westport, CN, 1977), pp. 79–87, who is most concerned to establish the secularity of Smith's position. The only extended discussion of the subject is in Gary M. Anderson, "Mr. Smith and the Preachers: The Economics of Religion in *The Wealth of Nations*," *Journal of Political Economy*, Vol. 6, #5 (1988), pp. 1066–88, a useful piece which attempts, however, to translate Smith's categories and motives into the desiccated categories of contemporary public choice theory, a procedure which verges on (unintended) self-parody.

2. *TMS*, III.v, pp. 161–70. For Smith's skeptical explanation of the appeal of Christianity, see *LJ* (B), p. 451. For overviews and analyses of Smith's theological views, see Walther Eckstein's introduction to his German edition of *TMS*, *Theorie der ethischen Gefühle*, 2 vols. (Leipzig, 1926), pp. xlv–li; and T. D. Campbell, *Adam Smith's Science of Morals* (London, 1971), pp. 221–33. Many commentators tend to assimilate Smith's deistic natural theology to Hume's confirmed atheism. The divergence in their positions, and Smith's discomfort with Hume's ultimate position, is brought out in T. D. Campbell and Ian Ross, "The Theory and Practice of the Wise and Virtuous Man: Reflections on

Adam Smith's Response to Hume's Deathbed Wish," *Studies in Eighteenth-Century Culture*, Vol. 11 (1981), pp. 65–74.

3. *WN*, V.i.g.1, p. 788.

4. *TMS*, II.ii.3.12, p. 91; III.ii.12, pp. 120–21; III.2.33–35, pp. 131–34; III.5.–III.6, pp. 163–78.

5. *WN*, V.i.g.1, pp. 788–89. The essence of Smith's analysis is confirmed by the work of subsequent historians of British religion. See James Obelkevich, "Religion," in F. M. L. Thompson (ed.), *The Cambridge Social History of Britain 1750-1950, Vol. 3, Social Agencies and Institutions* (Cambridge, 1990), pp. 313–17, 321–26.

6. *WN*, V.i.g.2, pp. 789–90.

7. *WN*, V.i.g.3, p. 790.

8. David Hume, *History of England* (1778), iii. pp. 30–31; quoted in *WN*, V.i.g.6, p. 791. For a sophisticated discussion of Hume's view of established religion in the larger context of his social and political thought, see Donald W. Livingston, *Hume's Philosophy of Common Life* (Chicago, 1984), pp. 311ff.

9. *WN*, V.i.g.8–9, pp. 792–94.

10. Voltaire, *Letters on England*, Letter 6, "On the Presbyterians."

11. *TMS*, VI.ii.1.17, p. 224; similarly, V.2.2–3, pp. 200–01.

12. See Paul Langford, *A Polite and Commercial People: England 1727-1783.* (Oxford, 1989), pp. 252ff.

13. The phrase "the moral environment of the poor" is drawn from Joel Schwartz, "The Moral Environment of the Poor," *The Public Interest*, #103 (1991), who cites this passage from Smith.

14. *WN*, V.i.g.10–12, pp. 794–96. For the role of Protestant Sunday schools in inculcating the virtues of self-control and punctuality and in creating "a culture of discipline, self-respect, and improvement," see Thomas Laqueur, *Religion and Respectability: Sunday Schools and Working Class Culture, 1780-1850* (New Haven, 1976), esp. pp. 214–41; and, more generally, F. M. L. Thompson, *The Rise of Respectable Society: A Social History of Victorian Britain, 1830-1900* (Cambridge, MA, 1988).

15. *WN*, V.i.g.12–16, pp. 796–97.

16. *WN*, V.i.g.34, pp. 807–08.

17. On the link between the reaction against enthusiasm and the rise of experimental science and natural religion, see the works of Michael Heyd, "The Reaction to Enthusiasm in the Seventeenth Century: Towards an Integrative Approach," *Journal of Modern History*, Vol. 53 (1981), pp. 258–80; "Protestantism, Enthusiasm and Secularization in the Early Modern Period," in *Religion, Ideology and Nationalism in Europe and America: Essays in Honour of Yehoshua Arieli* (Jerusalem, 1986), pp. 15–27. On the impact of natural religion on the British clergy, see Paul Langford, *A Polite and Commercial People: England 1727-1783* (Oxford, 1989), pp. 252ff. and 281.

18. *The Works of John Witherspoon* (Philadelphia, 1913), Vol. 3, p. 121, quoted in Roger L. Emerson, "The Social composition of enlightened Scotland: the select society of Edinburgh, 1754–1764," *Studies on Voltaire and the Eighteenth Century*, Vol. CXIV (1973), pp. 291–329, p. 310.

19. On the relationship of Smith to the Moderates, see John Dwyer, *Virtuous Discourse: Sensibility and Community in Late Eighteenth-Century Scotland* (Edinburgh, 1987); on the intellectual debt of the Moderates to stoicism see especially pp. 46ff.; and Richard Sher, *Church and University in the Scottish Enlightenment*, pp. 175–86. On Enlightened attempts to develop Christianity into rational religion, see Roy Porter, *The Enlightenment* (Atlantic Highlands, NJ, 1990), pp. 36ff.

20. *WN*, V.i.g.33–38, pp. 807–10.

21. Walter Bagehot, "Adam Smith as a Person" (1876), reprinted in *The Works of Walter Bagehot*, Vol. 3 (Hartford, 1889), pp. 269–306, p. 277.

CHAPTER 13
"A SMALL PARTY": MORAL AND POLITICAL LEADERSHIP IN COMMERCIAL SOCIETY

1. *TMS*, VI.i.15, p. 216.

2. On the overlap between classical and modern virtues in Smith and in the Scottish Enlightenment, see the compressed and penetrating comments of J. G. A. Pocock, "The political limits to premodern economics," in John Dunn (ed.), *The Economic Limits to Modern Politics* (Cambridge, 1990), pp. 121–41, pp. 134–40.

3. *TMS*, VI.iii.13, p. 242.

4. *TMS*, VI.1.13, p. 216.

5. *TMS*, VI.1.14, p. 216.

6. For a brilliant evocation of the origins and recurrent laments of this criticism, see Allan Bloom, "Commerce and 'Culture,'" in his *Giants and Dwarfs: Essays 1960–1990* (New York, 1990), pp. 277–94.

7. *TMS*, VI.1.15, p. 216.

8. *TMS*, VI.iii.13, p. 242.

9. *TMS*, I.iii.2, p. 62.

10. *TMS*, VI.iii.25, p. 247.

11. *TMS*, VI.iii.25, p. 248.

12. *TMS*, VII, iv, 24–25, p. 336.

13. In this purpose, Smith was continuing the tradition of his teacher, Francis Hutcheson. See Duncan Forbes, *Hume's Philosophical Politics* (Cambridge, 1978), p. 56; Richard F. Teichgraeber III, *"Free Trade" and Moral Philosophy: Rethinking the Sources of Adam Smith's Wealth of Nations* (Durham, 1986), pp. 123–33; and Richard Sher, *Church and University in the Scottish Enlightenment* (Princeton, 1985), pp. 166–68.

3. See the excellent article by Enzo Pesciarelli, "Smith, Bentham, and the development of contrasting ideas of entrepreneurship," *History of Political Economy*, Vol. 23, #3 (1989), pp. 521–36, which I have drawn upon in the discussion that follows.

4. *WN*, II.iv.15, p. 357.

5. *WN*, I.xi.10, p. 266.

6. *TMS*, VI.i.12, p. 215.

7. *WN*, V.i.e.18, p. 741.

8. *WN*, V.i.e.33, p. 756.

9. The relevant chapter can be found in *Jeremy Bentham's Economic Writings*, ed. Werner Stark (London, 1952), and as "Appendix C" to Smith's *Correspondence*, to which the following page references apply.

10. See Hans Jaeger, "Unternehmer," in Otto Brunner and Werner Conze (eds.), *Geschichtliche Grundbegriffe* (Stuttgart, 1975).

11. See Joseph A. Schumpeter, *The Theory of Economic Development* (New Brunswick, NJ, 1983, German original published in 1911), and more generally Schumpeter, *Capitalism, Socialism, and Democracy*, Third Edition (New York, 1950).

12. See, for example, Schumpeter, *Capitalism, Socialism and Democracy*, pp. 157ff.; and more recently, Ferdinand Mount, *The Subversive Family: An Alternative History of Love and Marriage* (London, 1983); and Michael Novak, *The Spirit of Democratic Capitalism* (New York, 1982), pp. 156–70. On the theme of the family in other works of the Scottish Enlightenment, see Gladys Bryson, *Man and Society: The Scottish Inquiry of the Eighteenth Century* (1945; reprinted, New York, 1968), pp. 172ff.; Dwyer, *Virtuous Discourse*; and Rosemarie Zagarri, "Morals, Manners, and the Republican Mother," *American Quarterly*, Vol. 42, #2 (1992), pp. 26–43.

13. See the brilliant analysis by J. G. A. Pocock, in his "Introduction" to the Hackett edition of Burke's *Reflections on the Revolution in France* (Indianapolis, 1987); on Burke's turn toward an Anglican defense of the state after 1789, see J. C. D. Clark, *English Society 1688–1832* (Cambridge, 1985), pp. 247ff.

14. On Hamilton's political economy, see Drew R. McCoy, *The Elusive Republic: Political Economy in Colonial America* (New York, 1982), pp. 146ff.

15. On List, see the article by Keith Tribe in *The New Palgrave*.

16. The most informed and important analysis of Marx along these lines is Leszek Kolakowski, *Main Currents of Marxism: Vol.1. The Founders* (Oxford, 1978).

17. For an excellent overview of this question—which took the form of Marx's wrestling with the "transformation problem"—see Jerrold Seigel, *Marx's Fate: The Shape of a Life* (Princeton, 1978), Part 3.

18. For some late-nineteenth-century British examples, see Ger-

trude Himmelfarb, *Poverty and Compassion: The Moral Imagination of the Late Victorians* (New York, 1991), pp. 68–75.

19. *TMS,* VI.ii.3, pp. 228–29.

Chapter 15
Some Unanticipated Consequences of Smith's Rhetoric

1. On citations of Smith's works in the parliamentary debates of the 1790s, see Kirk Willis, "The role in Parliament of the economic ideas of Adam Smith, 1776–1800," *History of Political Economy,* Vol. 11, #4 (1979), pp. 505–44. The quotation is from Francis Horner, in L. J. Horner (ed.), *Memoirs and Correspondence of Francis Horner* (Boston, 1852), Vol. I, pp. 237–38, cited in Donald Winch, "Science and the Legislator: Adam Smith and After," *The Economic Journal,* Vol. 93, (Sept. 1983), pp. 501–20, p. 512.

2. Walter Bagehot, "Adam Smith as a Person" (1876), reprinted in *The Works of Walter Bagehot,* Vol. 3 (Hartford, 1889), pp. 269–306, p. 303.

3. *WN,* IV.ix.51, p. 687.

4. See Laurence Dickey, "Historicizing the 'Adam Smith Problem': Conceptual, Historiographical, and Textual Issues," *Journal of Modern History,* Vol. 58, #3 (Sept. 1986), pp. 579–609, p. 600; and Arthur O. Lovejoy, " 'Nature' as Aesthetic Norm," in his *Essays in the History of Ideas* (Baltimore, 1948), pp. 69–77.

5. See Jacob Viner, *The Role of Providence in the Social Order: An Essay in Intellectual History* (Princeton, 1972); and Charles Taylor, *Sources of the Self: The Making of Modern Identity* (Cambridge, MA, 1989), Chapter 16.

6. *TMS,* VII.ii.1.21, p. 277.

7. Karl R. Popper, *The Poverty of Historicism,* Third Edition (New York, 1964), pp. 58–70.

8. *TMS,* III.5.5, p. 165.

9. *TMS,* III.5.6, p. 166.

10. *TMS,* III.3.25, p. 147.

11. *TMS,* VI.iii.25, pp. 247–48.

12. *TMS,* VI.ii.1.18, pp. 224–25.

13. On this conception of the self, see Alasdair MacIntyre, *After Virtue* (Notre Dame, 1981), p. 56; and Lionel Trilling, *Sincerity and Authenticity* (Cambridge, MA, 1972), p. 9.

14. See the brilliant historical portrait by Daniel Walker Howe, *The Political Culture of the American Whigs* (Chicago, 1979), esp. pp. 300–03.

15. Jeremy Bentham, *Deontology,* ed. A. Goldworth (Oxford, 1983), p. 130, cited and discussed in John Dinwaddy, *Bentham* (New York, 1989), pp. 49ff.

16. I have borrowed this formulation from Taylor, *Sources,* pp. 82–83. See also his discussion on pages 327ff.

17. John Stuart Mill, "Bentham" (1838), reprinted in John Stuart Mill, *Essays on Politics and Culture*, Gertrude Himmelfarb (ed.) (New York, 1962; reprinted Gloucester, MA, 1973), pp. 77–120, pp. 97–98.

18. On Mill as the progenitor of a new, "revisionary liberalism," see John Gray, "Mill's and Other Liberalisms," *Critical Review*, Vol. 2, #2/3 (1988), pp. 12–35, p. 26; and Gertrude Himmelfarb, *On Liberty and Liberalism: The Case of John Stuart Mill* (New York, 1974).

19. See the analysis in Himmelfarb, *On Liberty and Liberalism*, p. 59.

20. M. A. Abrams, *The Mirror and the Lamp: Romantic Theory and the Critical Tradition* (New York, 1953), pp. 20–21, and *passim*. For a skeptical view of Romantic individualism grounded in a careful analysis of the experience of several leading Romantics, see Gerald N. Izenberg, *Impossible Individuality: Romanticism, Revolution, and the Origins of Modern Selfhood, 1787–1802* (Princeton, 1992).

21. John Stuart Mill, *On Liberty*, Gertrude Himmelfarb (ed.) (New York, 1974), pp. 132–33.

22. Nancy L. Rosenblum, "Pluralism and Self-Defense," in Nancy L. Rosenblum (ed.), *Liberalism and the Moral Life* (Cambridge, MA, 1989), p. 210.

23. The term "imperial self" is taken from Quentin Anderson, *The Imperial Self* (New York, 1971). For an excellent summary of the inclinations and preferences of expressive individualism, see George Kateb, "Democratic Individuality and the Meaning of Rights," in Rosenblum (ed.), *Liberalism*, p. 191. On the history of expressive individualism, see Taylor, *Sources*, pp. 374ff. and *passim*. On its contemporary incidence, see Robert Bellah, *et al.*, *Habits of the Heart: Individualism and Commitment in American Life* (Berkeley, 1985), pp. 32–35 and *passim*.

CHAPTER 16

THE TIMELESS AND THE TIMELY

1. Max Weber, *Gesammelte Aufsätze zur Religionssoziologie*, Second Edition (Tübingen, 1922), p. 22.

2. *TMS*, VII.ii.2.13, p. 299.

3. For applications of economic models to the family, see Gary S. Becker, *The Economic Approach to Human Behavior* (Chicago, 1976); and Richard Swedberg (ed.), *Economics and Sociology: Redefining Their Boundaries* (Princeton, 1990), and pp. 325–27 of Swedberg's summary.

4. The quote is from David M. Winch, *Analytical Welfare Economics* (Harmondsworth, 1971), p. 25.

5. For a critique of the empirical validity of "public choice" theory, see Jeffrey Friedman, "The Democratic Welfare State," *Critical Review*, Vol. 4, #4 (1990), pp. 672–74, 698. See also Steven E. Rhoads, *The Economist's View of the World: Government, Markets, and Public Policy* (Cambridge, 1985), Chapters 9 and 11. Stephen Holmes provides an

extended critique of the postulate that self-interest explains much of human behavior and shows that Hume and Smith thought likewise in "The Secret History of Self-Interest," in Jane J. Mansbridge (ed.), *Beyond Self-Interest* (Chicago, 1990), pp. 267–86.

6. The works of Robert K. Merton have been especially important in this regard. See his "The Unanticipated Consequences of Purposive Social Action" (1936), reprinted in Merton, *Sociological Ambivilance* (New York, 1976); and "Manifest and Latent Functions," in *Social Theory and Social Structure*, Third, Enlarged Edition (New York, 1968). The theme of unanticipated consequences and its implications for sociology has been perhaps the most significant continuity in Merton's work.

7. For one of many statements of this recognition, see Nathan Glazer, *The Limits of Social Policy* (Cambridge, MA, 1988), especially the title essay.

8. See the critique by Albert O. Hirschman, *Rhetoric of Reaction: Perversity, Futility, Jeopardy* (Cambridge, MA, 1991); for a critique of some aspects of Hirschman's critique, see Jerry Z. Muller, "Albert Hirschman's Rhetoric of Recrimination," *The Public Interest*, #104 (1991), pp. 81–92.

9. For elements of such an analysis, see Alan Ehrenhalt, *The United States of Ambition* (New York, 1991).

10. For a useful treatment of Smith's political thought, and the links between Hume, Smith, Madison, and Hamilton, see Stephen Miller, "Adam Smith and the Commercial Republic," *The Public Interest*, #61 (Fall, 1980), pp. 106–22. Also germane to this theme are David F. Epstein's penetrating book, *The Political Theory of the Federalist* (Chicago, 1984); Roy Branson, "James Madison and the Scottish Enlightenment," *Journal of the History of Ideas*, Vol. 42 (1979), pp. 235–50; and Douglass Adair, "That Politics May Be Reduced to a Science: David Hume, James Madison and the Tenth Federalist," in *Fame and the Founding Fathers: Essays of Douglass Adair*, ed. Trevor Colbourn (New York, 1974).

11. See the excellent study by Jonathan Beecher, *Charles Fourier: The Visionary and His World* (Berkeley, 1988), esp. Chapter 11.

12. On Bentham's Panopticon, see the classic article by Gertrude Himmelfarb, "The Haunted House of Jeremy Bentham," in *Victorian Minds* (New York, 1968), as well as her subsequent reflections in "Bentham's Utopia," in *Marriage and Morals Among the Victorians* (New York, 1986), and *The Idea of Poverty* (New York, 1984), pp. 78–85. As one Bentham scholar has pointed out, however, Bentham's urge to control and regulate was moderated in most of his other policy recommendations by his respect for the principle that each man is ordinarily the best judge of how to promote his own welfare. See John Dinwiddy, *Bentham* (New York, 1989), pp. 95–96.

It is the central contention of Michel Foucault's influential *Disci-*

pline and Punish: The Birth of the Prison (New York, 1977) that Bentham's Panopticon project was in fact the institutional model for most of modern society. For useful expositions and critiques of this claim, see J. G. Merquior, *Foucault* (Berkeley, 1985), Chapter 7; and Michael Walzer, "The Politics of Michel Foucault," in David Couzens Hoy (ed.), *Foucault: A Critical Reader* (New York, 1986).

13. For a discussion of such approaches, see Susan Rose-Ackerman, *Rethinking the Progressive Agenda: The Reform of the American Regulatory State* (New York, 1992), Chapter 7, "Social Services: Proxy Shopping."

14. For a fine exposition of this approach, see Steven E. Rhoads, *The Economist's View of the World: Government, Markets, and Public Policy* (Cambridge, 1985), Chapter 4.

15. See George Stigler's 1964 Presidential Address to the American Economic Association, "The Economist and the State," reprinted in George Stigler, *The Economist as Preacher and Other Essays* (Chicago, 1982).

16. See for example the recent slew of books along these lines reviewed in William A. Galston, "Home Alone," *The New Republic* (Dec. 2, 1991), pp. 40–44.

17. *TMS*, II.ii.1.8, p. 81.

18. Compare the thoughtful essay by Jeffrey Friedman, "The New Consensus: II. The Democratic Welfare State," *Critical Review*, Vol. 4, #4 (1990), pp. 633–708, esp. pp. 686–90.

19. For a description and critique of this trend, see Steven E. Rhoads, "Economists on Tastes and Preferences," in James H. Nichols, Jr., and Colin Wright (eds.), *From Political Economy to Economics—and Back?* (San Francisco, 1990), pp. 79–104, esp. pp. 100–01.

20. See Rhoads, *Economist's View*, pp. 155ff., for examples.

21. Rhoads, *Economist's View*, p. 177.

22. The works of Michel Foucault have served as a catalyst in this development.

23. Joseph Schumpeter, *Capitalism, Socialism, and Democracy*, Third Edition (New York, 1950), Chapters 21 to 23: Albert O. Hirschman, *Shifting Involvements: Private Interest and Public Action* (Princeton, 1982), p. 106; and Rhoads, *Economist's View*, pp. 201–22.

Guide to Further Reading

Of essays and articles on Adam Smith there is no end: hundreds, perhaps thousands, have appeared in the two centuries since his death. This section is not intended as a complete and exhaustive guide to the literature on Adam Smith or to related topics explored in the text. That would probably be impossible, and it is far from clear that it would be desirable. For the most part, I have included only works which are worth reading, while criticizing those elements I believe are misleading. For a more comprehensive listing of works on Smith, see Martha Bolar Lightwood, *A Selected Bibliography of Significant Works about Adam Smith* (Philadelphia, 1984), which lists over 700 books and articles in English and only scratches the surface of the relevant literature.

SMITH'S WORKS

For most purposes, the best place to turn for reliable and accessible editions of Smith's works is to the *Glasgow Edition of the Works and Correspondence of Adam Smith,* commissioned by the University of Glasgow to commemorate the bicentenary of *The Wealth of Nations.* The edition is published in hardcover by Oxford University Press and in sturdy and remarkably affordable soft-cover editions by Liberty Press/Liberty Classics of Indianapolis,

Indiana. These are critical editions, based on the last version of each text which Smith was able to correct, with indications of the textual changes from edition to edition. They also include extensive footnotes which provide a great deal of useful information: references to the subject at hand elsewhere in the same work and in Smith's other writings, and, in some volumes, relevant quotations from works consulted by Smith, which are useful for judging the extent and limits of the novelty of his arguments and sometimes their polemical intent. Each volume includes an introduction by the volume's editors, which are more likely to be of use to those with some prior knowledge of Smith's work than to beginners. The six volumes of the Glasgow edition comprise not only everything published by Smith in his lifetime, but some posthumously published essays, the texts of several sets of lectures, and his correspondence.

Volume One of the Glasgow edition contains *The Theory of Moral Sentiments*, edited by A. L. Macfie and D. D. Raphael, first published in 1976, and with minor corrections in 1979. The other significant edition of the *TMS* is a German edition, *Theorie der ethischen Gefühle*, two volumes (Leipzig, 1926), edited by Walther Eckstein. This edition includes a learned introduction by Eckstein, and the second volume includes a long section of notes which give the original sources of many of Smith's quotations and identify the people and events mentioned in the text. The excellent introduction includes a section on the reception of the book at the time of its publication, a comparison of the various editions, and an extensive analysis of changes to the sixth edition. Especially good are the discussion of Smith's views on religion and Eckstein's refutation of "the Adam Smith problem"—a pseudo-problem which captivated nineteenth-century German scholars who sought to explain the purported contradiction between the supposedly benevolent view of man in the *TMS* and the purely egoistic and materialistic view of man in *WN*. Eckstein shows that "the Adam-Smith problem" was based on a careless and distorted reading of both works, since Smith did not view man as exclusively altruistic or benevolent in the *TMS* or as purely egoistic or materialistic in *WN*.

Volume Two of the Glasgow edition contains *An Inquiry into the Nature and Causes of the Wealth of Nations*, edited by R. H. Campbell and A. S. Skinner, first published in 1976, and with minor corrections in 1979. It comes in a two-volume set. A nineteenth-century edition of enduring value is that of the distinguished economist J. R. McColloch, originally published in Edinburgh in 1828 in four volumes. The first volume includes a long introduction which places Smith's work in the context of earlier works on political economy and offers a sympathetic critique of some of Smith's views. Most of the fourth volume comprises extensive notes by McColloch, some of which are analytic and others descriptive of economic developments since Smith's time.

The edition of *WN* edited by Edwin Cannan and first published in 1898 has much to recommend it. A long introduction by Cannan includes a description of the various editions of the book, long summaries from the (then recently discovered) 1763–64 set of lectures on jurisprudence, a summary of *WN* itself, and an analysis of Smith's intellectual debts to his teacher, Hutcheson, and to Mandeville. Cannan also provides numerous, useful notes. His most valuable addition, perhaps, was to provide brief summaries printed alongside each paragraph, which may help some readers follow the argument of the book, though others may find them distracting and annoying. The Cannan edition was reprinted by the University of Chicago in 1976 in one volume.

The Penguin Books edition of *WN*, first published in 1970, includes the first three books, omitting books four and five entirely, a selection meant to favor the narrowly "economic" parts of the work. The long introduction by Andrew Skinner, a distinguished student of Smith's work, includes an uninspired overview of the moral psychology of the *TMS*, a restatement of the economic doctrines of books I and II of *WN* (sometimes less clear than the original), a summary of Smith's policy prescriptions for state action, and a useful (though somewhat overly economistic) treatment of Smith's theory of historical stages.

Essays on Philosophical Subjects, edited by W. P. D. Wightman and J. C. Bryce, comprises Volume Three of the Glasgow edition, published in 1980. This volume includes Smith's long essay on "The History of Astronomy," which conveys his conception of the psychology of science and the nature of scientific development. Also included is Smith's "A Letter to the Authors of the Edinburgh Review" of 1756, which offers his judgment on significant intellectual developments in his own day. The volume also reprints Dugald Stewart's "Account of the Life and Writings of Adam Smith, L.L.D." First published in 1794, this first overview of Smith's life and work, by his distinguished student and successor, is arguably still the best in recapturing the characteristic features of Smith's thought, the moral concerns of *WN*, and the fact that the book was addressed to contemporary policy makers and that it was understood by contemporaries as an attack on mercantile interests. It is reprinted along with a useful introduction by Ian Ross.

Volume Four of the Glasgow edition contains *Lectures on Rhetoric and Belles Lettres*, edited by J.C. Bryce, and published in 1983. These lectures, delivered during 1762–63 at Glasgow University, cover a remarkably wide range of subjects (so wide that it is hard to imagine that Smith's listeners could follow his line of thought) from the Greek historians to contemporary French drama. For those interested in Smith as a social analyst, these lectures demonstrate his attention to the psychology of persuasion and his attempts to link rhetorical and literary forms to the historical and social contexts in which they arose. The volume also includes a wide-ranging speculative essay first published during Smith's lifetime, "Considerations Concerning the First Formation of Languages."

During his years at the University of Glasgow, Smith lectured regularly on "jurisprudence," a rubric which covered "justice, police, revenue and arms"—or, as we would now say, law, public policy, taxation, and defense. Smith expanded, revised, and reworked his lectures on the last three subjects and published them as *The Wealth of Nations*. That book suggests Smith's views of law and government in passing remarks and comments, but he never completed a projected work that would have been devoted to those topics. Dissatisfied with his manuscript, he ordered his literary executors to have it burned. Nevertheless, two sets of student notes on Smith's Glasgow lectures have turned up, one a summary and précis of the lectures given in 1763–64, known as *LJ* (B), the other a far more complete set of notes on the lectures given in 1762–63, known as *LJ* (A). These lectures form an invaluable part of Smith's *ouevre*, but they must be used with caution. For while they are the product of vast learning and reflection, they do not represent views which Smith himself was willing to publish, and every professor knows that lectures sometimes contain spontaneous, ill-considered, and undigested remarks which he would excise from a published version. Moreover, the *Lectures on Jurisprudence* are notes taken by students, which are by no means always an accurate reflection of what the lecture has meant to convey. One way of minimizing that drawback is to give greater weight to propositions which Smith advanced in both sets of lectures. Volume Five of the Glasgow edition, *Lectures on Jurisprudence,* edited by Ronald L. Meek, D. D. Raphael, and Peter G. Stein and published in 1978, includes both versions, as well as an introduction describing their history and a very useful collation of the two. Also included in this volume are several short manuscripts from about the same time, including an early draft of *The Wealth of Nations.*

Volume Six of the Glasgow edition, *The Correspondence of Adam Smith,* edited by Ernest Campbell Mossner and Ian Simpson Ross, was published in 1977, and in a slightly augmented edition in 1987. Smith's letters reveal relatively little about the development of his ideas, but they are useful for tracing his social contacts and for observing him in his roles first as a tutor to the children of the powerful and then as a policy adviser to statesmen. His letter of November 1779 to Lord Carlisle, President of the Board of Trade, on the subject of free trade with Ireland, is an excellent specimen of Smith's ability to bring detailed knowledge, general principles of economic policy, and a concern for the public interest to bear on contemporary affairs in the years after the publication of *The Wealth of Nations.* The volume contains a number of useful appendices, including a long and informed critique of *The Wealth of Nations* by the former colonial administrator and member of Parliament, Thomas Pownall, published in 1776; Jeremy Bentham's critique of Smith's strictures on usury; and some examples of customhouse documents which give a flavor of Smith's activities as Commissioner of Customs.

The availability of the Glasgow edition in paperback editions (with the exception of the volume of correspondence) means that the best editions are eminently affordable. Those seeking a one-volume introduction to Adam Smith may turn to *The Essential Adam Smith* (New York, 1986), edited by Robert L. Heilbroner, which includes long and intelligently selected excerpts from *The Theory of Moral Sentiments* and *The Wealth of Nations,* as well as shorter excerpts from Smith's other works. Despite the editor's acuity, however, much of interest and importance for understanding Smith as a historical analyst and social theorist is necessarily lost.

Smith's Life

At present, we lack a thorough, modern, scholarly biography of Smith. The situation will soon be remedied by Ian Simpson Ross, whose forthcoming biography will appear as a volume of the Glasgow edition. Stewart's biographical memoir remains a good place to start. Much richer in biographical detail (though scanty on Smith's intellectual development) is John Rae, *Life of Adam Smith*, first published in 1895, and reprinted along with Jacob Viner's "Guide to John Rae's *Life of Adam Smith*"—itself a very substantial contribution by a leading Smith scholar—by August Kelley (New York, 1965). Additional material on Smith's life appears in W. R. Scott, *Adam Smith as Student and Professor* (Glasgow, 1937). R. H. Campbell and A. S. Skinner, *Adam Smith* (New York, 1982), is a serviceable and up-to-date short biography by two distinguished scholars of Smith's work which emphasizes the Scottish and university contexts and makes extensive use of the newly published correspondence. It is stronger on the settings than on the intellectual substance of Smith's thought. A study by Gary M. Anderson, William F. Shughart II, and Robert D. Tollison, "Adam Smith in the Customhouse," *Journal of Political Economy*, Vol. 93, #4 (1985), pp. 740–59, shows that Smith sought out his post as Customs Commissioner and devoted himself to the enforcement of customs duties and the creation of a more efficient customs system.

Those interested in more specialized research on Smith will want to know what books he had in his library. To be sure, Smith did not own every book he read or read every book he owned, but the two categories overlap to an unusual extent. For information on Smith's library, see James Bonar, *A Catalogue of the Library of Adam Smith* (Second Edition, 1932; reprinted New York, 1966), and Hiroshi Mizuta, *Adam Smith's Library. A Supplement to Bonar's Catalogue with a Checklist of the Whole Library* (Cambridge, 1967).

General Works on Smith

A reliable short introduction to Smith and his work is D. D. Raphael, *Adam Smith* (New York, 1985), in the Oxford Past Masters series. Reflecting its author's expertise, the book is particularly good in its treatment of Smith's moral psychology

An indispensable collection of essays for a contextual understanding of *The Wealth of Nations* is Istvan Hont and Michael
Ignatieff (eds.), *Wealth and Virtue: The Shaping of Political Economy
in the Scottish Enlightenment* (Cambridge, 1983). Especially fine
are the introductory essay by the editors, "Needs and justice in
the *Wealth of Nations*," Hont's "The 'rich–country–poor country'
debate in Scottish classical political economy," and the essays by
J. G. A. Pocock and Donald Winch. John Robertson, "The
Scottish enlightenment at the limits of the civic tradition,"
focuses on David Hume's break with the tradition of civic
republicanism. The essay by Nicholas Phillipson, "Adam Smith
as a civic moralist," offers a somewhat inaccurate account of
Smith's moral theory and develops a very strained interpretation
of Smith as a "regionalist" thinker, based in part on the
misreadings of Ralph Lindgren (discussed below), in part on
textually unwarranted assertions.

Two leading scholars of Smith's work have published collec-
tions of their articles: Andrew Skinner, *A System of Social Science:
Papers Related to Adam Smith* (Oxford, 1979), and Alec L. Macfie,
The Individual in Society: Papers on Adam Smith (London, 1967).
Jacob Viner, *Essays on the Intellectual History of Economics*, edited
by Douglas A. Irwin (Princeton, 1991), is a collection of the most
relevant essays by a major student of Smith's life and economic
thought.

SMITH'S MORAL AND POLITICAL THOUGHT

Joseph Cropsey, *Polity and Economy: An Interpretation of the
Principles of Adam Smith* (The Hague, 1957; reprinted Westport,
CN, 1977), and his chapter on Smith in Leo Strauss and Joseph
Cropsey (eds.), *History of Political Philosophy* (Third Edition,
Chicago, 1987), are works of great intellectual penetration,
though the role of approbation and of self-approbation in
Smith's civilizing project are virtually ignored, and the impor-
tance of sub-political and non-economic institutions are slighted.

Hans Medick, *Naturzustand und Naturgeschichte der bürgerlichen Gesellschaft: Die Ursprünge der bürgerlichen Sozialtheorie als
Geschichtsphilosophie bei Samuel Pufendorf, John Locke and Adam
Smith* (Göttingen, 1973; reprinted 1981), is a perceptive work
which sees the Scots as transforming moral philosophy into so-

cial science by taking the normative claims to freedom and equality of the natural rights and contract theorists and giving them a basis in the development of historical institutions through a synthesis of jurisprudence, history, and philosophy. Medick attributes to Smith the belief that humanistic education could be brought to the entire population, which is more Hegelian and Habermasian than Smithian, and also attributes to him, without textual warrant, a greater egalitarianism than he in fact exhibited.

Donald Winch, *Adam Smith's Politics: An essay in historiographical revision* (Cambridge, 1978), begins with a sustained and reasoned attack on the tendency to view Smith's work with anachronistic hindsight by assimilating it too closely to nineteenth-century European liberalism. Winch makes the case that politics plays a more important role in Smith's work than is revealed by this anachronistic perspective, and that Smith's thought can best be understood in relation to eighteenth-century civic humanism on the one hand and to Hume's "sceptical Whiggism" on the other. In a number of subsequent essays, Winch has pointed to the centrality of Smith's attempt to create a "science of the legislator" in understanding his overall intentions: "Science and the Legislator: Adam Smith and After," *The Economic Journal,* Vol. 93 (Sept. 1983), pp. 501–20; "Adam Smith and the Liberal Tradition," in Knud Haakonssen (ed.), *Traditions of Liberalism* (St. Leonards, Australia, 1988), pp. 83–101. Winch disputes the emphasis on the Scottish perspective in understanding Smith in "Adam Smith's 'enduring particular result'; A political and cosmopolitan perspective," in Hont and Ignatieff (eds.), *Wealth and Virtue.*

J. Ralph Lindgren, *The Social Philosophy of Adam Smith* (The Hague, 1973), attempts to reconstruct Smith's social philosophy entirely without reference to historical context, based mostly on the texts themselves, allowing considerable room for transferring to Smith his own nostalgic view of the past and critical view of capitalism. Smith lived before the French and industrial revolutions, and Lindgren imagines that "before the integrity of cultural bonds were wrenched by these twin upheavals society and community were still a reality" (p. 109)—a view difficult to reconcile with Smith's judgment of medieval society or of the society of his own day. Lindgren provides insights into Smith's social psychology but presents a very strained reconstruction of

Smith's theory of government in Chapter 4, in which he holds that Smith believed that as government becomes more complex and institutionalized it becomes alienated from the moral sentiments of the community and undermines its own legitimacy. His dubious conclusion is that "Smith was convinced that the commercial society of his day was in imminent danger of collapse as a society."

Far more reliable is T. D. Campbell, *Adam Smith's Science of Morals* (London, 1971), which offers a systematic presentation of Smith's moral theory as it appears in the *TMS*. Richard F. Teichgraeber III, *"Free Trade" and Moral Philosophy: Rethinking the Sources of Adam Smith's* Wealth of Nations (Durham, 1986), focuses on Smith's debts to and reformulation of the thought of Grotius, Hutcheson, and Hume. Laurence Dickey, "Historicizing the 'Adam Smith Problem': Conceptual, Historiographical, and Textual Issues," *Journal of Modern History*, Vol. 58, #3 (Sept. 1986), pp. 579–609, explores the changes between editions of *The Theory of Moral Sentiments*. Norbert Waszek, "Two Concepts of Morality: A Distinction of Adam Smith's Ethics and Its Stoic Origin," *Journal of the History of Ideas* (Vol. 45, #4 (Oct. 1984), pp. 591–606, follows an important stoic theme in Smith's work. Though Adam Smith began as a philosopher, which for him meant primarily classical philosophy, scholarship on his work has suffered from a lack of attention by philosophers fully conversant with his Greek and Latin referents. That situation will be remedied by Charles L. Griswold, Jr., in his forthcoming book on Smith, tentatively titled *Liberalism, Virtue Ethics, and Moral Psychology: Adam Smith's Stoic Modernity*. For an insightful interim contribution focused on the relationship between the form and the content of Smith's ethics, see his "Rhetoric and Ethics: Adam Smith on Theorizing about the Moral Sentiments," *Philosophy and Rhetoric*, Vol. 24, #3 (1991), pp. 213–37.

David McNally, *Political Economy and the Rise of Capitalism: A Reinterpretation* (Berkeley, 1988), attempts to put Smith into context by stressing (indeed exaggerating) the relationship of *The Wealth of Nations* to Physiocratic doctrine, but it is often shrewd in making connections between *WN* and *TMS*. McNally errs in believing that Smith's appeal to landlord–legislators stemmed from a commitment to agrarian capitalism instead of seeing it as a strategic address to the holders of power. By ignoring the rhetorical aspects of Smith's attack on merchants and on the negative effects of the division of labor, and by failing to recognize that for Smith a society of "justice" was the most one could aim for and better than what had preceded it, he makes Smith seem more critical of existing reality than he in fact was. He also overstresses the primacy of agricultural growth in Smith by playing down Smith's belief that the greatest effectiveness of the division of labor was in manufacture, by ignoring Smith's references to the growing availability of manufactured consumer goods, and by neglecting the context of the consumer revolution.

Knud Haakonssen, *The Science of a Legislator: The Natural Jurisprudence of David Hume and Adam Smith* (Cambridge, 1981), offers a reconstruction of Smith's jurisprudence based largely on the *LJ*. The book traces the conceptual linkages between *TMS* and the *LJ* and provides the best reconstruction of Smith's conception of historical stages and historical development, demonstrating that there is more to it than the "four-stage theory," and that law, institutions, defense, geography, and accident all play a role in Smith's view of history. The book is an antidote in this regard to Ronald Meek, *Social Science and the Ignoble Savage* (Cambridge, 1976), a valuable study which places Smith's work in the context of other eighteenth-century theories of history but tends to make Smith's interpretation of history appear more economistic (and hence more proto-Marxist) than is warranted.

SMITH'S PLACE IN THE HISTORY OF ECONOMICS

Robert L. Heilbroner, *The Worldly Philosophers: The Lives, Times, and Ideas of the Great Economic Thinkers*, now in its sixth edition (New York, 1986), has rightfully achieved a monopoly on introductions to the history of economics. Joseph Schumpeter, *History of Economic Analysis*, edited by Elizabeth Boody Schumpeter (New York, 1954), pp. 181–94, offers a wry portrait of Smith and the appeal of *WN*, suggesting that "his very limitations made for success." The book remains indispensable on the relationship between *WN* and previous and subsequent economic thought.

Joyce Oldham Appleby, *Economic Thought and Ideology in Seventeenth-Century England* (Princeton, 1978)—despite some inaccurate comments on Smith and a propensity to read later economic views into the seventeenth century—recounts the economic debates of that century, including the views of advocates of freer internal and international trade. She traces the rise of protectionist arguments and legislation in the late seventeenth century to the interests of manufacturers and landlords. Just how developed and sophisticated European economic thought was in the century before the publication of *The Wealth of Nations* is demonstrated by Terence Hutchison, *Before Adam Smith: The Emergence of Political Economy, 1662–1776* (Oxford, 1988), after reading which no one will ever again imagine that Smith "created" economics. For a discussion of Smith's relationship to the economic thought of his time and his often unacknowledged borrowing from his contemporaries, see Salim Rashid, "Adam Smith's Acknowledgements: Neo-Plagiarism and the Wealth of Nations," *Journal of Libertarian Studies*, Vol. 9, #2 (1990), pp. 1–24; and "Adam Smith and the Market Mechanism," *History of Political Economy*, Vol. 21, #1 (1992), pp. 129–52.

The accuracy of Smith's conception of "the mercantile system" is disputed by D. C. Coleman, "Adam Smith, Businessmen, and the Mercantile System in England," *History of European Ideas*, Vol. 9, #2 (1988), pp. 161–70.

E. A. Wrigley, *Continuity, chance, and change: the character of the industrial revolution in England* (Cambridge, 1988), is a valuable exploration of the industrial revolution as characterized by the transition from an organically based economy to an inorganically based economy. Wrigley conflates Smith's view of population growth and the long-term tendency toward economic stasis with that of Ricardo and Malthus. (See Hont, "Rich Country Debate," for an alternative view of Smith, which explores his solution to these problems.) Donald Winch, "Science and the Legislator: Adam Smith and After," *The Economic Journal*, Vol. 93 (Sept. 1983), pp. 501–20, offers a detailed reconstruction of Smith's views on the all-important corn trade and examines some of the salient differences between Smith's work and that of Malthus and Ricardo.

George Stigler, "The Successes and Failures of Professor Smith," in *The Economist as Preacher and other Essays* (Chicago, 1982), is a brief and incisive analysis of Smith's main insights and errors, from the point of view of subsequent economic analysis. Samuel Hollander, *The Economics of Adam Smith* (Toronto, 1973), provides an analysis and restatement of *WN* in contemporary economic terms. Chapters 3 and 7 refute the view that Smith's work was deficient in its lack of attention to contemporary technological and industrial developments. For a similar attempt, which comes to rather different conclusions, see Mark Blaug, *Economic Theory in Retrospect*, Fourth Edition (Cambridge, 1985). Henry William Spiegel, *The Growth of Economic Thought*, Third Edition (Durham, NC, 1991), puts the development of economic ideas in their larger intellectual contexts and provides extensive bibliography.

Several of the most important works on economics by Smith's distinguished predecessors and contemporaries have been reprinted. John de Witt (actually Pieter de la Court), *The True Interest and Political Maxims of the Republic of Holland*, was published in English translation in London in 1746. It was reprinted by Arno Press in New York in 1972. David Hume's economic essays are included in Eugene F. Miller (ed.), *David Hume: Essays Moral, Political, and Philosophical* (Indianapolis, 1987), and are treated by Eugene Rotwein in his introduction to Hume's *Writings on Economics*, edited by Eugene Rotwein (Madison, 1970). On Josiah Tucker, see R. L. Schuyler (ed.), *Josiah Tucker: A Selection from His Economic and Political Writings* (New York, 1931), and George Shelton, *Dean Tucker and Eighteenth-Century Economic and Political Thought* (New York, 1981).

ECONOMICS AND POLITICS IN BRITAIN

Among the most important and useful works for understanding the British political and economic contexts in which Smith wrote are Paul Langford, *A Polite and Commercial People: England 1727–1783 (The New Oxford History of England)* (Oxford, 1989); and John Brewer, *The Sinews of Power: War, Money, and the English State, 1688–1783* (New York, 1989). On mercantilism, see: D. C. Coleman (ed.), *Revisions in Mercantilism* (London, 1969); D. C. Coleman, "Mercantilism Revisited," *The Historical Journal*, Vol. 23, #4 (1980), pp. 773–91; and Jacob Viner's article "Mercantilist Thought" in *The International Encyclopedia of the Social Sciences*, Vol. 4, pp. 435–43, which is reprinted in Viner, *Essays on the Intellectual History of Economics*. On the British economy in the eighteenth century, see: David S. Landes, *The Unbound Prometheus: Technological Change and Industrial Development in Western Europe from 1750 to the Present* (Cambridge, 1969), Chapter 2; T. S. Ashton, *An Economic History of England: the Eighteenth Century*

(London, 1955); and Neil McKendrick, John Brewer, and J. H. Plumb, *The Birth of a Consumer Society: The Commercialization of Eighteenth-Century England* (Bloomington, 1982).

INTELLECTUAL TRADITIONS

No scholar has made a more important contribution to an understanding of the intellectual traditions and contexts which influenced Smith's work than J. G. A. Pocock. Because his contribution has been a changing and dynamic one, however, readers familiar only with his best-known book may misjudge the significance of his contribution. In *The Machiavellian Moment: Florentine Political Thought and the Atlantic Republican Tradition* (Princeton, 1975), he traced the development of civic republicanism from its Greek roots through the eighteenth century, including its role in debates about the moral and cultural effects of commerce. Thereafter a host of other scholars discovered civic republican elements in every nook and cranny of eighteenth-century British and American thought. A thoughtful review essay by J. H. Hexter, "Republic, Virtue, Liberty, and the Political Universe of J. G. A. Pocock," in Hexter, *On Historians* (Cambridge, MA, 1979), points out that Pocock's book offered a one-sided perspective on early modern political thought and virtually ignored the role of competing traditions more conducive to liberty in the sense of the protection of the individual *from* the holders of political power. Pocock's subsequent essays, of which the most relevant are collected in *Virtue, Commerce, and History* (Cambridge, 1985), have explored the relationship of the language of civic republicanism to competing interpretative frameworks, including the tradition of civil jurisprudence and what he sees as a new "commercial humanism" focused on the improvement of "manners"—on which see especially the essay, "Virtues, rights, and manners: A model for historians of political thought." Also relevant is his essay, "Cambridge paradigms and Scotch Philosophers: a study of the relations between civic humanist and the civil jurisprudential interpretations of eighteenth-century social thought," in Hont and Ignatieff (eds.), *Wealth and Virtue*.

On the natural law tradition and its transformation in the seventeenth and eighteenth centuries, see Richard Tuck, "The 'modern' theory of natural law," in Anthony Pagden (ed.), *The Languages of Political Theory in Early-Modern Europe* (Cambridge, 1987), pp. 99–119; Peter Stein, "From Pufendorf to Adam Smith: the natural law tradition in Scotland," in Norbert Horn (ed.), *Europäisches Rechtsdenken in Geschichte und Gegenwart*, two volumes, Vol. 1 (Munich, 1982), pp. 667–79; and, more broadly, Peter Stein, *Legal Evolution: The Story of an Idea* (Cambridge, 1980). Thomas A. Horne, *Property Rights and Poverty: Political Argument in Britain, 1605–1834* (Chapel Hill, 1990), provides a very useful discussion of Smith's relationship to the tradition of natural jurisprudence which expands on and complements the essay by Hont and Ignatieff and shows that for Smith government policy was meant to provide cheapness of provision and commodities.

The development of neo-stoicism and its influence on Smith remains underexplored. On the manifold meanings and influences of stoicism in early modern Europe, see William J. Bouwsma, "The Two Faces of Humanism: Stoicism and Augustinianism in Renaissance Thought," in his *A Useable Past: Essays in European Cultural History* (Berkeley, 1990). On continential neo-stoicism, see Wilhelm Dilthey, *Gesammelte Schriften: II Band: Weltanschauung und Analyse des Menschen seit Renaissance und Reformation* (Stuttgart, 1957), and Gerhard Oestreich, *Neo-Stoicism and the early modern state* (Cambridge, 1982).

PSYCHOLOGICAL INSTITUTIONALISM

On the growing exploration of the passions in early modern France, see Anthony Levi, *French Moralists: The Theory of the Passions, 1585 to 1649* (Oxford, 1964), a treasury of sources and influences. Dale Van Kley, "Pierre Nicole, Jansenism, and the Morality of Enlightened Self-Interest," in Alan Charles Kors and Paul J. Korshin (eds.), *Anticipations of the Enlightenment in England, France, and Germany* (Philadelphia, 1987), pp. 69–85, elucidates an important link in the intellectual historical chain. For a rather jaundiced and Foucault-inspired interpretation of Locke which brings out the social role of approbation and disapprobation in his thought, see James Tully, "Governing Conduct," in Edmund Leites (ed.), *Conscience and Casuistry in Early Modern Europe* (Cambridge and Paris, 1988), pp. 12–71. F. B. Kaye's long introduction to his edition of Bernard Mandeville, *The Fable of the*

Bees or Private Vices, Publick Benefits (two volumes Oxford, 1924; reprinted Indianapolis, 1988), is a goldmine of information on earlier theorists of the passions and on Mandeville's influence on subsequent eighteenth-century thinkers. Perhaps the broadest and most lucid overview of the theme of approbativeness in eighteenth-century thought is Alfred O. Lovejoy, *Reflections on Human Nature* (Baltimore, 1961), which examines the development of the strategy of replacing the work of virtue and reason with the passions in seventeenth-century and eighteenth-century thought and treats Smith's *Theory of Moral Sentiments* as the culmination of that process. Works which offer broad explorations of the themes of the passions and their control in eighteenth-century French thought are Lester G. Crocker, *An Age of Crisis: Man and World in Eighteenth Century French Thought* (Baltimore, 1959), and Jean Ehrard, *L'Idée de nature en France a l'aube des Lumières* (Paris, 1970), pp. 223–41.

Eric Voegelin, *From Enlightenment to Revolution* edited by John H. Hallowell (Durham, NC, 1975), Chapters 2–3, presents a brilliant analysis of the psychological institutionalism of Smith's French contemporary, Helvétius, his relationship to Pascal, and his influence on Jeremy Bentham. Voegelin offers a scathing critique of all forms of psychological institutionalism, which he views as a secularist response to the disorder of the human soul created by the eclipse of the experience of "creaturely nothingness" which is a precondition for the religious "return to the ground of existence." As is often the case in reading Voegelin, one need not agree with his premises to profit from his analytic acumen. Though Smith met Helvétius in Paris and owned copies of his books *De l'Esprit* and *De l'Homme*, they seem to have undertaken parallel explorations of related themes leading to different conclusions rather than to have influenced each other in any significant way. But the comparison is worth exploring, not least because it would amplify the distinction between Smith's reliance on mechanisms which channel self-interest for the public good and Helvétius' attempt to manipulate men through institutional mechanisms of pleasure and pain into *identifying* the public interest as their private interest, on which see Keith Michael Baker, *Condorcet: From Natural Philosophy to Social Mathematics* (Chicago, 1975), pp. 214ff.

The most direct and by far the most important source of Smith's psychological institutionalism was David Hume. For a useful overview of the theme in Hume, see David Miller, *Philosophy and Ideology in Hume's Political Thought* (New York, 1981), pp. 101–20; the book includes a suggestive discussion of the overlap among the views of Hume, Smith, and Burke (pp. 196–205).

On the exploration of the social role of the passions in British and Scottish thought, see Milton L. Myers, *The Soul of Modern Economic Man: Ideas of Self-Interest Thomas Hobbes to Adam Smith* (Chicago, 1983). For the influence of the French moralists on Hume, see Peter Jones, *Hume's Sentiments: Their Ciceronian and French Context* (Edinburgh, 1982), pp. 1–43. L. A. Selby-Bigge (ed.), *British Moralists,* two volumes (Oxford, 1897), brings together selections by eighteenth-century writers and includes an introduction by the editor with an extensive discussion of eighteenth-century British moralist thought as a reaction to Hobbes and Mandeville. A useful collection is Louis Schneider (ed.), *The Scottish Moralists on Human Nature and Society* (Chicago, 1967), which includes an introduction that calls attention to the concern of the Scots with social psychology, the nonrational foundations of action, and unintended consequences. The volume is now out of print—perhaps some enlightened publisher may see fit to resuscitate it. On self-interest and the exploration of the emotions in the Scottish Enlightenment, see Stephen Holmes, "The Secret History of Self-Interest," in Jane J. Mansbridge (ed.), *Beyond Self-Interest* (Chicago, 1990), pp. 267–86.

Albert O. Hirschman, *The Passions and the Interests: Political Arguments for Capitalism Before Its Triumph* (Princeton, 1977), traces the changing conception of material self-seeking from a vice to a passion which could be used to counterbalance other passions, and to its redefinition as an interest which could be used to restrain the passions and make men more predictable and gentle and less aggressive and warlike. While, as Hirschman notes, Smith did not make this distinction between the passions and economic interest, Hirschman's contention that "Smith undercut the idea that passion can be pitted against passion" ignores the central role of this conception in *TMS.* An essay which goes beyond a coda to *The Passions and the Interests,* namely the title piece of Hirschman's *Rival View of Market Society and Other Recent Essays* (New York, 1986), is a marvelously learned and analytically acute discussion of recurrent patterns in the evaluation of the cultural and political effects of the market. On a related theme, see his *Shifting Involvements: Private Interest and Public Action* (Princeton, 1982), Chapter 3, "The General Hostility Toward New Wealth."

Nathan Rosenberg, "Some Institutional Aspects of the Wealth of Nations," *Journal of Political Economy*, Vol. 18, #6 (1960), pp. 557–70, is probably the best article ever written on Smith's purposes in writing *WN* and on the role of policy in channeling self-interest to the greater economic benefit of society. See also Rosenberg's contribution to *Essays on Adam Smith*, "Adam Smith on Profits—Paradox Lost and Regained," and his "Adam Smith and the Stock of Moral Capital," *History of Political Economy*, Vol. 22, #1 (1990), pp. 1–17.

THE ENLIGHTENMENT

On Enlightenment thought, the best survey remains Peter Gay, *The Enlightenment: An Interpretation*, two volumes (New York, 1966–69), which includes extensive bibliographical essays. Portraying the Enlightenment through the prism of its French protagonists, Gay overstates the antipathy to religion among enlightened intellectuals and understates the differences between national contexts. These weaknesses are remedied by Roy Porter and Mikulas Teich (eds.), *The Enlightenment in National Context* (Cambridge, 1981), and by Robert Wuthnow, *Communities of Discourse: Ideology and Social Structure in the Reformation, the Enlightenment, and European Socialism* (Cambridge, MA, 1989), which brings together a great deal of secondary literature on the social, economic, and political context of the Enlightenment, including its Scottish branch. But the discussion of how this information illuminates the thought of enlightened thinkers focuses almost entirely on Voltaire and Rousseau, with virtually no discussion of Scottish thought. A brief, learned, and reliable study which emphasizes the changing historiography on the Enlightenment since Gay's work is Roy Porter, *The Enlightenment* (Atlantic Highlands, NJ, 1990).

Charles Taylor's *Sources of the Self: The Making of Modern Identity* (Cambridge, MA., 1989), is a work of remarkable range and insight in which intellectual history is put at the service of moral philosophy. It is particularly valuable on the new evalua-

raries, religious and lay. On the conception of women and the educative role of the family as a theme in the Scottish Enlightenment, see Rosemarie Zagarri, "Morals, Manners, and the Republican Mother," *American Quarterly*, Vol. 44, #2 (June 1992), pp. 26–43.

Ronald Hamowy, *The Scottish Enlightenment and the Theory of Spontaneous Order* (Carbondale, IL, 1987), explores a major subclass of the theory of unanticipated consequences in the Scottish Enlightenment. Hamowy points out, quite rightly, that the theory could have deeply conservative consequences, since any existing institutional arrangement could be regarded as the product of evolutionary selection, a consequence which he argues was not recognized by Smith. Yet the fault may lie more with Hamowy's characterization of the Scots' position than with the Scots themselves. The notion that existing society could be regarded as a product of "spontaneous order" is a far more radical idea than the notion that particular socially beneficial institutions had come about without the deliberate intention of historical actors, and in this radical form it was not widely maintained by the Scots, and certainly not by Smith. The role of the legislator in reforming or creating institutions to channel the passions to socially beneficial goals was incompatible with such a view. Hamowy, explicitly following Friedrich Hayek, appears to have read back into the Scottish thinkers a far more radical (and implausible) conception than they in fact maintained.

THE RECEPTION OF SMITH'S WORK

We lack a study of the changing image of Smith comparable to John Rodden, *The Politics of Literary Reputation: The Making and Claiming of 'St. George' Orwell* (New York, 1989), though such a study would be instructive. On the British reception of *The Wealth of Nations* in the decade after its publication, see, most recently, John E. Crowley, "Neo-Mercantilism and The Wealth of Nations: British Commercial Policy after the American Revolution," *Historical Journal*, Vol. 33, #2 (1990), pp. 339–60, which contains references to earlier works on the issue. Emma Rothschild, "Adam Smith and conservative economics," *Economic History Review*, Vol. 45, #1 (1992), pp. 74–96, is marred by an image of Smith which is rather more radical than can legitimately be adduced from a balanced reading of his works. On Smith's broader influence on British political debate, discussions of public policy, and political science, see: Bernard Semmel, *The Rise of Free Trade Imperialism* (Cambridge, 1970); Gertrude Himmelfarb, *The Idea of Poverty: England in the Early Industrial Age* (New York, 1984); and Stefan Collini, Donald Winch, and John Burrow, *That Noble Science of Politics* (Cambridge, 1983). For Smith's influence on the American Founders, see William Grampp, "Adam Smith and the American Revolutionists," *History of Political Economy*, Vol 11, #2 (1979), pp. 179–80. On his reception across the Channel, see Melchior Palyi, "The Introduction of Adam Smith on the Continent," in John Maurice Clark, *et al.*, *Adam Smith, 1776–1926* (1928; reprinted New York, 1966). Norbert Waszek, *The Scottish Enlightenment and Hegel's Account of 'Civil Society'* (Dordrecht, 1988), reviews much of the literature on the Scottish Enlightenment and its reception in Germany.

Moral Philosophy and Social Science Today

Steven E. Rhoads, *The Economist's View of the World: Government, Markets, and Public Policy* (Cambridge, 1985), presents both an informed conspectus of the application of economic modes of thought to public policy and a thoughtful critique of the limits of the world view of contemporary economics. See also his essay, "Economists on Tastes and Preferences," in James H. Nichols, Jr., and Colin Wright (eds.), *From Political Economy to Economics—and Back?* (San Francisco, 1990), pp. 79–104. Thoughtful works on related themes include Albert O. Hirschman, "Against Parsimony: Three Easy Ways of Complicating Some Categories of Economic Discourse," in his *Rival View of Market Society and Other Essays* (New York, 1986); Richard H. Thaler, *The Winner's Curse: Paradoxes and Anomalies of Economic Life* (New York, 1992); and Alan Wolfe, *Whose Keeper? Social Science and Moral Obligation* (Berkeley, 1989).

Reference Works

Among the reference works which are particularly useful on the history of social, political, and economic thought are: *The New*

Palgrave: A Dictionary of Economics, edited by John Eatwell, Murray Milgate, and Peter Newman (New York, 1987); *The International Encyclopedia of the Social Sciences,* edited by David L. Sills (New York, 1968); the older but still useful *Encyclopedia of the Social Sciences,* edited by Edwin R. A. Seligman (New York, 1931); *The Dictionary of the History of Ideas,* edited by Philip P. Wiener (New York, 1973); and *Geschichtliche Grundbegriffe,* edited by Otto Brunner and Werner Conze (Stuttgart, 1975–). Joseph A. Schumpeter, *History of Economic Analysis,* edited by Elizabeth Boody Schumpeter (New York, 1954), is an encyclopedic work which delivers more than its title promises. It deals insightfully if sometimes idiosyncratically with the history of social science and social philosophy, as well as with the history of economics, from Plato through Keynes.

Acknowledgments

"THE DUTIES OF GRATITUDE," SMITH wrote in *The Theory of Moral Sentiments*, "are perhaps the most sacred of all those which the beneficent virtues prescribe to us." The intellectual, emotional, and material beneficence of others leaves me well placed to discharge this most sacred of duties.

In the footnotes, I have acknowledged my direct intellectual debts to those whose work I have used. But I owe a special though more indirect debt to those whose writings or personal influence motivated me to ask the questions which led to my study of Smith: to Daniel Bell, Irving Kristol, David Landes, Robert K. Merton, and Philip Rieff. I have profited from the learning of many of my colleagues in the Department of History at the Catholic University of America who have provided me with advice and information. I am particularly grateful to Jon Wakelyn, the former chairman of the department, for maintaining an atmosphere at once collegial and congenial to research. A number of scholars from a range of disciplines read and commented on an earlier draft of this book: I thank Charles L. Griswold, Jr., John A. Hall, Joel Schwartz, Fritz Stern, Rosemarie Zagarri, and especially Istvan Hont for their recommendations, which I have tried to put to good use. I have also profited from conversations on early modern history with Norbert Finzsch,

Arthur Herman, and Paul Rosenberg. I am grateful to Ian S. Ross for sending me copies of his published papers on Smith.

My larger project on capitalism in modern European thought, of which this volume is an unanticipated consequence, has been materially aided by fellowships from the Catholic University of America, the John M. Olin Foundation, and the Lynde and Harry Bradley Foundation. I am deeply grateful to all three organizations for their support.

Contrary to one of the most famous aphorisms of *The Wealth of Nations,* I have long benefited from the benevolence of butchers and would like to thank the vice president and the secretary–treasurer of Muller's Meats Limited, and above all its president, who taught me a good deal about commercial society though he doesn't know Smith from Adam.

This book is dedicated to my wife Sharon, my greatest source of happiness, who for two decades has been my constant spectator, yet remains partial to me. I am grateful also to our children, Elisha, Sara, and Seffy, who, as Smith would say, impose a useful restraint upon my conduct by their frequent presence—and are a great joy.

Peter Dougherty, erstwhile senior editor at The Free Press, is a man who believes that ideas are important enough to put effort into making them accessible. He responded with alacrity to the suggestion that I might divert my efforts to a work on Adam Smith, and his queries, recommendations, and urgings played an important role in the shaping of this book. It was a great pleasure to work with him, and I am gratified that he was able to pass the book into the able hands of Adam Bellow. I am also grateful to Everett Sims for his copy editing, and to Celia Knight, Production Supervisor at The Free Press, who supervised the metamorphosis from manuscript to book.

None of the above is responsible for the uses I have made of their advice, ideas, love or money. Though each has strengthened the book, its weaknesses reflect only my manifold imperfections.

Index